Fire Alarm

Fire Alarm

The Investigation of the U.S. House Select Committee on Benghazi

Bradley F. Podliska

LEXINGTON BOOKS
Lanham • Boulder • New York • London

Published by Lexington Books
An imprint of The Rowman & Littlefield Publishing Group, Inc.
4501 Forbes Boulevard, Suite 200, Lanham, Maryland 20706
www.rowman.com

6 Tinworth Street, London SE11 5AL, United Kingdom

British Library Cataloguing in Publication Information Available

Library of Congress Cataloging-in-Publication Data Available

ISBN 978-1-66690-616-5 (cloth : alk. paper)
ISBN 978-1-66690-617-2 (electronic)

♾™ The paper used in this publication meets the minimum requirements of American National Standard for Information Sciences—Permanence of Paper for Printed Library Materials, ANSI/NISO Z39.48-1992.

For Florian,
Yes, that's right. Pink, purple, all the colors – let them cross over, outside the lines.

Contents

List of Figures

List of Tables

Acknowledgments

If you turn to page III of the *Final Report of the Select Committee on the Events Surrounding the 2012 Terrorist Attack in Benghazi*, you will not see my name on the list of committee staff. But, like the others on the page, I arrived at 1036 Longworth House Office Building each day at 9 a.m. and worked until 5 p.m. on days Congress was out of session and until 6 p.m. on days Congress was in session. When I joined the House Select Committee on Benghazi in 2014, I believed that I would be able to provide answers to the families of Glen Doherty, Sean Smith, Christopher Stevens, and Tyrone Woods, and that belief continues today. Just like other tragedies—the September 11 terrorist attacks, the failed 1961 Bay of Pigs invasion, and the 1912 sinking of the *Titanic*—the Benghazi attack can and should be examined without fear or favor. *Fire Alarm: The Investigation of the U.S. House Select Committee on Benghazi* is the culmination of that belief.

I am thankful for that cadre of attorneys and Republican staffers—the good people—that saw wrongdoing in Congress, in which its members argued that it is the only employer in the country that has a legal loophole to fire military reservists. These attorneys, Peter Romer-Friedman, Joseph Napiltonia, Thomas Jarrard, Kathryn Piscitelli, and Mark Zaid, and those unnamed Republican staffers held Congress accountable. My commander and supervisor Colonel Tom Bayer and Mr Thomas Baus also had my back in this band of brothers. Jake Tapper and Adam Housley listened to my story, never losing sight of the military reserve angle, and reported the facts to the American people. Leon Neyfakh allowed me to provide my perspective on the investigation for his excellent podcast *Fiasco: Benghazi*.

I remain grateful for the patience and guidance of both academics and practitioners, who not only offered feedback on this book but work without fail to find the truth and prepare the next generation of students. For this, I would like to thank Robert Mahoney, James Campbell, Ryan White, Brian Price, John Minney, Brent Lawniczak, Christopher Weimar, Christopher Stamper, Robert Kerr, Lisa Kerr, Jon Henderickson, Keith Henderson, Joseph Beal, Joseph Osborne, Andrew Jasso, and Steven Alsop. Similarly, I would like to thank Jeffrey Kraus and Paul Lendway for their feedback on an earlier version of Chapter 3, which I presented at the 2021 Midwest Political Science Association annual conference. As with *Acting Alone*, I am thankful again for Joseph Parry, Carter Moran, Emilia Rivera, and the wonderful staff at Lexington Books. They have been professional and accommodating, making the process not only stress-free but a pleasure.

Michael Krozer not only provided experienced writing advice but also perfectly captured the essence of *Fire Alarm* with the book cover design. Dr R. J. Podliska took a boot camp level of scrutiny to editing the manuscript, displaying a level of attention to detail that would make a drill sergeant proud. Christopher Sprecher was kind enough to read multiple drafts and mentor me along the way. Tyson Chatagnier was instrumental in steering me on a methodologically correct path. Melia Pfannenstiel made time in her busy schedule to read through and edit my manuscript. Megan Varney helped me with the art of style and grammar. Cynthia Jones, Kelli McConnell, and Bailey Wood also provided invaluable insight.

For those friends, who go back to my Maryland, Wisconsin, Virginia, Texas, and Germany days, I am always laughing about the stories we share on our spins around the sun—Justin Vaughn, Jared Wold, Ed Blythe, Michael Helfrich, Michael Tully, Howard Liao, Adam Clampitt, Jason Mecler, Bethany Widick, Tiffany Bailey, Lisa Rosenthal, Mark Nastase, Tina Nastase, Elizabeth Starek, and Bob Sholtis. Brant Munday and Keith Ramsay, you were taken too soon.

I wrote this book to honor my family. I am appreciative of their support, trust, and all that they have done since my 2010 *Acting Alone* book dedication. Most lovingly, I dedicate this book to the one who is Holden and Nettie's best friend, loves unicorns and dragon rides, and brings meaning to my life.

Introduction

THE PUZZLE: HOW DID INVESTIGATING A TERRORIST ATTACK ON AMERICANS TURN PARTISAN?

In October 2015, Republican presidential candidate Donald Trump and Democratic presidential candidate Hillary Clinton agreed on one topic: the House Select Committee on Benghazi was partisan. Trump described the work of the Benghazi Committee as "very partisan," and Clinton labeled it a "partisan farce."[1]

This rare agreement among the candidates referred to the tenth and final congressional investigation into the September 11, 2012, attack on a U.S. diplomatic compound and a Central Intelligence Agency (CIA) annex in Benghazi, Libya, perpetrated by Ansar al-Sharia, a U.S. State Department–designated terrorist organization. Three years after people across the world followed coverage surrounding the horrifying attack that claimed the lives of Information Officer Sean Smith, CIA operatives Glen Doherty and Tyrone Woods, and Ambassador Chris Stevens, the sixth U.S. ambassador to be killed in a terrorist attack, the persistent congressional investigations failed to yield a detailed assessment of the decisions and actions that President Barack Obama considered the "worst mistake" of his presidency.[2]

The timing of the Benghazi attack, weeks within the 2012 presidential election, prompted strong reactions from each candidate. Immediately following the storming of the diplomatic compound and before mortars hit the CIA annex, the 2012 Republican presidential nominee Mitt Romney lit the fuse of a years-long political fight. Romney issued a statement attacking President Obama: "It's disgraceful that the Obama Administration's first response was not to condemn attacks on our diplomatic missions, but to sympathize with those who waged the attacks." President Obama fired back, "Governor Romney seems to have a tendency to shoot first and aim later."[3]

The title of this book has a dual meaning: the first signifies the attackers setting fire to the Benghazi compound, while the second represents the series of congressional "fire alarm" investigations.[4] The attack became partisan fodder, starting with ad hominem accusations between opposing presidential candidates and transitioning into a four-year legislative-executive war of attrition.

A Congress responsive to such an alarm may rapidly address the crisis to assure the public that appropriate protection and rescue procedures are in place, in the event of a similar attack. Unfortunately, following the failure of U.S. agencies to anticipate and respond to the Benghazi attack, Congress failed to seize an opportunity to address identifiable shortfalls, choosing instead to seize the opportunity for partisan electoral gain.

The final investigation related to the 2012 Benghazi attack, conducted by the House Select Committee on Benghazi ("Benghazi Committee"), ended 134 days before the 2016 presidential election and nearly four years after the attack. At the end of the Benghazi Committee proceedings, 72 percent of Americans believed its purpose was political gain. However, only 40 percent of Americans believed the Benghazi hearings had "gone too far" and 59 percent were dissatisfied with the manner in which Secretary of State Hillary Clinton had handled the Benghazi attack.[5]

Partisanship derived from investigating a terrorist attack on Americans presents a puzzle. How did a terrorist attack become so partisan? Does partisanship extend to congressional investigations? Why were Americans dissatisfied with the investigation?

Solving this puzzle appears straightforward: Congress instituted an investigatory framework of partisan control, encompassing the speaker of the House to the most junior committee staff member to facilitate electoral advantage for the party in control. Rather than investigating crises—such as the Benghazi terrorist attack or the January 6, 2021, attack on the U.S. Capitol—as a non-partisan, fact-based, solution-oriented constitutional oversight obligation, Congress consistently shirks its responsibility to understand and address the causes and consequences of crises through investigations. Instead, it conducts investigations as though they are operations within a war for electoral success. Simply put, congressional investigations are taxpayer-funded political attacks.

PROBLEMS AND PITFALLS IN EXISTING RESEARCH

The academic literature on Congress, parties, and oversight is comprehensive, temporally supported, and nearly empirical law in concluding that

Figure 0.1 Taxonomy of Congressional Investigation. *Source*: Figure created by author.

contemporary congressional investigations are partisan, and Congress, as a whole, is divided along party lines more than at any other point in history.[6] The historical path of Congress reining in a president dates back to 1792 but has become pronounced following Watergate and the 1994 congressional reforms.[7] Existing research on congressional investigations is categorized as Congress acting under its own initiative to examine the executive branch (i.e., a "police patrol") or Congress responding to a crisis or complaint (i.e., a "fire alarm").[8] Figure 0.1 illustrates this taxonomy.

A gap in the existing research is an assessment of the internal dynamics of partisan congressional investigations in practice to include the selection of leadership, the role of staff, and the ability to trace an investigation's primary focus or target. Figure 0.2 illustrates an extension of the taxonomy of a congressional investigation down to its level of committee internal dynamics.

A second issue with current research is the lack of a model or the ability to account systematically for the partisan nature of congressional investigations regardless of which party is in power or the issue under investigation. Current research includes quantitative analysis of congress and partisanship,

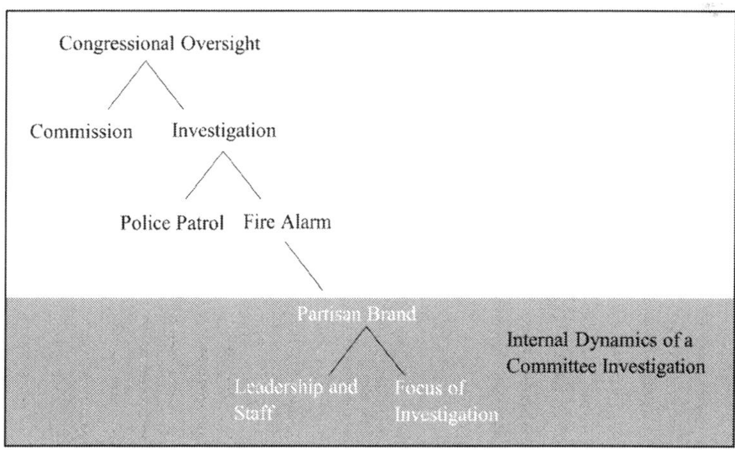

Figure 0.2 Taxonomy of Congressional Investigation with Internal Dynamics. *Source*: Figure created by author.

a cooperative versus confrontational investigation model, and in-depth case studies, but it lacks a generalizable model to explain and predict partisan investigations.[9]

A third shortcoming is the assumption that a congressional investigation is a cost-free opportunity to politically damage the opposition party. In a divided government, where the party in control of Congress does not control the White House, Congress uses its available tools in an attempt to reduce the president's popularity.[10] Such attempts align with crises or scandals and require strict party discipline to be effective.[11] But, is it truly cost-free? Can the investigating party harm its own long-term electoral fortunes, if even indirectly?

CONTRIBUTIONS OF THIS STUDY

To address these problems with current research, this study focuses on three questions in solving the puzzle of partisanship:

1. Why is an investigation, performed as Congress's oversight function, partisan?
2. What does a partisan model, which accounts for internal dynamics, look like?
3. What are the political costs for the targeted party, and the party conducting the investigation?

Fire Alarm contributes to the existing research on congressional investigations and the 2012 Benghazi terrorist attack in three ways. First, this study offers a firsthand account of the Benghazi Committee investigation. Based on my background in intelligence analysis, I was hired in 2014 to serve as a staff member for the Benghazi Committee.[12] As a Capitol Hill outsider, this position provided me with direct access to investigation materials and majority party members, as well as an opportunity to view congressional proceedings through a new lens. The understudied, publicly available 989-page *Final Report of the Select Committee on the Events Surrounding the 2012 Terrorist Attack in Benghazi* includes 11 volumes of witness interview transcripts and 3 volumes of primary source documents.[13] Drawing from this report and materials from the ten House and Senate committee investigations of the Benghazi terrorist attack, I detail the Benghazi attack, reactions from military and political figures within the Obama administration, and the perspective of an investigation insider.

Second, this study draws upon the history of investigations and institutional changes, particularly after Watergate and the 1994 Republican takeover of Congress, to present a new theoretical framework that I label the partisan model of congressional investigations. It is a model based on political gain, not oversight of the executive branch. Following a process-tracing method, I identify committee member selection, high-profile committee events, investigative staff assignments, and temporally proximate electoral candidates as the key elements of partisan investigation.[14] Importantly, this model applies to both Democratic and Republican parties, when each operate in the majority party role.[15]

Finally, this book provides answers to questions surrounding the attack that were previously overlooked due to the partisan-driven scope of the investigation. By addressing these gaps, this research provides a more complete understanding of events before, during, and after the attack that claimed the lives of four Americans and facilitates an assessment of shortfalls and potential remedies to avoid future loss of life.

ROADMAP

Chapter 1 begins by establishing the context of the Libyan security environment in 2012 and attempts by the U.S. State Department to understand and shape the environment. Through the perspective of congressional investigators, it details the events of September 11, 2012, and the Obama administration's response in the hours after members of Ansar al-Sharia stormed the diplomatic compound in Benghazi. The recounting of the attack is geographically organized by areas of responsibility to demonstrate the bureaucratic deficiencies in crisis response across time zones and long distances as well as the individual actions of leaders with decision-making authority. The chapter concludes by presenting an accounting of the Obama administration's development of a post-attack narrative, through an analysis of remarks and speeches by administration officials.

Chapter 1 does not provide a comprehensive assessment of available secondary sources, such as media reports, pertaining to the Benghazi attack. Instead, this analysis relies upon primary source material from U.S. House of Representatives and Senate reports, hearings, and witness interviews, specifically the abundant material produced through Benghazi Committee proceedings. These records reveal investigatory gaps regarding White House, State Department, and Pentagon actions, which I expand upon in subsequent chapters.

Chapter 2 reviews the literature on presidential-congressional friction and congressional investigations and develops an explanation for the partisanship that prejudiced the Benghazi investigation. Congressional investigations can be effective tools to reign in presidential power, but I argue that after 1994 such investigations are guided by partisan political motivations. I detail the history of institutional changes and propose a new model that accounts for the relationship between the party in control of Congress and the party in control of the executive branch, the selection and roles of members and staff, and the focus of the investigation. Three hypotheses follow the explanation of the partisan model, and the chapter concludes with an explanation of this study's research design and case study methodology.

Chapter 3 focuses on the internal, partisan dynamics of the Benghazi Committee. I first review the previous nine congressional investigations leading up to May 8, 2014, when the House of Representatives voted to establish the Benghazi Committee to "conduct a full and complete investigation and study and issue a final report of its findings to the House."[16] Following a chronology beginning with the first Benghazi Committee hearings, I apply the partisan model to member and staff selections and the focus of the investigation. Referring back to leaders identified in chapter 1, I trace the attendance of members and staff to witness interviews. The chapter concludes with an evaluation of my hypotheses.

Chapter 4 focuses on the political costs to both parties, through three phases of the investigation: the neutral phase, the "Clinton-hyper-focus" phase, and the "other agency" phase, before examining the impact of the Benghazi Committee on the 2016 presidential election. After analyzing the cost to Democrats in the 2016 election, I focus on a less intuitive calculation—the political cost for Republicans. While congressional investigations provide the party in control an arena to mount political attacks, it is not a cost-free endeavor, as they can exacerbate intra-party divisions and divert attention from conducting the investigation. This chapter concludes with an analysis of group decision-making and missed opportunities to garner lessons due to the partisan nature of the investigation.

The final chapter summarizes results from the partisan model, highlighting the role of party loyalty, staff selection, and temporally proximate political rivals in investigations. The chapter concludes by highlighting the impact of such partisanship on domestic and foreign policy, offers potential areas for future research, and recommends ways to improve the integrity of congressional investigations.

NOTES

1. Donald Trump, "Donald Trump calls Benghazi Committee 'very partisan,'" *CNN*, October 25, 2015, https://www.cnn.com/videos/politics/2015/10/25/donald-trump-benghazi-committee-partisan-sot-state-of-the-union.cnn, accessed January 11, 2022; Jonathan Easley, "Republican; Benghazi probe 'designed to go after' Hillary," *The Hill*, October 14, 2015, https://thehill.com/blogs/ballot-box/presidential

-races/256982-gop-lawmaker-benghazi-probe-designed-to-go-after-hillary, accessed January 11, 2022.

2. David D. Kirkpatrick and Steven Lee Myers, "Libya Attack Brings Challenges for U.S.," *New York Times*, September 13, 2012, https://www.nytimes.com/2012/09/13/world/middleeast/us-envoy-to-libya-is-reported-killed.html, accessed January 11, 2022; Frederic Wehrey, *The Burning Shores: Inside the Battle for the New Libya* (New York: Farrar, Straus and Giroux, 2018), 267.

3. Philip Rucker, "Romney Repeats Sharp Criticism of Obama after Benghazi, Cairo attacks," *Washington Post*, September 12, 2012, https://www.washingtonpost.com/politics/decision2012/romney-repeats-sharp-criticism-of-obama-on-libya-egypt-attacks/2012/09/12/31074af4-fcdf-11e1-b153-218509a954e1_story.html, accessed January 11, 2022.

4. The fire alarm description of the attack is derived from a Diplomatic Security agent in the Benghazi mission compound tactical operations center, who sounded the alarm as the attack began. The terrorists, in their attack, used gasoline to light furniture on fire, filling the villa with black smoke. See Wehrey, *Burning Shores*, 130–31.

5. CNN/ORC poll, October 14–17, 2015, http://i2.cdn.turner.com/cnn/2015/images/10/21/rel11e.-.benghazi.pdf, accessed January11, 2022.

6. Douglas Kriner, "Can Enhanced Oversight Repair the Broken Branch," *Boston University Law Review* 89 (2009): 765–93; Lance Cole and Stanley Brand, *Congressional Investigations and Oversight: Case Studies and Analysis* (Durham, NC: Carolina Academic Press, 2011); Douglas Kriner and Eric Schickler, *Investigating the President: Congressional Checks on Presidential Power* (Princeton: Princeton University Press, 2016); Nolan McCarty, Keith T. Poole, and Howard Rosenthal, *Polarized America: The Dance of Ideology and Unequal Riches* (Boston: MIT Press, 2006); Alex Kuzoian, "This 60-second Animation Shows How Divided Congress Has Become Since 1949," *Business Insider*, September 11, 2019, https://www.businessinsider.com/animation-rise-partisanship-congress-house-representatives-60-years-2016-4, accessed January 11, 2022.

7. See John H. Aldrich and David W. Rohde, "The Transition to Republican Rule in the House: Implications for Theories of Congressional Parties," *Political Science Quarterly* 112, no. 4 (1997–1998): 541–67; Christopher J. Deering and Stephen S. Smith, *Committees in Congress*. 3rd ed. (Washington, DC: CQ Press, 1997); Barbara Sinclair, *Unorthodox Lawmaking: New Legislative Processes in the U.S. Congress*. 2nd ed. (Washington, DC: CQ Press, 2000); Barbara Sinclair, *Party Wars: Polarization and the Politics of National Policy Making* (Norman: University of Oklahoma Press, 2006); Irving Younger, "Congressional Investigations and Executive Secrecy: A Study in the Separation of Powers," *University of Pittsburgh Law Review* 20 (1959): 756–58.

8. Mathew McCubbins and Thomas Schwartz, "Congressional Oversight Overlooked: Police Patrols versus Fire Alarms," *American Journal of Political Science* 28, no. 1 (1984): 165–79; Steven J. Balla and Christopher J. Deering, "Police Patrols and Fire Alarms: An Empirical Examination of the Legislative Preference for Oversight," *Congress & the Presidency* 40, no. 1 (2013): 27–40.

9. For current research examples of quantitative, case study, or model-based analysis, see Kriner and Schickler, *Investigating the President*; Douglas Kriner and Eric

Schickler, "Investigating the President: Committee Probes and Presidential Approval, 1953 – 2006," *The Journal of Politics* 76, no. 2 (2014): 521–34; Douglas Kriner and Francis Shen, "Responding to War on Capitol Hill: Battlefield Casualties, Congressional Response, and Public Support for the War in Iraq," *American Journal of Political Science* 58, no. 1 (2014): 157–74; Cole and Brand, *Congressional Investigations and Oversight*; Frank John Smist, *Congress Oversees the United States Intelligence Community, 1947–1994* (Knoxville: University of Tennessee Press, 1994).

10. See David C.W. Parker and Matthew Dull, "Divided We Quarrel: The Politics of Congressional Investigations, 1947–2004," *Legislative Studies Quarterly* 34, no. 3 (2009): 319–45; David C.W. Parker and Matthew Dull, "Rooting Out Waste, Fraud, and Abuse: The Politics of House Committee Investigations, 1947 to 2004," *Political Research Quarterly* 66, no. 3 (2013): 630–44; Kriner, "Can Enhanced Oversight," 765–93; Kriner and Schickler, *Investigating the President.*

11. See Brendan Nyhan, "Scandal Potential: How Political Context and News Congestion Affect the President's Vulnerability to Media Scandal," *British Journal of Political Science* 45, no. 2 (2015): 435–66; Miguel M. Pereira and Nicholas W. Waterbury, "Do Voters Discount Political Scandals over Time?," *Political Research Quarterly* 72, no. 3 (2019): 584–95; Sinclair, *Party Wars*; Douglas Kriner and Liam Schwartz, "Divided Government and Congressional Investigations," *Legislative Studies Quarterly* 33, no. 2 (2008): 295–321.

12. My name as an investigator with the Benghazi Committee has been redacted from the "Committee Staff" page of the Benghazi *Final Report.* See Select Committee on the Events Surrounding the 2012 Terrorist Attack in Benghazi, *Final Report of the Select Committee on the Events Surrounding the 2012 Terrorist Attack in Benghazi: House of Representatives; Together with Additional and Minority Views* (114th Cong., 2d sess., 2016. H. Rept. 114-848), (III). But, the Benghazi Committee Democrats in the "Minority Views" section of the *Final Report* listed me as a member of "Chairman Gowdy's staff." See Select Committee, *Final Report*, 910. LegiStorm records also confirm me as a staff member. See LegiStorm, "House Select Committee on Benghazi – Staff Salaries," *LegiStorm*, n.d., https://www.legistorm.com/office/House_Select_Committee_on_Benghazi/2911.html, accessed January 20, 2022.

13. The official Benghazi Committee records are available on the govinfo.gov website. See "House Select Committee on the Events Surrounding the 2012 Terrorist Attack in Benghazi," *govinfo.gov*, n.d., https://www.govinfo.gov/committee/house-benghazi?path=/browsecommittee/chamber/house/committee/benghazi/collection/OTHER-1, accessed January 20, 2022.

14. For process tracing, see Alexander George and Andrew Bennett, *Case Studies and Theory Development in the Social Sciences* (Cambridge, MA: MIT Press, 2004), 205–14; Andrew Bennett, "Processing Tracing and Causal Inference," In *Rethinking Social Inquiry: Diverse Tools, Shared Standards*, 2nd edition, edited by Henry E. Brady and David Collier (Lanham, MD: Rowman & Littlefield, 2010).

15. To put it simply, the model explains and predicts any post-1994 investigation, including both the investigations of the Benghazi Committee and the Democrat-run House Select Committee to Investigate the January 6th Attack on the U.S. Capitol.

16. Select Committee on Benghazi, "About," n.d., https://archives-benghazi-republicans-oversight.house.gov/about, accessed January 16, 2022.

Chapter 1

Benghazi Attack and Obama Administration Response

INTRODUCTION

The 2012 terrorist attack on the U.S. diplomatic compound in Benghazi, Libya, represents a breakdown in crisis response procedures and underscores the risks of faulty assumptions. This chapter uses congressional sources to examine the State Department's efforts to present Libya as a centerpiece of Clintonian "smart power" and chronicle the attack and Obama administration response. Organizing events into actions by geographic-based groups in Benghazi, Washington, DC, and Stuttgart, Germany, allows an assessment of individual and group decision-making within the White House, State Department, Pentagon, and CIA. The final section focuses on the Obama administration's portrayal of the attack as inspired by the anti-Islamic film *Innocence of Muslims*, with particular attention to the narrative shared across American media by U.S. ambassador to the United Nations Susan Rice

THE SECURITY ENVIRONMENT IN LIBYA

With the pro-democracy Arab Spring protests and uprisings starting in 2010, the Obama administration sought to use the power of the State Department to turn North African countries into stable democracies. For Hillary Clinton, this represented "smart power," in which the U.S. would "lead with diplomacy, support with development, and when necessary as a last resort, not a first choice, [use the military]."[1] Libya and the removal of Dictator Muammar Qadhafi was to be an example of how the Middle East and North Africa could be transformed. Clinton testified about this approach, "We can kill [terrorist] leaders, but until we help establish strong democratic institutions, until we do a better job communicating our values and building relationships, we are going to be faced with this level of instability."[2]

Clinton sent then-special envoy J. Christopher Stevens to Benghazi in April 2011 to meet with insurgency leaders fighting Qadhafi.[3] In this effort, Clinton visited Libya in October 2011, the same month Qadhafi was killed, to "see what [the U.S.] could do" to transition Libya to having elections and a secure environment.[4] Libya's transitional or interim government was the Transitional National Council, which was succeeded by the General National Congress in August 2012.[5] The administration was working with the interim government to achieve one of its goals in Libya: find and take possession of as many weapons, including any remaining chemical weapons from the Qadhafi regime, as possible.[6]

Qadhafi had neglected Benghazi, and Benghazi was where the uprising started. For this reason and to ensure those in Benghazi believed they were valued in Libya's future, Stevens advocated for a diplomatic presence there.[7] Stevens proposed that a Benghazi Mission compound be established for three months past the projected July 2012 elections and serve the following functions: (1) as a "platform for POL/ECON [political/economic] reporting," (2) assist with weapons collection efforts, and (3) develop commercial outreach.[8] Principal Officers (POs) would use the compound to meet with local leaders (both political and militia), foreign diplomats, non-governmental organizations, business owners, and even "regular Libyans." In short, the compound would serve as an outreach center for the community. The POs would then report on the state of Benghazi and eastern Libya.[9]

In 2012, Libya was a violent place. Extremists, including Al Qaeda, took advantage of a post-Qadhafi security vacuum in Libya and expanded their operations there.[10] Between April and June 2012, there were 21 security incidents. On April 6, 2012, an improvised explosive device (IED) was thrown over the Benghazi Mission compound wall, and on April 10, an IED was thrown at a convoy of the UN Special Representative to Libya. On May 22, a rocket-propelled grenade (RPG) was fired at the International Committee of the Red Cross. On June 6, there was another IED attack on the compound, and on June 11, there was an RPG attack on the UK Ambassador. Other countries abandoned Libya, the United States did not.[11] Adding to the insecurity of the United States's position in Libya was the fact that the Intelligence Community (IC) had "gaps" in its ability to understand the extremist threat or provide warning.[12]

In terms of responsibility for embassy security, the chain of responsibility for embassy security went from Secretary of State Clinton to Under Secretary for Management Patrick Kennedy to Assistant Secretary for Diplomatic Security (DS) Eric Boswell to Principal Deputy Assistant Secretary for Diplomatic Security Scott Bultrowicz to Deputy Assistant Secretary for

International Programs Charlene Lamb.[13] Kennedy was responsible for the security of diplomatic facilities overseas, and Lamb was responsible for managing DS programs that protected the missions and personnel.

In carrying out its responsibilities, the State Department was required to follow the Security Environment Threat List (SETL) rating, which determines what security measures are needed to meet Overseas Security Policy Board (OSPB) and Secure Embassy Construction and Counterterrorism Act (SECCA) standards. The December 2011 SETL rated Libya as "critical" for political violence and "high" for terrorism and crime.[14] Subject to these standards, the State Department was required to put in place effective countermeasures. However, the State Department signed a lease for its Benghazi compound on August 3, 2011, and in order to bypass federal law and State Department standards, it designated the compound as "temporary."[15] Independent Panel on Best Practices member Todd Keil, who had served previously as a DS Regional Bureau director, referred to the "temporary" designation of the compound as a "purposeful effort to skirt the standards."[16] Lamb acknowledged the shortcoming, saying the temporary status posed "a huge challenge" for DS, especially "without having local resources to spend [the] money effectively."[17]

On December 27, 2011, five DS agents were authorized for Benghazi, but this number of DS agents was only achieved for a total of 23 days in 2012.[18] On January 2 and 5, 2012, Benghazi Mission security officials requested, via memo, jersey barriers, lighting, sandbags, observation platforms, guard posts, egress locks on window bars, arm barriers, concrete, barbed wire, and a security specialist.[19] Also, on January 5, Kennedy approved an extension of the compound lease through the end of 2012.[20] The Bureau of Diplomatic Security was not consulted.[21] On January 10, 2012, security officials requested five DS agents, via memo, to protect the compound. Lamb did not approve the request.[22] On January 26 and February 23, 2012, its request for sandbags, lighting, arm barriers, and guard posts was approved. However, there was no response for the other requests.[23]

On June 14, 2012, Benghazi Mission officials held an emergency meeting after five major security incidents involving RPG and IED attacks. It requested five DS agents for Benghazi. There was no response to the request.[24] On July 9, 2012, Tripoli Embassy officials requested four DS agents, but Lamb did not respond.[25] On August 27, 2012, a DS agent in his turnover notes informed DS agents in Benghazi that they "are on their own."[26] The problematic security situation was compounded in August 2012 when Kennedy terminated the Department of Defense Site Security Team's (SST) responsibility in augmenting embassy security.[27] The Embassy in Tripoli had relied on SST personnel, and those personnel had traveled to Benghazi on three occasions in March, April, and June 2012 to assist with protecting the compound.[28]

For security, the State Department relied on a militia group, the February 17 Martyrs Brigade, and an unarmed local guard.[29] The goal for Clinton's planned October 2012 visit was to make the compound a permanent consulate.[30]

THE BENGHAZI ATTACK

On September 11, 2012, there were only three DS agents on the compound (plus an additional two DS agents that Stevens brought with him), three armed February 17 members, and five local guards.

Benghazi Events

At 9:42 p.m. Eastern European Time (EET) on September 11, the attack on the Benghazi Mission compound commenced. The February 17 members and local guards ran away as soon as the attack started. A DS agent at the compound called the Annex and requested assistance.[31] The CIA Annex Global Response Staff (GRS) team began gathering their weapons at 9:46 p.m., while Chief of Base "Bob," the Deputy Chief of Base, and the GRS Team Lead met.[32] The Chief of Base began calling local partner militias, including calling the February 17 militia to acquire a gun truck.[33] One GRS team member testified that the Chief of Base told the Annex response team, "Stand down. You need to wait."[34] However, another GRS team member and the Deputy Chief of Base testified that there was no stand-down order, just a delay as the Chief of Base made calls to try to obtain assistance.[35] At 10:05 p.m., the GRS team departed the Annex, and, due to a roadblock, did not arrive at the compound until 10:45 p.m.[36] At 11:16 p.m., the GRS and the State personnel departed the compound.[37]

At 12:34 a.m. and 1:10 a.m., militants attacked the CIA Annex.[38] Then, there was a lull for four hours.[39] The Annex was reinforced with a six-person team from Tripoli, including Doherty and two Defense Department personnel at 5:05 a.m., right before a mortar attack at 5:17 a.m.[40] CIA Annex personnel left the Annex at 6:37 a.m. and made their way to Benghazi Airport.[41] At 10:19 p.m., more than 24 hours after the initial attack, the Benghazi personnel arrived in Germany from Tripoli.[42]

Washington, DC, Actions

At 4:32 p.m. Eastern Daylight Time (EDT), the National Military Command Center (NMCC) informed Secretary of Defense Leon Panetta and Chair, Joint Chiefs of Staff Martin Dempsey of the attack. At 5:00 p.m. (EDT), Panetta and Dempsey met with Obama at the White House for a previously scheduled meeting. Obama ordered military force to be used. From 6:00 to 8:00 p.m., Panetta, Dempsey, U.S. Africa Command Commander Carter Ham, and others met at the Pentagon.[43] At 7:00 p.m., Panetta ordered assets moved, about three hours after the attack.[44] He specifically ordered the following units to deploy: (1) two Fleet Antiterrorism Security Team (FAST) platoons, stationed in Rota, Spain; (2) a U.S. European Command Special Operations Forces Commander's In-extremis Force (CIF), training in Central Europe; and (3) a United States-based special operations force (SOF).[45] At a 7:30 p.m. (EDT) White House conference call with agency representatives, the focus of the meeting suggested that the White House, Pentagon, and State Department had shifted away from responding to the Benghazi attack and more toward responding to Tripoli and unrest in the region.[46] The NMCC issued initial guidance to deploy forces at 8:39 p.m. and at 8:53 p.m.[47] One FAST team was to deploy to Benghazi and the other to Tripoli.[48]

Ham detailed the reasons for a delayed military response—a mission shifting from one of an attack on the compound to one of a hostage rescue operation to one of pursuing the attackers.[49] Ham was clear that the plan was to get forces to Sigonella Naval Air Station, Italy, which was termed an intermediate staging base to "build situational understanding, and then employ those forces."[50] The U.S. Africa Command Deputy Commander for Military Operations vice-admiral Charles Leidig confirmed Ham's decision. Leidig stated that an "execute order" was never given during the time of the attack.[51] The CIF and United States-based SOF forces were to stage in Sigonella and a FAST team was to "eventually" move into Tripoli.[52] U.S. Africa Command Director of Operations (J3) admiral Richard Landolt defined this period of gaining situational understanding as from midnight to 4 a.m. (EET).[53] Landolt summed up the reason for a lack of military response, "We weren't anticipating a second attack."[54]

During a Senate hearing on February 7, 2013, Dempsey testified, "Nothing stopped us, nothing slowed us."[55] The best military response was ground forces, and it would have taken between 13 and 15 hours for those forces to arrive.[56] In that same hearing, Dempsey, in a response to Senator John McCain's question about why the military wasn't prepared pre-September 11 to respond to a volatile situation in Libya, stated, "[The military] never received a request for support from the State Department."[57]

Figure 1.1 illustrates the chain of command of the key military leaders.[58]

Stuttgart, Germany, Actions

At U.S. Africa Command, Leidig, 17 minutes after the attack started, directed an unarmed, unmanned aerial vehicle (UAV) from Derna, Libya, to fly over the Benghazi compound.[59] It arrived at 10:53 p.m. (EET).[60] But U.S. Africa Command was reliant on U.S. European Command military assets, and the

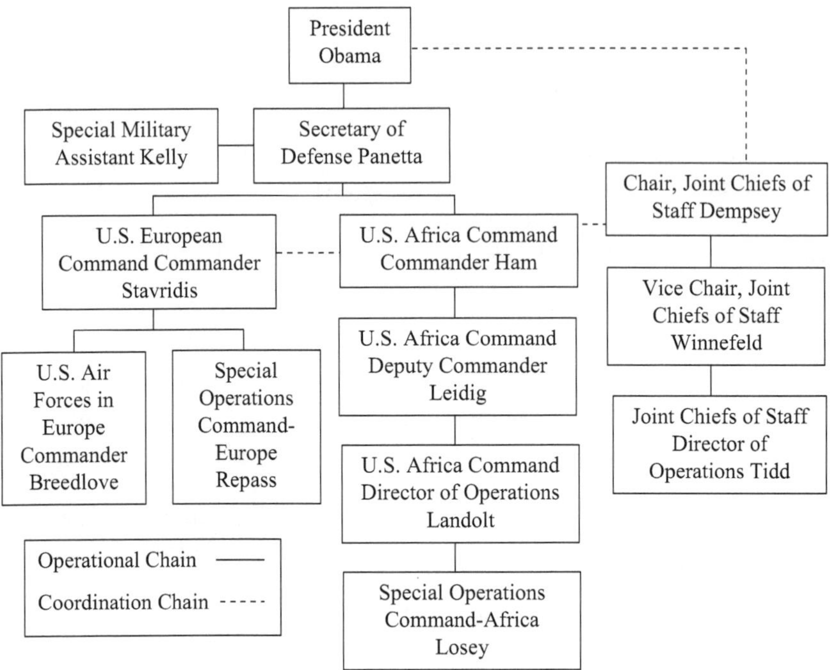

Figure 1.1 Chain of Command. *Source*: Figure created by author.

assets, as ordered by Panetta and Dempsey, were scattered throughout Europe (i.e., not positioned for crisis response).[61] The FAST platoons were stationed in Rota, Spain, but the C-130 transport planes used to move the platoons were based in Ramstein Air Base, Germany. None of the C-130s were on alert.[62] The FAST teams were further delayed about 30 minutes, as they were told to change from their uniforms to civilian clothes.[63] The CIF, which was typically available in Germany and is designed for quick reaction crisis response, was on a training exercise in Croatia.[64] Adding to the delay, the CIF had to drive 180 miles to retrieve a forklift in order to load their plane.[65] The CIF was the first of the U.S. European Command assets to be ready to deploy at 7 a.m. (EET), more than 9 hours after the attack. Major General Michael Repass, commander of Special Operations Command Europe, testified that the CIF was the first unit available because of his "own volition" he made sure the CIF was ready "about 5 or 6 hours ahead of contingency plan standards and requirements."[66]

Military forces did not start moving until 12:05 a.m., more than five hours after Secretary Panetta's orders.[67] Diplomatic clearance was approved mid-morning (EET).[68] At 2:15 p.m. (EET), a C-17 departed Ramstein and then departed Tripoli at 7:17 p.m. (EET) for its return to Germany.[69] The C-17 pilot testified that he could have been in Benghazi within four hours of being ordered to go, and he was "surprised," given the alert status that his crew was on, that issues such as diplomatic clearance, airplane security (Air Force Ravens security forces), and a necessary $30,000 cash payment to the Libyans had not been worked out.[70] Diplomatic clearance was approved at 9:38 a.m. (EET), but the pilot confirmed he would have been willing to take off without it.[71]

Military options not used included F-16s and other unspecified capabilities at Souda Bay, Greece.[72] The Air Force had two squadrons, each with 21 F-16s, at Aviano Air Base in Italy. However, the F-16s needed refueling for the 2-hour, 1,000-mile flight to Libya. Air refuelers were based in Mildenhall, England.[73] In fact, early on the morning of September 12, the F-16s were ready for takeoff, but given the lack of refuelers, the F-16s would have needed to refuel via "hot-pit" at Sigonella.[74]

Likely unknown to the operators at Aviano, Ham made the decision to not employ the F-16s, due to factors such as the presence of surface-to-air missiles in Libya, distinguishing friend from foe on the ground, and having to reconfigure the F-16s from training to combat status.[75] Additionally, Dempsey, in the Senate Committee on Armed Services (SASC) hearing on February 2, 2013, testified that the F-16s would have taken "up to 20 hours" to get to Benghazi and were "the wrong tool for the job."[76] In that same hearing, Dempsey also acknowledged assets at Souda Bay, Greece, had the capability to respond but did not respond due to "time, distance, and alert posture."[77] Ham, who was in charge of the military response, and Leidig were not aware of any aircraft assets at Souda Bay.[78] Souda Bay is a one-and-half-hour flight from Benghazi.[79]

In toto, a U.S. military response did not occur for 23 hours, when a FAST team arrived in Tripoli at 8:56 p.m. (EET) on September 12.[80] This lack of response was due to a combination of factors, including geographic distance, cross-combatant command coordination between U.S. Africa Command and U.S. European Command, and approval from national authorities in Washington.[81] Leidig specifically stated that Ham at no point gave him "specific guidance on any specific options or things to do."[82]

Brigadier General Robert Lovell, who served as the Deputy Director for Intelligence and Knowledge Development with U.S. Africa Command and was in the Joint Operations Center (JOC) during the attack, cited another reason for the lack of a military response as being due to "a lot of looking to the State Department for what it was that they wanted" and "looking back to the United States for more [communication and leadership]."[83] Leidig confirmed this perspective, "the State Department never made any request to AFRICOM for any military assistance that night."[84] Ambassador Anthony Holmes was the U.S. Africa Command deputy to the commander for civil-military activities, and he would have been the State Department adviser at U.S. Africa Command. Leidig testified that Holmes was not present in the JOC, despite being notified of the attack.[85] A State Department political adviser was in the JOC during the attack but did not provide "anything of substance."[86]

Tripoli Actions

Notified of the attack, six security personnel, including Doherty and two Defense Department personnel, departed Tripoli on a chartered Libyan aircraft.[87] Four SST members remained behind in Tripoli, due to a concern about a potential attack there. Later, Rear Admiral Brian Losey, commander of Special Operations Command-Africa, reinforced the order for the SST members to stay in Tripoli, given they were the only ones in Tripoli with "any security experience whatsoever."[88]

The end result was the death of four Americans, Christopher Stevens, Sean Smith, Glen Doherty, and Tyrone Woods, and the beginning of a political controversy during a presidential contest.

Individual Leader Actions

The actions of executive branch leaders are first listed in order of line of succession and then, in the case of the Department of Defense, in order of rank. Table 1.1 lists the individual actions of each leader from the time of the attack at 3:42 p.m. (EDT) on September 11 until the State and CIA personnel were on a flight from Tripoli to Germany, at 4:19 p.m. (EDT) on September 12.[89]

President Barack Obama

On September 11, 2012, at 5 p.m. (EDT), President Obama met with Panetta and Dempsey at the White House. Panetta testified that Obama ordered all available assets to respond.[90] The meeting lasted between 15 and 30 minutes.[91] Panetta and Dempsey did not have any further contact with Obama that night.[92] At 10:27 p.m., Obama called Clinton.[93] Communications director for the National Security Council Tommy Vietor told national media that Obama was in the White House that night but not in the Situation Room.[94]

Vice President Joseph Biden

Biden did not play a significant role, if any role at all, in response to the Benghazi attacks. In fact, for the most important meeting of the crisis—the initial White House meeting on how to respond to attacks—Biden was not present, despite being scheduled to attend. On the morning of September 11, 2012, Biden attended a 9/11 ceremony at the Flight 93 National Memorial

Table 1.1 Individual Leader Actions, September 11–12

September 11–12 (EDT)	*Obama*	*Biden*	*Clinton*	*Panetta*	*Dempsey*	*Petraeus*	*Ham*	*Stavridis*
5:00 p.m.	Meeting	Absent		Meeting	Meeting			
5:38 p.m.			Talk on Phone			Talk on Phone		
6:00 p.m.				Meeting	Meeting		Meeting	
6:49 p.m.			Calls Libyan president					
7:00 p.m.				Orders FAST, CIF, SOF deployment				
7:05 p.m.			State Department conference call					
7:30 p.m.	White House conference call with agency liaisons		White House conference call with agency liaisons	White House conference call with agency liaisons		White House conference call with agency liaisons		
8:30 p.m.					GCC conference call		GCC conference call	GCC conference call
8:39 p.m.					FAST and CIF authorizations			
8:53 p.m.					SOF authorization			
10:08 p.m.			Issues statement					
10:27 p.m.	Phone call		Phone call					
11:38 p.m.			Emails status update					

(*continued*)

Table 1.1 (Continued)

September 11–12 (EDT)	*Obama*	*Biden*	*Clinton*	*Panetta*	*Dempsey*	*Petraeus*	*Ham*	*Stavridis*
11:45 p.m.				Calls Pastor Jones				
12:05 a.m.							Orders C-17 deployment	
1:00 a.m.								CIF ready
1:19 a.m.					FAST diplomatic clearance		FAST diplomatic clearance	FAST diplomatic clearance
8:15 a.m.							C-17 departs Germany	C-17 departs Germany
10:00 a.m.							C-130 departs Rota with FAST	C-130 departs Rota with FAST
2:00 p.m.								CIF arrives at staging base
2:56 p.m.							FAST arrives in Tripoli	FAST arrives in Tripoli
3:28 p.m.					SOF arrives at the staging base			
4:19 p.m.							Personnel evacuate to Germany	Personnel evacuate to Germany

in Shanksville, PA.[95] He delivered remarks from 10:30 to 10:37 a.m. (EDT). After the remarks, Biden made an unscheduled stop at the Shanksville Volunteer Fire Department, inviting the firefighters to the White House for a beer.[96] Biden's communications and actions after the fire department stop are unknown. Biden was scheduled to return to Washington and attend the previously scheduled 5 p.m. meeting with Obama, Panetta, and Dempsey, but he did not attend the meeting.[97] No Benghazi Committee witnesses provided testimony that Biden played a significant role.[98]

Secretary of State Hillary Clinton

Shortly after 4 p.m. (EDT), Clinton was notified of the attack.[99] Deputy chief of staff for policy for the secretary of State Jacob Sullivan testified that Foreign Service Officer Steve Mull entered Clinton's office to tell her of the attack. Clinton spent the evening speaking with Obama, National Security Adviser Thomas Donilon, CIA Director David Petraeus, Libyan President Mohamed Magariaf, and Deputy Chief of Mission in Libya Gregory Hicks. She also communicated with Patrick Kennedy, DS, and Near Eastern Affairs (NEA) officials, as well as her senior leadership team. She participated in the 7:30 p.m. (EDT) conference call between the White House, Defense Department, and IC.[100] Clinton testified, "Regarding what I was doing on September 11, I was at the State Department all day and late into the night."[101] At some point (before the attack on Annex), with most of her core staff still at State Department headquarters, Clinton went home and continued to work.[102] She testified, "I did not sleep all night. I was very much focused on what we were doing."[103] This included making phone calls to Dempsey and Donilon early into the morning of September 12.[104]

In the aftermath of the attack, Clinton accepted and agreed to implement the Accountability Review Board (ARB) 29 recommendations.[105]

Secretary of Defense Leon Panetta

Panetta was notified of the attack by 4:32 p.m. (EDT), while he was at the Pentagon.[106] Obama, Panetta, and Dempsey then met at the White House at 5 p.m. for a previously scheduled meeting. Panetta testified he informed Obama of the attack at the beginning of the meeting and that Obama ordered all available assets to respond.[107] At 6 p.m., Panetta, Dempsey, Ham, vice chair of the Joint Chiefs of Staff Admiral James Winnefeld, Chief of Staff Jeremy Bash, and Senior Military Assistant General John Kelly met to identify assets.[108] Panetta relied on the recommendations of Dempsey and Ham in terms of what units were available.[109] As specified in a 7:19 p.m. email from Bash, Panetta ordered the FAST teams, CIF, and a "hostage rescue" team to deploy.[110] Panetta stated, "I issued the orders, and . . . my approach was:

Move those forces as quickly as we can."[111] According to Kelly, Panetta did not put limitations or restrictions on the deploying forces.[112] Panetta did not know the reason for the approximately three-hour delay between the NMCC initial guidance and the notification to deploy.[113] Panetta stated that he was at the Pentagon until 11 p.m. or 12 a.m. (EDT) and that he received updates throughout the night.[114]

Panetta testified it would have taken at least 9–12 hours for military assets to deploy to Libya.[115] But, he also made it clear that it was not his job to follow the "particulars of . . . who was where when, at what time."[116]

General Martin Dempsey, Chair Joint Chiefs of Staff

Dempsey was at the White House for a previously scheduled 5 p.m. (EDT) meeting with Obama and Panetta, and at 6 p.m., he met with Panetta and Ham to identify assets. At 8:30 p.m., Dempsey, Ham, and Admiral James Stavridis, Commander of U.S. European Command held a conference call. At 8:39 p.m., Dempsey ordered the CIF and FAST teams to respond. At 8:53 p.m., Dempsey ordered United States-based SOFs to respond. This was 5 hours after the attack and three-plus hours after Obama directed a response. Dempsey, like Panetta, stated that he was working until after the attack was over and went to bed after midnight (EDT). He then received a briefing at 4 a.m., when the evacuees departed Benghazi for Tripoli.[117]

General Carter Ham, Commander of U.S. Africa Command

In the days leading up to the anniversary of September 11 and with concerns about tensions in the region, Ham put U.S. Africa Command personnel on "heightened awareness," but he made the decision not to put strike aircraft, including the F-16s at Aviano, on "heightened alert," believing they would not be an "appropriate" crisis response resource.[118]

Coincidentally, Ham was visiting the Pentagon from U.S. Africa Command headquarters in Stuttgart, Germany, at the time of the attack.[119] For military leadership, Ham was the first to be informed of the attack, and he informed Dempsey. He and Dempsey briefed Panetta, before Panetta and Dempsey departed for their 5 p.m. White House meeting.[120] After the attack and during Panetta and Dempsey's meeting at the White House, Ham, who was at the Pentagon, began communicating with the U.S. Africa Command JOC, which was also communicating with the NMCC, in order to develop situational awareness.[121]

Ham was in operational control of the military response to the attack.[122] Ham met with Panetta, Dempsey, and others at 6 p.m. (EDT) to review what assets could be used to respond. By 7 p.m., Panetta ordered assets to be deployed, and Ham testified he understood what Panetta's order meant. At

8:02 p.m., Ham informed U.S. Africa Command of what assets to deploy.[123] Ham left the Pentagon between 10:30 and 11 p.m. to go to his hotel and then returned to the Pentagon around 5 or 6 a.m., after he was notified of the attack on the Annex.[124]

Admiral James Stavridis, Commander of U.S. European Command

U.S. Africa Command did not have assigned forces and was reliant on U.S. European Command (USEUCOM) forces and bases, under the command of Stavridis.[125] According to Repass, Stavridis was in Mons, Belgium, serving in his dual role as Supreme Allied Commander Europe, during the night's events and not a key player.[126]

CIA Director David Petraeus

Petraeus was working at CIA headquarters, when his chief of staff and the director of the National Clandestine Service (NCS) notified him of the attack.[127] Clinton called him at 5:38 p.m. (EDT) to inform him of the attack and that the ambassador was missing.[128] Petraeus also talked to Donilon several times that night, and he talked to the Chief of Station in Libya twice.[129] After the GRS team returned to the Annex from the Mission compound, Petraeus went home but continued working.[130] Petraeus viewed the feed from UAV flying over Benghazi at his CIA office and at his house.[131] In his conversations with Donilon, he reviewed which military assets could respond, but in general, he saw his role as gaining situational awareness and "[staying] out of [the CIA in Libya's] hair."[132] Petraeus was awakened from his bed, after the mortar attack on the Annex, and informed that CIA officers in Libya were going to "burn the base" (i.e., destroy classified material and evacuate).[133]

THE OBAMA ADMINISTRATION POST-ATTACK RESPONSE

In the aftermath of the attack, the Obama administration drew criticism for falsely claiming the Benghazi attack was due to a protest gone awry. The controversy can be traced back to events on the morning of September 11 in Cairo, Egypt. The U.S. Embassy there was dealing with protests about an anti-Islamic, U.S.-produced video, "Innocence of Muslims." The U.S. Embassy released a statement: "The Embassy of the United States in Cairo condemns the continuing efforts by misguided individuals to hurt the religious feelings of Muslims—as we condemn efforts to offend believers of all religions."[134]

September 11 Actions

State Department spokeswoman Victoria Nuland at 6:09 p.m. (EDT) first crafted a statement to be used with the press: "We have no information regarding a connection between [the Cairo protests and Benghazi attack]."[135] However, the narrative changed at a 7:30 p.m. (EDT) interagency conference call or secure video teleconference (SVTC) hosted by the White House and led by Deputy National Security Adviser Denis McDonough.[136] Participants included Clinton, White House Deputy National Security Adviser for Strategic Communications Ben Rhodes, Bash, Kelly, State Department Chief of Staff and Counselor to Clinton Cheryl Mills, Sullivan, Kennedy, Director of the National Counterterrorism Center Matthew Olsen, and National Security Staff Member Benjamin Fishman.[137] After the SVTC, the Obama administration first disavowed the Cairo statement, and then it conflated an anti-Islamic video protest in Cairo with unrest in the region, including the attack at Benghazi.[138] The narrative was encapsulated in a Sullivan-written and Clinton-issued statement at 10:08 p.m. (EDT), which stood as the official U.S. government response to the attacks: "Some have sought to justify this vicious behavior as a response to inflammatory material posted on the Internet."[139] Immediately after the Clinton statement, Republican Presidential Candidate Mitt Romney criticized the Obama administration for "sympathiz[ing] with those who waged the attacks."[140]

Clinton was telling a different story privately, never mentioning a protest. In a phone call to Libyan president Magariaf, she stated that "Ansar as-Sharia [*sic*]" claimed responsibility. In an email to her daughter, Clinton claimed "an Al Queda-like [*sic*] group" conducted the attack.[141]

September 12 Actions

At 7:00 a.m., the Executive Coordinator of the Presidential Daily Brief delivered a Situation Report to Chief of Staff Jacob Lew and gave a copy to an usher to deliver to Obama. The report contained a line "the presence of armed assailants from the outset suggests this was an intentional assault and not the escalation of a peaceful protest."[142] Later that morning, Obama, with Clinton present, issued Rhodes-drafted remarks in the Rose Garden:

> We reject all efforts to denigrate the religious beliefs of others. But there is absolutely no justification to this type of senseless violence. . . . No acts of terror will ever shake the resolve of this great nation, alter that character, or eclipse the light of the values that we stand for.[143]

Clinton, in a speech drafted by Sullivan, Dan Schwerin, and Megan Rooney, repeated Obama's claim: "Some have sought to justify this vicious behavior, along with the protest that took place at our Embassy in Cairo yesterday, as a response to inflammatory material posted on the Internet."[144]

Privately, Clinton continued to state it was a terrorist attack, telling Egyptian prime minister Hesham Kandil: "We know that the attack in Libya had nothing to do with the film."[145] As shown in Table 1.2, for September 12, the administration used the Sullivan-drafted September 11 statement for its narrative.[146]

September 13 Actions

In the morning, Clinton repeated the claims from her September 11 statement and September 12 remarks in her September 13 "Remarks at the Opening Plenary of the U.S.-Morocco Strategic Dialogue" speech: "I also want to take a moment to address the video circulating on the Internet that has led to these protests in a number of countries."[147] Rhodes copied phrases from Clinton's September 13 remarks and emailed out "Talking Points on Movie" at 12:02 p.m. (EDT) for government officials to use when speaking about the attack.[148]

September 14 Actions

For the first time, the IC became involved in the administration's post-attack narrative. At 11:15 a.m. (EDT), CIA's Office of Terrorism Analysis drafted and sent out for coordination six unclassified bullet points or talking points in response to a request from the House Permanent Select Committee on

Table 1.2 Administration Statements, September 11–12

10:08 p.m. September 11 State Department Statement	*September 12 Obama Rose Garden Remarks*	*September 12 Clinton State Department Remarks*
Some have sought to justify this vicious behavior as a response to inflammatory material posted on the Internet.	–	Some have sought to justify this vicious behavior, along with the protest that took place at our Embassy in Cairo yesterday, as a response to inflammatory material posted on the Internet.
The United States deplores any intentional effort to denigrate the religious beliefs of others.	We reject all efforts to denigrate the religious beliefs of others.	–
There is never any justification for violent acts of this kind.	But there is absolutely no justification for this type of senseless violence. None.	But let me be clear—there is no justification for this, none.

Intelligence (HPSCI). This is what is referred to as the HPSCI talking points. Later that afternoon, the CIA's Office of Public Affairs (OPA) sent the talking points to Rhodes, Vietor, and other administration officials. The first bullet in the talking points contained the word "attacks" in describing what occurred in Benghazi.[149] By 5:09 p.m., CIA's OPA sent revised talking points, in which the word "demonstration" had replaced "attacks."[150] Later that evening and in an email, Nuland objected to a bullet that stated CIA had produced "pieces on the threat of extremists linked to al-Qa'ida in Benghazi and eastern Libya."[151]

Rhodes also spent Friday coordinating which administration official would appear on Sunday political talk shows. He first selected Clinton, who declined via her staff, and his second choice Donilon also declined.[152] So, in the afternoon, he called Rice and asked her. She reluctantly accepted.[153]

After Rhodes lined up Rice to appear on the Sunday talk shows, he began to coordinate the talking points for her appearance. In what would trigger the creation of the Benghazi Committee, Rhodes sent out an email at 8:09 p.m. ("Subject: RE: PREP CALL with Susan: Saturday at 4:00 p.m. ET"), stating that one of the "Goals" was to convey the following: "To underscore that these protests are rooted in an Internet video, and not a broader failure of policy."[154] Notably, Rhodes copied Clinton's September 13 Moroccan speech to write the talking points for Rice. Admitting he was unaware of any intelligence linking a video to the attacks, Rhodes wrote the "Goals" and "Top-lines" talking points independent of the HPSCI talking points.[155] In fact, Rhodes clarified that only the Q&A on page two of his 8:09 p.m. email was taken from the HPSCI talking points.[156] The Q&A was as follows:

> Q: What's your response to the Independent story that says we have intelligence 48 hours in advance of the Benghazi attack that was ignored? Was this an intelligence failure?
>
> A: We are not aware of any actionable intelligence indicating that an attack on the U.S. Mission in Benghazi was planned or imminent. The currently available information suggests that the demonstrations in Benghazi were spontaneously inspired by the protests at the US Embassy in Cairo and evolved into a direct assault against the US Consulate and subsequently its annex.[157]

September 15 Actions

On Saturday morning at 11:08 a.m. (EDT), Deputy CIA Director Michael Morell, who had attended a Deputies Committee meeting earlier that morning, put the final edits on the HPSCI talking points and sent them to administration officials, including Rhodes.[158] Rhodes made one final edit at 11:26 a.m. (EDT), replacing the term "Consulate" with "diplomatic post."[159] Meanwhile, Rice spent the morning preparing for her Sunday talk show appearances. She reviewed intelligence reports and a briefing book that Communications Director Erin Pelton had prepared for her.[160] At 2:44 p.m. (EDT), Sullivan sent the HPSCI talking points to Susan Rice's office and stated the office should "confirm w Ben [Rhodes] that Susan [Rice] can deploy tomorrow."[161]

During a 4:00 p.m. (EDT) conference call, Rhodes, Vietor, Pelton, Deputy to the U.S. Permanent Representative to the United Nations Rexon Ryu, Chief of Staff Salman Ahmed, Special Assistant to the President and Director of Broadcast Media Dag Vega, and Senior Adviser to President David Plouffe prepared Rice for her talk show appearances.[162] During the preparation session, Benghazi was "barely mentioned," no White House, State Department, or Defense Department experts participated, and the talking points only had six bullet points and five questions and answers.[163] Rice stated, "I don't have any recollection of talking about [the Benghazi attacks] in any depth" and "I don't recall us talking about the [HPSCI] talking points."[164] The conference call was short, lasting only 30–45 minutes.[165]

September 16 Actions

The preparation culminated in Rice claiming on the Sunday talk shows that the attack was due to an anti-Islamic video. On ABC's *This Week*, Rice stated, "But our current best assessment, based on the information that we have at present, is that, in fact, what this began as, it was a spontaneous—not a premeditated—response to what had transpired in Cairo."[166] Rice further stated, "What happened this week in Cairo, in Benghazi, in many other parts of the region . . . was a result—a direct result of a heinous and offensive video." In her testimony to the Benghazi Committee, Rice confirmed that she "quite possibly" misspoke in drawing a link between the video and the Benghazi attack.[167] Rice's comments infuriated Magariaf, who also appeared on *Face the Nation*, who then refused to cooperate in the investigation.[168]

As shown in Table 1.3, it took until September 13 for the administration to consolidate its messaging, and then it used this messaging through Rice's Sunday talk show appearances.[169] For the talk shows, Rice used Rhodes's phrases that he had copied from Clinton's September 13 Moroccan remarks, much more so than the HPSCI talking points.

Post-September 16 Actions

The administration continued its messaging through September 20.[170] Olsen forced a narrative change when he testified before the Senate Homeland Security and Governmental Affairs Committee on September 19. Olsen

Table 1.3 Administration Statements, September 13–16

September 13 Clinton Moroccan Statement	*September 14 Rhodes Email*	*September 16 Rice Talk Show Statements*	*IC Talking Points*
I also want to take a moment to address the video circulating on the Internet that has led to these protests in a number of countries.	To underscore that these protests are rooted in an Internet video and not a broader failure of policy.	That what happened initially [in Benghazi] was that it was a spontaneous reaction to what had just transpired in Cairo as a consequence of the video (*FOX News Sunday*).	The currently available information suggests that the demonstrations in Benghazi were spontaneously inspired by the protests at the U.S. Embassy in Cairo and evolved into a direct assault against the U.S. diplomatic post and subsequently its annex.
Let me state very clearly—and I hope it is obvious—that the U.S. government had absolutely nothing to do with this video. We absolutely reject its content and message.	Third, we've made our view on this video crystal clear. The U.S. government had nothing to do with it. We reject its message and contents.	What happened this week in Cairo, in Benghazi, in many other parts of the region . . . was a direct result—a direct result of a heinous and offensive video that was widely disseminated, that the U.S. government had nothing to do with, which we made clear is reprehensible and disgusting (ABC's *This Week*).	–
To us, to me personally, this video is disgusting and reprehensible. It appears to have a deeply cynical purpose: to denigrate a great religion and to provoke rage. But as I said yesterday, there is no justification, none at all, for responding to this video with violence.	We find it disgusting and reprehensible. But there is absolutely no justification at all for responding to this movie with violence.	This is a response to a hateful and offensive video that was widely disseminated throughout the Arab and Muslim world. Obviously, our view is that there is absolutely no excuse for violence and that what has happened is condemnable (NBC's *Meet the Press*).	–

viewed what happened in Benghazi "as a terrorist attack from the outset" and testified to that fact.[171] He also did not mention a video.[172]

Post-2012 Presidential Election Actions

On December 18, 2012, the ARB, chaired by Ambassador Thomas Pickering and Admiral Michael Mullen, released its report, making 5 findings and 29 recommendations (24 of which were unclassified). It determined that the security in Benghazi was "inadequate" and "grossly inadequate to deal with the attack that took place" due to "leadership and management deficiencies."[173] Boswell and Lamb resigned on the same day as the report's release.[174]

Clinton, in testifying before the Senate Foreign Relations Committee on January 23, 2013, and in response to Senator Ron Johnson asking why she had not called evacuees to determine there was no protest before the attack, responded, "Was it because of a protest or was it because of guys out for a walk one night who decided they would go kill some Americans? What difference, at this point, does it make?"[175] The comment would become controversial, as Republicans used it to state that Clinton was indifferent to the deaths of Americans. Both before the Senate Foreign Relations Committee and later the same day before the House Foreign Affairs Committee, Clinton unambiguously stated "the terrorist attacks in Benghazi" at the beginning of her prepared statements.[176]

CONCLUSION

The tragedy in Libya is best understood through the strategic context of a State Department effort to facilitate a democratic transition in Libya in 2011–2012. This improbable effort relied on faulty assumptions and an optimistic analysis of the domestic and regional security environment. Obama administration officials believed the Arab Spring uprisings presented a window of opportunity to liberate Libyans from decades of brutal, authoritarian rule and to address the root causes of the population's mounting grievances through democracy. However, U.S. policy in Libya misunderstood the complex political, economic, and social dynamics and failed to identify the growing strength of extremist networks in Libya and across northern Africa as a key destabilizing factor. Moreover, the September 11, 2012, attack revealed the geographic constraints of executing U.S. policy and crisis response in Africa, as decision-makers within the bureaucracy spanned from Tripoli to Stuttgart to Washington, DC, and assets were not available to respond for 23 hours.

As President Obama, Vice President Biden, and Secretary Clinton looked to Panetta, Dempsey, and General Ham for a response, plans and decisions rested on poor communication and the incorrect assessment that the compound was not actively under attack. Following this failure to understand and adapt to the ongoing situation, President Obama and Secretary Clinton turned to the speechwriting abilities of Rhodes and Sullivan to craft a post-attack narrative. The narrative began on September 11 with Clinton stating, "Some have sought to justify this vicious behavior as a response to inflammatory material posted on the Internet" and ended on September 16 with Rice affirming, "That what happened initially [in Benghazi] was that it was a spontaneous reaction to what had just transpired in Cairo as a consequence of the video."[177]

Tragedies such as the Benghazi attack require careful, considerate study to derive lessons learned to address security lapses. However, the national consensus to investigate this tragedy became an unproductive partisan battle. The following chapter presents an explanation for the devolution of investigating such tragedies to score-settling among political parties.

NOTES

1. "Hearing 4," Hearing before the Select Committee on the Events Surrounding the 2012 Terrorist Attack in Benghazi House of Representatives, October 22, 2015, 361. Notably, the Obama administration used military force in Libya and did not seek authorization from Congress. Exceeding the 60-day limit of the War Powers Resolution, Obama argued that his military actions did not meet the definition of "hostilities" as defined by the resolution. See Louis Fisher, "Military Operations in Libya: No War? No Hostilities?," *Presidential Studies Quarterly* 42, no. 1 (2012): 181.

2. "Benghazi: The Attacks and the Lessons Learned," Hearing before the Committee on Foreign Relations U.S. Senate, January 23, 2013, S. Hrg. 113–184, 17.

3. "Hearing 4," Hearing before the Select Committee, 283.

4. "Benghazi: The Attacks," Hearing before the Committee on Foreign Relations, 23; "Benghazi, Instability, and a New Government: Success and Failures of U.S. Intervention in Libya," Hearing before the Committee on Oversight and Government Reform House of Representatives, May 1, 2014, Serial No. 113–110, 4.

5. Select Committee on the Events Surrounding the 2012 Terrorist Attack in Benghazi, *Final Report of the Select Committee on the Events Surrounding the 2012 Terrorist Attack in Benghazi: House of Representatives*; *Together with Additional and Minority Views* (114th Cong., 2d sess., 2016. H. Rept. 114-848), 294; Jacob Sullivan, *Interviews of Witnesses Before the Select Committee on the Events Surrounding the 2012 Terrorist Attack in Benghazi: House of Representatives* (114th Cong., 2d sess., Volume 6, 2016), 520–21.

6. "Benghazi: The Attacks," Hearing before the Committee on Foreign Relations, 22; "Hearing 4," Hearing before the Select Committee, 291; Select Committee, *Final Report*, 301.

7. Select Committee, *Final Report*, 304–305.

8. Select Committee, *Final Report*, 306.

9. Select Committee, *Final Report*, 314–16. Notably, the security environment and small staff precluded an abundance of reporting. See Select Committee, *Final Report*, 316.

10. Matt Olsen, *Interviews of Witnesses Before the Select Committee on the Events Surrounding the 2012 Terrorist Attack in Benghazi: House of Representatives* (114th Cong., 2d sess., Volume 9, 2016), 178–81.

11. Select Committee, *Final Report*, 134, 554. It should be noted that other countries, such as Italy, France, Turkey, and Malta, also maintained a diplomatic presence in Libya. See *Report of the U.S. Senate Select Committee on Intelligence Review of the Terrorist Attacks on U.S. Facilities in Benghazi, Libya, September 11–12, 2012, together with Additional Views*. 113th Cong., 2d sess., 2014. S. Report. 113–134, 26.

12. "Review of the Benghazi Attacks and Unanswered Questions," Hearing before the Committee on Oversight and Government Reform House of Representatives, September 19, 2013, Serial No. 113–59, 10; Select Committee, *Final Report*, 348.

13. "Benghazi: Exposing Failure and Recognizing Courage," Hearing before the Committee on Oversight and Government Reform House of Representatives, May 8, 2013, Serial No. 113 30, 85; "The Security Failures of Benghazi," Hearing before the Committee on Oversight and Government Reform House of Representatives, October 10, 2012, Serial No. 112–193, 99; Select Committee, *Final Report*, 348.

14. Select Committee, *Final Report*, 309.

15. By December 2014, the State Department had 285 diplomatic facilities worldwide and none of them were designated as temporary compounds. See "Hearing 2," Hearing before the Select Committee on the Events Surrounding the 2012 Terrorist Attack in Benghazi House of Representatives, December 10, 2014, 37–38.

16. One of the ARB recommendations was the establishment of a five-member independent panel to evaluate State Department operations in high risk, high threat areas. Keil was a member of the panel. "Hearing 1," Hearing before the Select Committee on the Events Surrounding the 2012 Terrorist Attack in Benghazi House of Representatives, September 17, 2014, 43.

17. Charlene Lamb, *Interviews of Witnesses Before the Select Committee on the Events Surrounding the 2012 Terrorist Attack in Benghazi: House of Representatives* (114th Cong., 2d sess., Volume 8, 2016), 231.

18. Select Committee, *Final Report*, 318, 536.

19. Select Committee, *Final Report*, 317–18.

20. Kennedy noted that security for a complex is based on its size, the movement of its personnel (i.e., how often those personnel leave the complex), the volatility of the area, the threats, and host-nation capability. See Patrick Kennedy, *Interviews of Witnesses Before the Select Committee on the Events Surrounding the 2012 Terrorist Attack in Benghazi: House of Representatives* (114th Cong., 2d sess., Volume 11, 2016), 1386–88.

21. Select Committee, *Final Report*, 313.

22. Select Committee, *Final Report*, 319. According to DS Desk Officer Brian Papanu, Lamb only approved three DS agents in Benghazi because she thought they

were being used inappropriately as drivers. See "Review of the Benghazi Attacks," Hearing before the Committee on Oversight and Government Reform, 271–72.

23. Select Committee, *Final Report*, 318.

24. Select Committee, *Final Report*, 325–26.

25. Select Committee, *Final Report*, 329–30. Lamb testified that the lack of security in Benghazi was not due to a lack of budget. See "Security Failures of Benghazi," Hearing before the Committee on Oversight and Government Reform, 97.

26. Select Committee, *Final Report*, 333.

27. Select Committee, *Final Report*, 15. Kennedy based his decision on input from the Bureau of Diplomatic Security and Lamb. See "Benghazi: Where is the State Department Accountability?," Hearing before the Committee on Foreign Affairs House of Representatives, September 18, 2013, Serial No. 113–93, 86; Kennedy, *Interviews of Witnesses*, 1171–72, 1175.

28. Select Committee, *Final Report*, 546–47.

29. Select Committee, *Final Report*, 338.

30. "Benghazi: Exposing Failure," Hearing before the Committee on Oversight and Government Reform, 40, 89; Sullivan, *Interviews of Witnesses*, 548–49; Select Committee, *Final Report*, 328.

31. Select Committee, *Final Report*, 31–32, 36.

32. Mike Rogers and C.A. Ruppersberger, *Investigative Report on the Terrorist Attacks on U.S. Facilities in Benghazi, Libya, September 11–12, 2012* (Washington, DC: U.S. House of Representatives Permanent Select Committee on Intelligence, 2014), 4; Select Committee, *Final Report*, 38.

33. Select Committee, *Final Report*, 38–40.

34. Select Committee, *Final Report*, 46–47.

35. Select Committee, *Final Report*, 42, 48. Petraeus testified that no one presented evidence of a stand down order to him, and that the chief of base made a prudent decision to try to obtain local militia support. See David Petraeus, *Interviews of Witnesses Before the Select Committee on the Events Surrounding the 2012 Terrorist Attack in Benghazi: House of Representatives* (114th Cong., 2d sess., Volume 11, 2016), 940, 1036.

36. Select Committee, *Final Report*, 49–51.

37. Select Committee, *Final Report*, 71.

38. Select Committee, *Final Report*, 75–76.

39. Select Committee, *Final Report*, 78.

40. Select Committee, *Final Report*, 101, 103; "Department of Defense's Response to the Attack on U.S. Facilities in Benghazi, Libya, and the Findings of its Internal Review following the Attack," Hearing before the Committee on Armed Services United States Senate, February 7, 2013, S. Hrg. 113–164, 75.

41. Select Committee, *Final Report*, 112.

42. Select Committee, *Final Report*, 113.

43. Jeremy Bash, *Interviews of Witnesses Before the Select Committee on the Events Surrounding the 2012 Terrorist Attack in Benghazi: House of Representatives* (114th Cong., 2d sess., Volume 8, 2016), 647–48.

44. Select Committee, *Final Report*, 70–71.

45. Select Committee, *Final Report*, 573; "Department of Defense's Response," Hearing before the Committee on Armed Services, 3–4, 12. Panetta stated that he did not know there was a compound in Benghazi before the attack. See Leon Panetta, *Interviews of Witnesses Before the Select Committee on the Events Surrounding the 2012 Terrorist Attack in Benghazi: House of Representatives* (114th Cong., 2d sess., Volume 8, 2016), 336.

46. Select Committee, *Final Report*, 125.

47. Select Committee, *Final Report*, 93, 574; Panetta, *Interviews of Witnesses*, 324; Carter Ham, *Interviews of Witnesses Before the Select Committee on the Events Surrounding the 2012 Terrorist Attack in Benghazi: House of Representatives* (114th Cong., 2d sess., Volume 10, 2016), 1432.

48. Charles Joseph Leidig, Jr., *Interviews of Witnesses Before the Select Committee on the Events Surrounding the 2012 Terrorist Attack in Benghazi: House of Representatives* (114th Cong., 2d sess., Volume 10, 2016), 623; Bash, *Interviews of Witnesses*, 653. The FAST team originally slated to deploy to Benghazi was redirected to Tripoli, after U.S. personnel in Benghazi moved from there. See Leidig, *Interviews of Witnesses*, 618.

49. Ham, *Interviews of Witnesses*, 1317, 1329. As a note, the FAST platoon commander testified that FAST units are not designed for hostage rescue but rather for securing facilities. See FAST Platoon Commander, *Interviews of Witnesses Before the Select Committee on the Events Surrounding the 2012 Terrorist Attack in Benghazi: House of Representatives* (114th Cong., 2d sess., Volume 6, 2016), 35, 86. Petraeus also testified that only the CIF was capable of performing a hostage rescue mission, see Petraeus, *Interviews of Witnesses*, 909–10.

50. Ham, *Interviews of Witnesses*, 1328; Leidig, *Interviews of Witnesses*, 597–98; Richard Landolt, *Interviews of Witnesses Before the Select Committee on the Events Surrounding the 2012 Terrorist Attack in Benghazi: House of Representatives* (114th Cong., 2d sess., Volume 10, 2016), 928; James Winnefeld, *Interviews of Witnesses Before the Select Committee on the Events Surrounding the 2012 Terrorist Attack in Benghazi: House of Representatives* (114th Cong., 2d sess., Volume 9, 2016), 659–60.

51. Rear Admiral Brian Losey, commander of Special Operations Command-Africa, confirmed he did not receive orders to deploy special operation forces under his command. He stated that the only forces that were available for "reposturing" was the CIF under U.S. European Command, and he did not take operational control of the CIF after they arrived at the ISB. See Brian Losey, *Interviews of Witnesses Before the Select Committee on the Events Surrounding the 2012 Terrorist Attack in Benghazi: House of Representatives* (114th Cong., 2d sess., Volume 11, 2016), 208, 215, 233.

52. Select Committee, *Final Report*, 100, 123; Leidig, *Interviews of Witnesses*, 598–99.

53. Landolt, *Interviews of Witnesses*, 941.

54. Landolt, *Interviews of Witnesses*, 931.

55. "Department of Defense's Response," Hearing before the Committee on Armed Services, 66.

56. "Department of Defense's Response," Hearing before the Committee on Armed Services, 52–53.

57. "Department of Defense's Response," Hearing before the Committee on Armed Services, 28.

58. The chain of command is hierarchical, but as detailed, Panetta, Dempsey, and Ham worked in collaboration.

59. Select Committee, *Final Report*, 573; Ham, *Interviews of Witnesses*, 1273; Leidig, *Interviews of Witnesses*, 565. The UAV was relieved later in the night by a second UAV. See Leidig, *Interviews of Witnesses*, 605.

60. "Department of Defense's Response," Hearing before the Committee on Armed Services, 12.

61. Select Committee, *Final Report*, 114. Joint Chiefs of Staff Director of Operations (J3) Admiral Kurt Tidd confirmed that the Joint Staff asked U.S. Africa Command and U.S. European Command what forces were available to respond. See Kurt Tidd, *Interviews of Witnesses Before the Select Committee on the Events Surrounding the 2012 Terrorist Attack in Benghazi: House of Representatives* (114th Cong., 2d sess., Volume 9, 2016), 1411.

62. Select Committee, *Final Report*, 58.

63. "Department of Defense's Response," Hearing before the Committee on Armed Services, 79. The FAST platoon commander testified that the Marines changed three times their uniforms and civilian clothes. See FAST Platoon Commander, *Interviews of Witnesses*, 41.

64. Select Committee, *Final Report*, 59.

65. Michael Repass, *Interviews of Witnesses Before the Select Committee on the Events Surrounding the 2012 Terrorist Attack in Benghazi: House of Representatives* (114th Cong., 2d sess., Volume 10, 2016), 442–43.

66. Repass, *Interviews of Witnesses*, 445.

67. Select Committee, *Final Report*, 71, 574.

68. Select Committee, *Final Report*, 118–19. The C-17 pilot stated that he would have been willing to take off without the diplomatic clearance approval. See C-17 Pilot, *Interviews of Witnesses Before the Select Committee on the Events Surrounding the 2012 Terrorist Attack in Benghazi: House of Representatives* (114th Cong., 2d sess., Volume 9, 2016), 1198–99.

69. Select Committee, *Final Report*, 112–13. The C-17 pilot testified that his crew was the only European theater crew in "BRAVO" standby alert status (i.e., allowed one hour to report from time of alert and then two hours 45 minutes for mission preparation) from September 10–12. An intelligence officer informed the C-17 pilot that unbeknownst to the pilot, someone had fired a missile at the C-17 as it took off from Tripoli. See C-17 Pilot, *Interviews of Witnesses*, 1116, 1152, 1155, 1173–74, 1183.

70. C-17 Pilot, *Interviews of Witnesses*, 1192, 1194–95.

71. C-17 Pilot, *Interviews of Witnesses*, 1198–99.

72. Select Committee, *Final Report*, 60, 64. Former Defense Intelligence Agency (DIA) Director Michael Flynn volunteered to Benghazi Committee investigators that the military "could have used a lot more imagination" in responding to the attack,

that DIA issued intelligence reports detailing both protests and an al Qaeda attack, and that he wasn't asked to review the Intelligence Community talking points. See Michael Flynn, *Interviews of Witnesses Before the Select Committee on the Events Surrounding the 2012 Terrorist Attack in Benghazi: House of Representatives* (114th Cong., 2d sess., Volume 6, 2016), 936, 977–78, 985–86, 996.

73. Select Committee, *Final Report*, 59.

74. F-16 Crew Chief, *Interviews of Witnesses Before the Select Committee on the Events Surrounding the 2012 Terrorist Attack in Benghazi: House of Representatives* (114th Cong., 2d sess., Volume 11, 2016), 522–24, 530–31, 546–47.

75. Select Committee, *Final Report*, 60; Howard McKeon, *Majority Interim Report: Benghazi Investigation Update* (Washington, DC: House Armed Services Committee, 2014), 19; Ham, *Interviews of Witnesses*, 1281. Leidig agreed with Ham's decision not to use the F-16s. See Leidig, *Interviews of Witnesses*, 609. Ham did acknowledge and Losey and Petraeus confirmed that the special operations personnel in Tripoli and Benghazi had the capability of directing the action of strike aircraft for a close air support mission. See Ham, *Interviews of Witnesses*, 1304–305; Losey, *Interviews of Witnesses*, 210; Petraeus, *Interviews of Witnesses*, 964. Former Joint Staff Vice Director of Operations Major General Roberson, a veteran F-16 pilot, testified that a F-16 show of force flight potentially would have worked, but less so with experienced enemy combatants, who were conditioned to it. See McKeon, *Majority Interim Report*, 20. Commander of U.S. Air Forces in Europe General Philip Breedlove testified that enemy combatants would likely have responded to it by leaving, as they associate "the sound of fighters with bombs going off." See Philip Breedlove, *Interviews of Witnesses Before the Select Committee on the Events Surrounding the 2012 Terrorist Attack in Benghazi: House of Representatives* (114th Cong., 2d sess., Volume 10, 2016), 75–76.

76. "Department of Defense's Response," Hearing before the Committee on Armed Services, 38.

77. "Department of Defense's Response," Hearing before the Committee on Armed Services, 29. Dempsey was referring to the U-28, a single-engine aircraft that is part of Air Force Special Operations Command. See Leidig, *Interviews of Witnesses*, 653.

78. Ham, *Interviews of Witnesses*, 1307–308; Leidig, *Interviews of Witnesses*, 653–54.

79. The Benghazi Committee wrote three sentences in its report on this issue and did not identify the assets on Souda Bay nor why they did not respond. See Select Committee, *Final Report*, 64.

80. Select Committee, *Final Report*, 574. The FAST platoon commander testified that his unit was notified at 2:30 a.m., ready at 5:45 a.m., the C-130s arrived around 12 p.m., and they took off around 4 p.m. (all times EET). See FAST Platoon Commander, *Interviews of Witnesses*, 39–40, 85. Given that personnel had already been evacuated from Benghazi, the other FAST team deployed to Souda Bay "to posture in response to any additional regional unrest." See "Department of Defense's Response," Hearing before the Committee on Armed Services, 91.

81. Mullen served as the ARB panel's military expert, and he concluded that the "military did everything they possibly could that night [of September 11]." See

"Review of the Benghazi Attacks," Hearing before the Committee on Oversight and Government Reform, 35–36.

82. Leidig, *Interviews of Witnesses*, 606.

83. "Benghazi, Instability," Hearing before the Committee on Oversight and Government Reform, 54, 64. Lovell clarified that U.S. Africa Command was "different" than a traditional combatant command. It was structured to support interagency efforts, specifically the State Department. See "Benghazi, Instability," Hearing before the Committee on Oversight and Government Reform, 57. Kelly was also critical of the State Department, speculating that a delayed military response was due to having to wait on the State Department to obtain diplomatic clearance. See John Kelly, *Interviews of Witnesses Before the Select Committee on the Events Surrounding the 2012 Terrorist Attack in Benghazi: House of Representatives* (114th Cong., 2d sess., Volume 9, 2016), 1271, 1283.

84. Leidig, *Interviews of Witnesses*, 671.

85. Leidig, *Interviews of Witnesses*, 612–13. Leidig, on the other hand, stayed at the JOC for a continuous 48 hours. See Leidig, *Interviews of Witnesses*, 588, 613.

86. Leidig, *Interviews of Witnesses*, 615.

87. Select Committee, *Final Report*, 55, 573.

88. McKeon, *Majority Interim Report*, 23.

89. Select Committee, *Final Report*, 70–71, 559–61, 573–74.

90. "Department of Defense's Response," Hearing before the Committee on Armed Services, 39.

91. Panetta, *Interviews of Witnesses*, 312–13, 393.

92. "Department of Defense's Response," Hearing before the Committee on Armed Services, 39–40, 42–43.

93. Select Committee, *Final Report*, 560.

94. Fox News, "Ex-White House spokesman downplays controversy over Benghazi talking points," *Fox News*, May 2, 2014, https://www.foxnews.com/politics/ex-white-house-spokesman-downplays-controversy-over-benghazi-talking-points, accessed January 10, 2022. Petraeus testified that Donilon informed him that he (Donilon) was keeping Obama informed throughout the night. See Petraeus, *Interviews of Witnesses*, 990.

95. Megan Slack, "Marking the Eleventh Anniversary of 9/11," *Obama White House*, September 11, 2012, https://obamawhitehouse.archives.gov/blog/2012/09/11/marking-eleventh-anniversary-911, accessed November 18, 2021.

96. Lucy Madison, "Biden Beer Invitation: 'No Malarkey,'" *CBS News*, September 11, 2012, https://www.cbsnews.com/news/biden-beer-invitation-no-malarkey/, accessed November 18, 2021.

97. Lynn Sweet, "President Obama Official Schedule and Guidance, Sept. 11, 2012. 9–11 Observance," *Chicago Sun-Times*, November 19, 2013, https://chicago.suntimes.com/politics/2013/11/19/18547803/president-obama-official-schedule-and-guidance-sept-11-2012-9-11-observance, accessed November 18, 2021. The attendees were Obama, Panetta, and Dempsey. See Select Committee, *Final Report*, 69, 559. Panetta did not recall Biden attending the meeting. See Panetta, *Interviews of Witnesses*, 315–16.

98. Biden was not on the list to speak publicly on TV shows for the administration and is not list as one of the "Significant Persons" in the Benghazi Committee report (Biden's name is cited a total of one time in the report). See Select Committee, *Final Report*, 197, 423, Appendix B. Biden attended the September 14 memorial service at Joint Base Andrews, where he allegedly made a controversial remark. See Jake Tapper, "Father of Slain Former SEAL, New Report, Raise Questions About Response to Benghazi Attack," *ABC News*, October 26, 2012, https://abcnews.go.com/blogs/politics/2012/10/father-of-slain-former-seal-new-report-raise, accessed November 18, 2021. During the vice presidential debate on October 11, 2012, Biden wrongly stated, "We weren't told they wanted more security. We did not know they wanted more security there." See Glenn Kessler, "Fact Check: State Department Contradicts Biden," *Washington Post*, October 11, 2012, https://www.washington-post.com/news/post-politics/wp/2012/10/11/fact-check-state-department-contradicts-biden/, accessed January 10, 2022.

99. "Benghazi: The Attacks," Hearing before the Committee on Foreign Relations, 13.

100. Sullivan, *Interviews of Witnesses*, 528–29, 662–65; "Benghazi: The Attacks," Hearing before the Committee on Foreign Relations, 14, 58; "Benghazi: Exposing Failure," Hearing before the Committee on Oversight and Government Reform, 96.

101. "Benghazi: The Attacks," Hearing before the Committee on Foreign Relations, 13.

102. "Hearing 4," Hearing before the Select Committee, 393–94.

103. "Hearing 4," Hearing before the Select Committee, 393.

104. "Benghazi: The Attacks," Hearing before the Committee on Foreign Relations, 14, 58. Dempsey testified he did not have any conversations with Clinton between the time of the attack on the compound and the mortar attack on the Annex. See "Department of Defense's Response," Hearing before the Committee on Armed Services, 53, 94.

105. "Benghazi: The Attacks," Hearing before the Committee on Foreign Relations, 8, 38–39.

106. Panetta, *Interviews of Witnesses*, 310.

107. Panetta, *Interviews of Witnesses*, 311–12.

108. Panetta, *Interviews of Witnesses*, 313, 316.

109. Panetta, *Interviews of Witnesses*, 388; Ham, *Interviews of Witnesses*, 1284.

110. Select Committee, *Final Report*, 83, 560; Panetta, *Interviews of Witnesses*, 314, 319.

111. Panetta, *Interviews of Witnesses*, 322.

112. Kelly, *Interviews of Witnesses*, 1266.

113. Bash, *Interviews of Witnesses*, 807.

114. "Department of Defense's Response," Hearing before the Committee on Armed Services, 78, 95; Panetta, *Interviews of Witnesses*, 337, 403.

115. "Department of Defense's Response," Hearing before the Committee on Armed Services, 17; Panetta, *Interviews of Witnesses*, 409, 459.

116. Panetta, *Interviews of Witnesses*, 371.

117. "Department of Defense's Response," Hearing before the Committee on Armed Services, 78, 95.

118. Ham, *Interviews of Witnesses*, 1267–68.

119. Ham, *Interviews of Witnesses*, 1271.

120. McKeon, *Majority Interim Report*, 14; Ham, *Interviews of Witnesses*, 1272–73.

121. Ham, *Interviews of Witnesses*, 1276.

122. "Department of Defense's Response," Hearing before the Committee on Armed Services, 79; Ham, *Interviews of Witnesses*, 1281.

123. Panetta, *Interviews of Witnesses*, 323.

124. Ham, *Interviews of Witnesses*, 1362–63.

125. Select Committee, *Final Report*, 57–58.

126. Repass, *Interviews of Witnesses*, 461.

127. Petraeus, *Interviews of Witnesses*, 995.

128. Petraeus, *Interviews of Witnesses*, 903, 1038; Select Committee, *Final Report*, 559.

129. Petraeus, *Interviews of Witnesses*, 908, 990, 995, 997.

130. Petraeus, *Interviews of Witnesses*, 908, 1042.

131. Petraeus, *Interviews of Witnesses*, 915.

132. Petraeus, *Interviews of Witnesses*, 998, 1046.

133. Petraeus, *Interviews of Witnesses*, 1047.

134. New York Times, "What They Said Before and After the Attack in Libya," *New York Times*, September 12, 2012, https://archive.nytimes.com/www.nytimes.com/interactive/2012/09/12/us/politics/libya-statements.html, accessed November 15, 2021.

135. Sullivan, *Interviews of Witnesses*, 722.

136. Select Committee, *Final Report*, 152–55.

137. Benjamin Fishman, *Interviews of Witnesses Before the Select Committee on the Events Surrounding the 2012 Terrorist Attack in Benghazi: House of Representatives* (114th Cong., 2d sess., Volume 8, 2016), 622, 626; Bash, *Interviews of Witnesses*, 682–84; Kelly, *Interviews of Witnesses*, 1338; Cheryl Mills, *Interviews of Witnesses Before the Select Committee on the Events Surrounding the 2012 Terrorist Attack in Benghazi: House of Representatives* (114th Cong., 2d sess., Volume 6, 2016), 196; Olsen, *Interviews of Witnesses*, 187–88.

138. Select Committee, *Final Report*, 152–55; Bernadette Meehan, *Interviews of Witnesses Before the Select Committee on the Events Surrounding the 2012 Terrorist Attack in Benghazi: House of Representatives* (114th Cong., 2d sess., Volume 7, 2016), 990.

139. Select Committee, *Final Report*, 152, 159, 428; Rhodes, *Interviews of Witnesses*, 870–72; Meehan, *Interviews of Witnesses*, 992. The Benghazi Report erroneously states on pages 156 and 157 that Speechwriters Schwerin and Rooney helped draft the September 11 statement. Both testified that they did not recall working on it. See Dan Schwerin, *Interviews of Witnesses Before the Select Committee on the Events Surrounding the 2012 Terrorist Attack in Benghazi: House of Representatives* (114th Cong., 2d sess., Volume 7, 2016), 144–45; Megan Rooney, *Interviews of Witnesses*

Before the Select Committee on the Events Surrounding the 2012 Terrorist Attack in Benghazi: House of Representatives (114th Cong., 2d sess., Volume 7, 2016), 50–51. Sullivan testified that he either wrote the statement alone or together with Nuland. See Sullivan, *Interviews of Witnesses*, 671–72, 674. Nuland could not recall drafting the statement. See Victoria Nuland, *Interviews of Witnesses Before the Select Committee on the Events Surrounding the 2012 Terrorist Attack in Benghazi: House of Representatives* (114th Cong., 2d sess., Volume 2, 2016), 190. Sullivan would work closely with Rhodes on crafting a narrative over the next several days. Rhodes stated that Sullivan was his "normal point of contact" at State. See Ben Rhodes, *Interviews of Witnesses Before the Select Committee on the Events Surrounding the 2012 Terrorist Attack in Benghazi: House of Representatives* (114th Cong., 2d sess., Volume 8, 2016), 864. The 10:08 p.m. statement represented the first of what would be referred to as the "talking points." Clinton testified that she was not involved in the talking points process. See "Benghazi: The Attacks," Hearing before the Committee on Foreign Relations, 21. However, Clinton made it clear that it was her decision to release a statement: "Back in my office [after the 7:30 pm SVTC], I told the team it was time to make a public statement." See Hillary Clinton, *Hard Choices* (New York: Simon & Schuster, 2014), 396.

140. Select Committee, *Final Report*, 424.

141. Select Committee, *Final Report*, 428.

142. Select Committee, *Final Report*, 575, 579–80. The insertion of the line would become controversial within the CIA, as the executive coordinator unilaterally decided to insert the line over the objections of analysts. See Select Committee, *Final Report*, Appendix H.

143. Select Committee, *Final Report*, 163; Barack Obama, "Remarks on the Attack on the U.S. Mission in Benghazi, Libya," September 12, 2012, https://www.govinfo.gov/content/pkg/DCPD-201200713/pdf/DCPD-201200713.pdf, accessed November 15, 2021.

144. Select Committee, *Final Report*, 163–64; Rooney, *Interviews of Witnesses*, 51–52; Schwerin, *Interviews of Witnesses*, 140.

145. Select Committee, *Final Report*, 429. When Representative Jim Jordan (R-OH) pressed Clinton on her contradictory statements during her October 22, 2015, hearing, she stated, "Well, Congressman, there was a lot of conflicting information that we were trying to make sense of. The situation was very fluid. It was fast moving." See "Hearing 4," Hearing before the Select Committee, 311.

146. Table 1.2 quotes are from Select Committee, *Final Report*, 152, 163.

147. Select Committee, *Final Report*, 429.

148. Rhodes, *Interviews of Witnesses*, 891–93, 1009.

149. Select Committee, *Final Report*, 186–87.

150. Changing "attacks" to "demonstrations" was factually incorrect, as intelligence reporting used the word "attacks" to describe what happened in Benghazi. See Select Committee, *Final Report*, 188–89, 206.

151. Zeke Miller and Alex Rogers, "Timeline: The Benghazi Emails: How the Obama Administration Created the Benghazi Talking Points," *Time*, May 16, 2013, https://swampland.time.com/2013/05/16/timeline-the-benghazi-emails/, accessed November 18, 2021.

152. Select Committee, *Final Report*, 196; Rhodes, *Interviews of Witnesses*, 897. Clinton, when asked about her decision to decline the Sunday talk shows, stated, "Well, I have to confess here [before the House Foreign Affairs Committee] in public, going on the Sunday shows is not my favorite thing to do. There are other things that I would prefer to do on Sunday mornings." See "Terrorist Attack in Benghazi: The Secretary of State's View," Hearing before the Committee on Foreign Affairs House of Representatives, January 23, 2013, Serial No. 113–11, 29.

153. Select Committee, *Final Report*, 198; Susan Rice, *Interviews of Witnesses Before the Select Committee on the Events Surrounding the 2012 Terrorist Attack in Benghazi: House of Representatives* (114th Cong., 2d sess., Volume 8, 2016), 1090–92. Clinton and Rice had a meeting that morning, but when asked what she recalled about the meeting, Rice stated, "Nothing." See Rice, *Interviews of Witnesses*, 1093. Clinton stated that she did discuss a Sunday talk show proposal with Rice. See "Terrorist Attack in Benghazi," Hearing before the Committee on Foreign Affairs, 94.

154. Select Committee, *Final Report*, 200; Rhodes, *Interviews of Witnesses*, 1012–16. In his interview with the Benghazi Committee, Rhodes admitted that the "protested rooted in an Internet video" was "not intended to assign responsibility for Benghazi." See Rhodes, *Interviews of Witnesses*, 930.

155. Select Committee, *Final Report*, 203; Rhodes, *Interviews of Witnesses*, 955–56, 968.

156. Rhodes, *Interviews of Witnesses*, 957.

157. Rhodes, *Interviews of Witnesses*, 1013.

158. Petraeus testified that he did not believe anyone at the White House applied pressure to change the talking points to fit a politically favorable narrative. He did not know the talking points would be used beyond the HPSCI Committee, and he viewed the drafting of the talking points as an "afterthought." See Petraeus, *Interviews of Witnesses*, 938, 975–76, 1079, 1084.

159. Miller and Rogers, "Timeline: The Benghazi Emails."

160. Rice, *Interviews of Witnesses*, 1096; Erin Pelton, *Interviews of Witnesses Before the Select Committee on the Events Surrounding the 2012 Terrorist Attack in Benghazi: House of Representatives* (114th Cong., 2d sess., Volume 9, 2016), 79.

161. Rexon Ryu, *Interviews of Witnesses Before the Select Committee on the Events Surrounding the 2012 Terrorist Attack in Benghazi: House of Representatives* (114th Cong., 2d sess., Volume 5, 2016), 1373.

162. Rice, *Interviews of Witnesses*, 1102; Rhodes, *Interviews of Witnesses*, 918.

163. Select Committee, *Final Report*, 204–205; Rhodes, *Interviews of Witnesses*, 1012–14.

164. Select Committee, *Final Report*, 204–205; Rice, *Interviews of Witnesses*, 1105–106.

165. Rice, *Interviews of Witnesses*, 1103.

166. Jake Tapper, "Ambassador Susan Rice: Libya Attack Not Premeditated," *ABC News*, September 16, 2012, https://abcnews.go.com/blogs/politics/2012/09/ambassador-susan-rice-libya-attack-not-premeditated/, accessed October 22, 2021; Rhodes, *Interviews of Witnesses*, 1020.

167. Rhodes, *Interviews of Witnesses*, 1022; Rice, *Interviews of Witnesses*, 1173.

168. Select Committee, *Final Report*, 210; "Benghazi: Exposing Failure," Hearing before the Committee on Oversight and Government Reform, 70.

169. Table 1.3 quotes are from Select Committee, *Final Report*, 214–15, 220, 429–31, 434; Rhodes, *Interviews of Witnesses*, 1012–14, 1028. For a transcript of Rice's comment on the talk shows, see Rhodes, *Interviews of Witnesses*, 1018–45.

170. Select Committee, *Final Report*, 236.

171. Olsen, *Interviews of Witnesses*, 222, 271.

172. Select Committee, *Final Report*, 236–38. Olsen did not coordinate his testimony with anyone outside of the NCTC. See Olsen, *Interviews of Witnesses*, 244–46. Petraeus stated that the "internal sense in the CIA on the morning of [September] 12" was that there was no protest, but then 12 intelligence reports "[came] in" that indicated a protest or gathering. See Petraeus, *Interviews of Witnesses*, 1011, 1051–52.

173. State Department, *Accountability Review Board Report*, December 18, 2012, https://2009-2017.state.gov/documents/organization/202446.pdf, accessed March 6, 2022.

174. Dana Hughes, "Four State Department Officials Relieved of Duties After Benghazi Report," *ABC News*, December 19, 2012, https://abcnews.go.com/blogs/politics/2012/12/three-state-department-officials-resign-after-benghazi-report, accessed December 3, 2021.

175. "Benghazi: The Attacks," Hearing before the Committee on Foreign Relations, 28.

176. "Benghazi: The Attacks," Hearing before the Committee on Foreign Relations, 6; "Terrorist Attack in Benghazi," Hearing before the Committee on Foreign Affairs, 5.

177. Select Committee, *Final Report*, 152; Rhodes, *Interviews of Witnesses*, 1040.

Chapter 2

Congressional Investigations

INTRODUCTION

Both Democrats and Republicans use congressional investigations as an arena to mount political attacks against members of the opposing party. Investigations expend taxpayer resources and reduce the time and energy Congress allocates to addressing important issues that affect Americans. This chapter presents a theoretical model to explain partisanship in congressional investigations. The following sections review the relationship between the executive and legislative branches and chronicle the history of congressional oversight and identify prominent shifts in that oversight, such as after Watergate and following Republicans gaining control of the 104th Congress. The latter shift, solidified by an institutional construct, resulted in investigations that seek to enforce party control within Congress to inflict political damage on a rival in the White House. Next, I organize congressional investigations into a taxonomy to explain the internal dynamics of an investigation, as introduced in the "Problems and Pitfalls in Existing Research" section of the Introduction chapter, and offer an explanatory model for partisan investigations. Finally, I evaluate hypotheses stemming from this model and introduce the research design for studying the Benghazi Committee investigation from 2014 to 2017.

THEORETICAL ARGUMENTS FOR PRESIDENT AND CONGRESSIONAL OVERSIGHT

Congress has little power over a president's short-term crisis decisions, but it can have a considerable impact in several ways over time. Congress controls the power of the purse and decides how and when to appropriate funds.[1] Notable examples include Congress denying President Gerald Ford's request for military assistance to the South Vietnamese in 1975, halting aid to Angola in 1975, and prohibiting funding in 1982 for the Contra rebels in Nicaragua.[2]

Congress can also stymie a president through legislative "inaction." President Woodrow Wilson's failure to win Senate ratification of his League of Nations initiative after World War I and President Harry Truman's efforts to pass the Marshall Plan are two examples. Passing the monumental Marshall Plan required help from Republicans in Congress, as well as a British foreign secretary and the Soviet Union.[3] President Truman's ability to convince the eightieth Congress to enact the European Recovery Program of 1948, based on Secretary of State George Marshall's 1947 Harvard commencement speech, was a testament to presidential appeal.[4]

Rallying public support as a strategy to stop a president from taking unilateral action in both domestic and international issue areas is another tactic Congress may employ.[5] In holding hearings, giving floor speeches, and taking to the airwaves, Congress can raise constitutional and policy concerns, which in turn may cause a president to reconsider his potential action.[6] In particular, members of Congress, as opposed to law professors or media elites, can be successful in generating a public narrative that the president is overstepping constitutional grounds and intruding on areas of congressional propriety.[7]

Another option and, arguably, one of the most effective tools for Congress to assert its influence over a president is its constitutional responsibility of oversight. Rule X, clause 2 of the *Rules of the House of Representatives* details these oversight responsibilities. Notably, the majority party writes the rules. Committees are tasked to "determine whether laws and programs . . . are being implemented and carried out in accordance with the intent of Congress and whether they should be continued, curtailed, or eliminated."[8] Committees may review and study how well laws are being executed, how well federal agencies are carrying out their responsibilities, and "any conditions or circumstances" that require "new or additional" legislation.[9] Keeping the executive branch in check is a fundamental and necessary function of Congress's constitutional duties.[10] Oversight is the "hammer," the ex post control, that Congress can synchronize with its "anvil" of legislation, an ex ante control to reign in a rogue executive branch.[11]

In its investigatory oversight role, Congress brings "institutional legitimacy" and shapes public opinion.[12] In one experiment, 83 percent of respondents supported Congress's ability to check executive excess via investigation.[13] Investigations generate news coverage that can turn the public against a president's agenda.[14] On the other hand, presidents, not facing the threat of investigation, are more likely to use military force as opposed to those facing intense scrutiny.[15]

An investigation or the threat of an investigation often initiates a legislative-executive branch legal battle. Congress can subpoena individuals and vote to hold individuals in criminal or civil contempt.[16] The president, in turn, often invokes the principle of executive secrecy and simply refuses to turn over documents or to make witnesses available to Congress.[17] The executive branch may also prohibit the U.S. Government Accountability Office (GAO), Congress's nonpartisan auditing entity, from examining the CIA and other intelligence agencies.[18] Congress, in turn, can hold up presidential nominations, as a means to gain information from a president.[19]

Presidents can point to leaks of classified information and the harm to national security as a reason not to comply with congressional demands. After all, congressional members have constitutional protections, specifically the "Speech and Debate Clause" of the U.S. Constitution, which precludes members from being questioned about their legislative duties.[20] Members can leak the classified information, and presidents will have few options to find and prosecute the offending members. This is even more concerning in the light of partisanship, in which party members have little, if any, incentive to hold their fellow party members accountable.[21] If a president ignores or refuses to comply with an investigation's findings, as the recommendations are non-binding or lacking in appropriation authority, Congress does have the ability to impeach an executive branch official in the House and remove the individual through a Senate trial.[22]

History of Congressional Oversight

This executive-legislative oversight battle dates to 1792, four years after the ratification of the Constitution, when Congress demanded President George Washington turn over papers related to the failed St. Clair military expedition.[23] Federalist members rallied behind Secretary of War Henry Knox and Treasury Secretary Alexander Hamilton to block the publication of the investigatory report.[24]

Since the first investigation of a president, Congress periodically pursues aggressive and passive oversight and can display effective oversight, as well as ineptitude.[25] Congress reasserted itself when the president overstepped the boundaries of his authority, as Congress felt President Theodore Roosevelt did with the Spanish American War, as well as with his Interior Department and Forestry Bureau.[26] As Lance Cole and Stanley Brand argue, Congress hit a high point when the Senate exposed executive branch criminality with its 1923–1924 Teapot Dome investigation.[27] Thirty years later, Congress hit a low point with its House Un-American Activities Committee (HUAC) and Senator Joseph McCarthy (R-WI) investigations. The latter ended with McCarthy's Chief Counsel Roy Cohn attempting to take personal revenge on the Army for drafting his friend and committee staff colleague.[28]

CASE STUDY: OVERSIGHT OF THE VIETNAM WAR

The Vietnam War offers a model of purposeful oversight of the executive branch. Representative Thomas Morgan's (D-PA) Foreign Affairs Committee, including the subcommittees, was active in investigating the Vietnam War.[29] Morgan, a party loyalist, was not critical of President Lyndon Johnson's handling of the Vietnam War.[30]

For March and April 1968 hearings, Morgan called witnesses from the Agency for International Development (USAID), State Department, and the Defense Department. Morgan's questioning of the witnesses was perfunctory. In approximately 200 pages of hearings, Morgan either just introduced a witness or asked an open-ended question (i.e., deferred to the witness). In fact, one witness, USAID's assistant administrator for Vietnam James Grant stated that "the news media have repeatedly overstated the adverse effects of the Tet offensive in Vietnam."[31] Another witness stated, "[After the Tet offensive], there certainly were no massive [Army of the Republic of Vietnam] desertions that occurred."[32] One would view the hearings as neutral, if not pro-administration.

In December 1968, Morgan submitted the "Measuring Hamlet Security in Vietnam" report based on a study mission by Representative John V. Tunney (D-CA). The report was highly critical of the South Vietnamese government's control of hamlets and the method used to collect and analyze data to assess the government's control. Tunney labeled the evaluation system as "Garbage In, Garbage Out."[33] In June 1971, Morgan submitted the "Report of Special Study Mission to Asia" based on the study mission of Representative Lester Wolff (D-NY). Wolff examined the U.S. military assistance program (MAP) and how reduced United States' direct involvement would affect six Asian nations. The report was critical of the South Vietnamese government, calling it a "failure."[34]

Even though the Senate was not loyal to Johnson, he enjoyed remarkable deference during the first years of the war.[35] Senator J. William Fulbright (D-AR) and his Committee on Foreign Relations started an eight-year investigation of the Vietnam War in January 1966.[36] Paul Light writes, "[Fulbright's] investigation [of the Vietnam War] was not only long, broad, complex, linked, and composed of multiple, nearly simultaneous hearing sets, it was also thorough, operated with significant freedom to investigate, was mostly nonpartisan, produced intense media coverage that included dozens of televised hearings, and generated enormous visibility."[37] Fulbright also allowed President Richard Nixon a year of deference before scrutinizing his criticism of the war.[38]

Fulbright was not a party loyalist, but his close relationship with Senator Richard Russell (D-GA), a frequent Johnson opponent on domestic issues with a very low party loyalty score, convinced the American public that Vietnam was a conflict not worth fighting.[39] In 1965, Russell stated that he had "never been able to see any strategic, political, or economic advantage to be gained in Vietnam" and he warned against a war in Vietnam.[40] Russell's disagreement with Vietnam manifested itself in the 1969 National Commitments Resolution, which reasserted Congress in the decision-making process for sending U.S. troops overseas.[41]

However, Russell remained a steadfast Johnson loyalist until "his last year of significant influence before being overtaken by declining health."[42] As chair of the Senate Appropriations Committee, Subcommittee on Department of Defense from 1963 to 1971, Russell held Vietnam War hearings and was instrumental in passing funding for the Vietnam War.[43] For the eight appropriations bills he chaired, all passed on unanimous votes. In fact, with the exception of the 1969 authorization bill, all of the defense bills cleared the Senate in a day and by voice vote.[44]

By 1973, after learning of Nixon's bombings of Cambodia, Congress overrode a Nixon veto and passed the War Powers Resolution. The resolution requires the president to notify Congress within 48 hours of committing military forces to conflict, prohibits forces from remaining more than 60 days, and allows for an additional 30 days to withdraw forces. The resolution remains controversial, with presidents of both parties failing to adhere to it and the Supreme Court not ruling on its constitutionality.[45]

The Select Committee on Presidential Campaign Activities, also known as the Senate Watergate Committee, was a defining moment or critical antecedent in executive-legislative relations.[46] Congress, with the combined efforts of the media and judicial system, investigated criminal activities associated with the 1972 presidential election, and due to its findings, President Richard Nixon was forced to resign.[47] Congress then passed legislation, such as the Freedom of Information Act, the Ethics in Government Act, and the Government in Sunshine Act, and aimed to strengthen its oversight authorities and increase transparency and ethical standards within the government.

Congress also turned to reign in executive branch power. Following publication of the intelligence agencies conducting domestic surveillance on antiwar and dissident groups in the United States, Congress launched investigations scrutinizing the Intelligence Community (IC) through the Senate's Church Committee (1975–1976) and the Pike Committee (1975–1976) in the

House.[48] The Church Committee, in particular, conducted what is considered to be "one of the most sweeping and intensive investigations in the history of the Senate."[49] It released 6 reports and 7 volumes of hearings and made 183 recommendations on improving intelligence while protecting civil liberties.[50] The Pike Committee pursued a confrontational approach with the executive branch, with the House voting to suppress the final report, but it was leaked.[51] The strong public outcry stemming from these findings prompted Congress to create permanent intelligence committees, authorize intelligence budgets on an annual basis, and require presidential submission of covert action proposals.[52]

The Watergate investigation had a third profound effect on executive-legislative relations. Congress positioned itself as an adversary to the president and investigations became the preferred method to reign in executive branch power. Prior to Watergate, high publicity investigations were uncommon—1.1 investigations per year during the Truman and Dwight Eisenhower presidencies and 0.6 investigations per year from the John Kennedy presidency through the Ford presidency.[53] The House took measures after Watergate to ensure a narrative for a media more willing to drum up scandals.[54] It shifted power to party leadership.[55] Party leaders handpicked committee chairs, based on loyalty, not seniority, and to ensure legislation met party approval, leaders increased the power of subcommittee chairs and rank-and-file members to work directly with leadership.[56]

Republican control of Congress following the 1994 elections marked a critical juncture in how the majority party wielded power.[57] To maintain and build momentum, Speaker of the House Newt Gingrich (R-GA) emphasized order and discipline within the party.[58] Gingrich took deliberate steps to enforce this order. He selected the committee chair, and the chair was subject to a secret party vote.[59] Gingrich cut committee staff by a third (reducing the expertise available), imposed term limits on committee chairs (ensuring no individual member concentrated power), removed the minority party from deliberations, and created task forces as an alternative legislative path to committees.[60] The committee chair position, in particular, was made feckless and weak with chairs having little authority over individual members. For instance, individual members can attend hearings or interviews, as they choose, and can ask questions at those hearings or interviews, as they like.[61]

Table 2.1 is a list of the 104th Congress reforms.[62]

Ironically, the reforms resulted in less ability to perform rigorous or detail-oriented oversight of the executive branch. First, by 2008 Senators received an average of 4.1 committee assignments, an increase from 2.1 in 1947.[63] With more committees and reduced time in Washington, the number of Senate committee hearing days dramatically declined in 1995, averaging less

Table 2.1 104th Congress Reforms

House Reforms	*Senate Reforms*
1. Six-year terms limits for committee and subcommittee chairs 2. Eight-year term limit for Speaker of the House. 3. Elimination of three standing committees (DC, Merchant Marine & Fisheries, Post Office & Civil Service) 4. Most committees limited to five subcommittees 5. Joint referrals eliminated; speaker designates "lead" committee 6. Majority party leaders have greater authority over committee chair selection 7. Members' committee votes published 8. Subcommittee staff hired by the committee chair 9. Committee staff was reduced by a third. Oversight gains authority to establish committee staff sizes.	1. Six-year term limits for committee chairs 2. Six-year term limits for party leaders other than floor leader and president pro tempore 3. Senators are prohibited from reclaiming seniority upon return to committee 4. Secret ballot elections for committee chairs in committee and party conferences; majority leader can nominate chair in case of conference rejection. 5. Party adopts legislative agenda before the beginning of each Congress and before committee chair selection.

than 1,000 days per year from 1995 to 2008. The decline was notable for the national security committees, the Armed Services and Foreign Relations Committees, which each on average held less than 80 hearing days per year.[64]

CASE STUDY: OVERSIGHT OF THE CLINTON ADMINISTRATION

Senator Fred Thompson's (R-TN) investigation of President Bill Clinton is a good example of the effectiveness of Newt Gingrich's institutional changes. During the 105th Congress, the Republicans controlled both the House and Senate, and they viewed the 1996 presidential campaign as controversial. According to the Republicans, the Clinton/Gore campaign team and the Democratic National Committee relied on "illegal contributions" and raised more than $44 million in excess of the presidential campaign spending limits.[65] The result was an investigation involving 15 committees. Light summed it up: "The Senate Intelligence Committee finally wrested primary investigatory control after battling nine full committees, three special congressional bodies, two presidential commissions, and two subcommittees."[66]

The investigations continued. The Governmental Affairs Committee, chaired by Thompson, held 32 days of hearings and issued 3 reports on technology transfers to China.[67] Thompson began the investigation on January 7, 1998, with the committee having two purposes: (1) to repeal, amend, or adopt new laws and (2) to "find the facts and reveal them for the American people."[68] The investigation ended on May 5, 1998, when the committee voted along party lines, 8 to 7, to approve the final report, "Investigation of Illegal or Improper Activities in Connection with 1996 Federal Election Campaigns." In the end, Thompson recommended Attorney General Janet Reno or an independent counsel use the findings to "aggressively pursue any and all indications of criminal wrong-doing."[69] Thompson believed China made a concerted effort to influence administration policy and obtain American technology but found no evidence that Clinton administration officials knew of the covert actions.[70]

Thompson and Ranking Member Senator John Glenn (D-OH) had frequent, public disagreements about the investigation. The *New York Times* cited the "partisan rancor" of the hearings, and Glenn dismissed the investigation as a "diversion" from Congress' own hypocrisy when it came to campaign fundraising.[71] Thompson admitted in the "Additional Views" section of the report that Congress "is a much more partisan institution than it used to be."[72] Notably, Senator Joseph Lieberman (D-CT) cited the partisan staff in suggesting preference for a Special Committee "joint, nonpartisan" staff or a Governmental Affairs "joint bipartisan" staff.[73]

Congressional investigations during President Barack Obama's tenure were emblematic of the intense partisanship. When controlling the House and Senate, Democrats conducted three major investigations: the BP oil spill; the National Highway Traffic Safety Administration (NHTSA) and Toyota recall; and the Fort Hood shooting. A Democratic-controlled Senate and Republican-controlled House during the 112th and 113th Congresses pursued 12 investigations: the "Fast and Furious" ATF gun operation; the Solyndra bankruptcy; the Benghazi terrorist attack; the Internal Revenue Service (IRS) scandal; Libya and violations of the War Powers Resolution (WPR); the Veterans Affairs (VA) scandal; Health and Human Services Secretary Kathleen Sebelius and Enroll America; the Environmental Protection Agency (EPA) investigations; rewriting a drilling moratorium report; Associated Press (AP) phone records; Food and Drug Administration (FDA) and a meningitis outbreak; and the Fort Hood shooting.[74] During these 12 investigations, the Democratic Senate held 21 hearings compared to 107 hearings in the Republican House.[75] The public airing of grievances between parties represents what Melanie Marlowe calls "a sorry state" as "members use their question time to further a campaign strategy, not to elicit information for legislative evaluation."[76]

A TAXONOMY OF CONGRESSIONAL INVESTIGATIONS

The relationship between legislative reforms and investigations of the executive branch allows for a taxonomy, beginning with the type of investigation: congressional or commission. Congressional investigations are either a fire alarm or police patrol style of oversight. The partisan brand is a defining facet of a fire alarm investigation. Categories of the partisan brand, shown in Figure 2.1, are investigative leadership and staff and focus of the investigation.

Commission vs Congressional Investigation

When an issue of national importance arises, Congress may establish a commission or select a committee to study or investigate it. If selecting a commission, Congress appoints individuals on a temporary basis to investigate and issue a report. Since 1989, the perception of the 150 congressional commissions is most often that of a neutral arbiter, due to their bipartisan or nonpartisan nature.[77]

The other decision path for Congress is to study or investigate via one of its committees, which is the focus of this book.[78] In doing so the committees follow the post-1994 reform model. Party power and control is the defining factor. This imperative has been taken to new heights (of dysfunction) as political parties have become increasingly polarized.[79] As such, investigations have moved from fact-finding and reform missions to ones involving

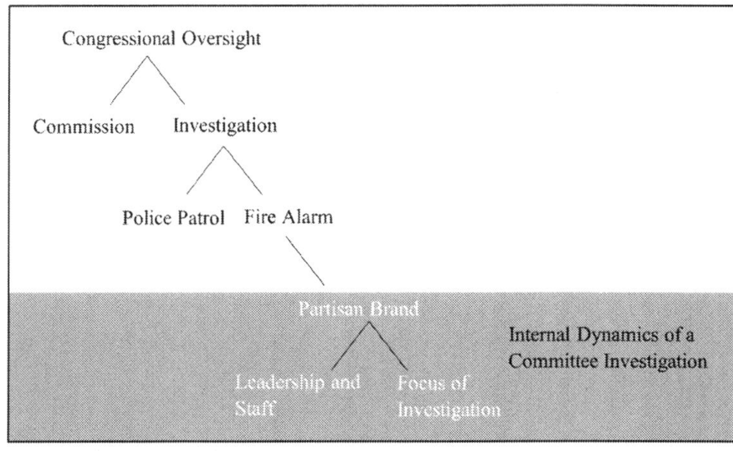

Figure 2.1 Taxonomy of Congressional Investigation with Internal Dynamics. *Source*: Figure created by author.

committee members asking politically charged questions to trigger news media coverage.[80] These investigations can be characterized as "political combat," in which the goal is not government reform but rather taking down political opponents.[81]

Party-led investigations of the president conducted in this manner are effective.[82] Political parties use them in both chambers on a consistent basis to "significantly diminish the president's standing among the public."[83] The result is clear: as the number of investigative hearings increases from 0 to 20 days a month, presidential approval decreases by about 2.5 percent.[84] Moreover, individual members that lead the investigation can gain publicity, bolster their electoral chances, and increase their political power.[85]

Congressional Investigation: Fire Alarms and Police Patrols

Congress has two methods at its disposal in conducting its investigation. It can either take on the role of "police patrol" or "fire alarm." Steven Balla and Christopher Deering define police patrol oversight as "[occurring] when legislators, on their own initiative, examine a sample of agency activities, with the aim of detecting, remedying, and discouraging bureaucratic behavior that is inconsistent with legislative preferences."[86] With police patrol, Congress takes the initiative to examine the executive branch in a centralized and controlled method. Its aim is to prevent violations, and when it does find violations, it remedies them through legislation.

Conducting police patrol oversight of the executive branch is a daunting task. The biggest issue is that representatives are not policy experts.[87] Moreover, as Marlowe writes, "the size, scope, and diffuse nature of government power and decision-making make it impossible for Congress to grasp what is going on in a coherent and productive way."[88] After all, there are 432 federal agencies to monitor.[89] Balla and Deering in examining eight committees across four post-Watergate time periods of both divided and unified government find that Congress carries out more routine, ongoing police patrol hearings than fire alarm hearings.[90] But, in terms of national security, the Senate Armed Services and Foreign Relations Committees tended to hold less than 20 days of hearings per year, especially after 1985. Police patrols for the Armed Services Committee consumed less hearing days than fire alarms by the 1990s.[91]

With fire alarm investigations, Congress responds to a crisis or a complaint. Its examination is decentralized and reliant on outside groups for information.[92] More formally, Balla and Deering define fire alarm oversight as legislators establishing "structures and processes that enable outside parties to examine agency decision making and alert legislative officials about particular actions with which they are dissatisfied."[93]

Fire alarms, in terms of international affairs, occur for the following type of events: (1) military and international crises, (2) the use of military force, (3) major treaties, and (4) scandals or incompetence.[94] Crises often lead to scandals, which are made prominent by the news media, which in turn spur investigations.[95]

Since the Watergate investigation in 1974, Congress has become more active in conducting high-profile investigations of the president—launching 42 investigations before Watergate and 58 after Watergate.[96] These post-Watergate high-profile investigations tend to be fire alarm investigations (77 percent of House investigations and 56 percent of Senate investigations).[97]

A variety of reasons prompt fire alarm investigations—legislating better policy, forwarding partisan and member agendas, and protecting Congress' oversight prerogative.[98] For example, the 2010 BP Deepwater Horizon oil explosion and spill was the largest environmental disaster in history, and Congress quickly pursued an investigation of the spill through 10 different committees and a legislative response through dozens of proposed bills.[99]

Fire Alarm: Partisan Brand

Fire alarm investigations offer a party the opportunity to enhance its partisan brand. Since Nixon's tenure in office, congressional electoral constituencies demonstrate greater polarization. Voters reward representatives with re-election for opposing a president from the opposing party and rejecting moderation and bipartisanship in exchange for party loyalty.[100]

The desire to win elections and regain power provides the minority party with an incredible incentive to engage in the proven tactic of partisan investigation and criticism of the president and the president's majority party.[101] This criticism is predictably applicable to both domestic and international issues.[102] Likewise, the president's party in Congress has an incentive to derail and obfuscate any investigation, as the president is inexorably linked via popular support and "the partisan brand" to the member's own electoral fortunes.[103]

The president and Congress serve different constituents.[104] While presidents have a broad range of legislative tools available to push their agenda (e.g., bargaining, personal appeals, and structuring choices), it may not matter as a divided government reduces the probability of significant legislation passing.[105] In fact, the opposition may use investigations to generate public support for new legislation.[106] A divided government, or one in which the opposition party controls Congress, is inherently more partisan and ideologically divisive.[107]

The empirical evidence is overwhelming: if the opposition party controls the legislature, it will conduct vigorous, numerous investigations.[108] It will conduct more public hearings.[109] This is especially true with post-Watergate reforms. Prior to 1975, the probability of the House initiating more than 12 investigations in a session was only 11 percent—when a president was of the opposite party. Stunningly, after 1975, this probability, under the same parameters, increases to 85 percent.[110]

The House is especially active.[111] Following an opposition party gaining control, congressional hearings increase five-fold and the duration of the hearings quadrupled.[112] This translates to a 40 percent increase in probability that the House will generate more than 12 committee investigations in a session.[113] When a committee is deemed responsible for protecting the reputation of the party, the probability of a committee exceeding the mean number of investigations increases more than 45 percent.[114]

The opposite effect occurs under unified government, one party owns both the White House and Congress. Investigations are less intense and of shorter duration.[115] For example, the Republican-controlled House Oversight and Government Reform Committee held just 37 hearings from 2003 to 2004 under the George W. Bush presidency versus 135 from 1993 to 1994 under the Clinton presidency.[116] From 2003 to 2006, the Republicans held fewer hearings on the Iraq War than the Democrats held in 15 months after taking control of Congress in 2007.[117] In examining the Iraq War between 2003 and 2010, Douglas Kriner and Francis Shen found that nearly 71 percent of Republicans gave no speeches critical of the Bush administration while one-third of Democrats gave 10 or more critical speeches.[118] The Democrats, under unified government from 2009 to 2010, averaged 30.5 days of investigative hearings, as opposed to 73.2 days during divided government from 2007 to 2014.[119]

A legislature's complacency is due to the party's collective fortunes in the next election—if the president is tarnished, congressional members, by party association, will also be tarnished.[120] If the president is elevated and protected, congressional members, by party association, will also be elevated.

Partisan Brand: Leadership and Focus of Investigation

Congress gives a president wide latitude, especially in terms of foreign policy or national security matters.[121] For example, Congress rarely, if ever, stops a president from deploying the military or using force.[122] Moreover, if a president's poll numbers increase as a result of foreign policy success, Congress is less likely to target the president for investigation.[123]

However, congressional leadership, working with third parties and the media, will target politically unpopular presidents or presidential candidates to trumpet a scandal close to a national election.[124] The targeting is most effective when executed during slow news cycles.[125] The opposition is particularly vulnerable in the case of a foreign policy or national security disaster.[126]

Putting the investigatory spotlight on one's opponent requires party leadership to maintain strict discipline. For every standard deviation increase in majority party cohesion, there is double the number of new investigations and more than double the number of high publicity (i.e., number of *New York Times* articles) investigations.[127] Maintaining strict discipline also provides the opportunity for party leaders to use investigations to raise money for their candidates.[128] Moreover, individual members can use investigations as national stages to build their reputation and increase their own electoral chances at the senatorial or presidential level.[129]

A PARTISAN MODEL OF CONGRESSIONAL INVESTIGATIONS

Frank John Smist, in *Congress Oversees the United States Intelligence Community*, offers two models of congressional oversight. The conservative "institutional" model seeks a cooperative relationship with the executive branch, hires Washington insiders as staff, and conducts a low-profile, non-confrontational inquiry. The adversarial "investigative" model seeks to uncover wrongdoing, hires Washington outsiders as staff, and conducts a high-profile confrontational investigation.[130] I propose a third partisan model based on whether the majority party in Congress is the president's political party enlists vetted Washington insiders to maintain tight control over staff and conducts widely publicized, confrontational investigations driven by the advancement of the partisan brand rather than improvement of government practices.

Committee Leadership and Staff

With the 104th Congress in 1995, House leadership began selecting party loyalists as committee chairs. The committee chair supported the party position 89.1 percent of the time in the House and 86 percent of the time in the Senate.[131] Informational committees (Banking, Education and Labor, Foreign Affairs, Judiciary, and Intelligence committees) are especially susceptible to party control.[132] The investigations and subsequent policy impacts often have consequences beyond the purview of these committees, so leadership chooses its members carefully.[133]

As shown in Table 2.2, for foreign policy investigations of "historical significance" from 1945 to 2012, both the party unity score of the committee chair and the number of investigations have increased since 1945, particularly since 1995.[134]

Congressional committee staff perform many functions—drafting and advocating for legislative proposal, conducting investigations, and serving as policy

Table 2.2 Foreign Policy Investigations of Historical Significance, 1945–2012

Cold War Period (1945–1971)	
Number of Investigations	11
Number of Committees	25
Number of Democratic-Led Committee Investigations	21
Number of Republican-Led Committee Investigations	4
Number of Committee Investigations per Year	0.96
Average Party Unity Score of Committee Chairman	74.66
End of Cold War Consensus Period (1972–1994)	
Number of Investigations	11
Number of Committees	27
Number of Democratic-Led Committee Investigations	25
Number of Republican-Led Committee Investigations	2
Number of Committee Investigations per Year	1.22
Average Party Unity Score of Committee Chairman	84.20
Republican Majority Period (1995–2012)	
Number of Investigations	4
Number of Committees	26
Number of Democratic-Led Committee Investigations	0
Number of Republican-Led Committee Investigations	26
Number of Committee Investigations per Year	1.53
Average Party Unity Score of Committee Chairman	88.48

experts for oversight functions.[135] But importantly, committee staff are not using their policy expertise or analytical skills to conceptualize problems, only to solidify the positions taken by their boss.[136] Moreover, while some committee staff do become experts in an issue area, the majority of staff members are generalists, and even those learning a particular issue often do not have as much expertise on the subject as their counterpart in the executive branch.[137]

Legislation, dating from 1946 to 1969, provided committees with 10 full-time staff members (four professional staff members and 6 clerks), and in 1970, legislation increased the professional staff size to 6 members and allowed committees to request additional staff.[138] The result was large staff increases, a purposeful design that allowed the legislative branch to compete with the executive branch in terms of personnel.[139] Moreover, members and their staff have in-house organizations to assist in oversight efforts.[140]

When Republicans gained majority control of the House in 1995, leadership cut committee staff. As illustrated in Table 2.3, the number of House committee staff members dramatically decreased from 2,267 in 1989 to 1,266 in 1995, while Senate committee staff declined from 1,116 to 796 from 1989 to 1995. These numbers have remained low. For example, the Senate cut its SSCI staff by 15 percent to just 34 staff members in 2007.[141] Meanwhile, House and Senate personal staffing levels remain relatively stable.[142]

Table 2.3 Congressional Staff, 1979–2015

	1979	*1989*	*1993*	*1995*	*1999*	*2009*	*2015*
House Committee	2,027	2,267	2,147	1,266	1,267	1,324	1,164
House Personal	7,067	7,569	7,400	7,186	7,216	6,907	6,030
Senate Committee	1,410	1,116	994	796	910	913	951
Senate Personal	3,593	3,867	4,138	4,247	4,272	3,884	3,917

Source: Information from *Vital Statistics on Congress*, https://www.brookings.edu/wp-content/uploads/2019/03/Chpt-5.pdf.

As members increased the number of hearings and held longer investigations to justify increasing staff sizes, the intended downsizing had an opposite effect.[143] Staffers focused less on research and objectivity and more on compiling "gotcha" questions for members to use for dramatic effect against a witness. Another consequence was the transfer of experienced staffers from a standing committee to the investigating committee and hiring loyal operatives to ensure investigation findings aligned with the party narrative.

Focus of Investigation

The focus of the investigation is the opposite party, specifically that party's president or presidential candidate. Investigations combined with scandal are effective against a rival's presidential candidate. First, an opposition party and the press can align on the creation or enhancement and co-production of a scandal.[144] Control of investigations, particularly in the House, allows the majority party to highlight distinctions between itself and a president from the opposing party and to increase the prospect of electoral success.[145] More precisely, if a scandal, particularly a moral scandal, can be tied to one's opponent within 12 months of an election, it can "significantly decrease their electoral prospects."[146]

HYPOTHESES

The partisan model of congressional investigations proposes that the majority party in Congress uses investigations as a tool to advance the interests of the party, rather than the maintenance of executive power as a co-equal branch of government. Following the work of John Aldrich and David Rohde, Barbara Sinclair, and Deering and Stephen Smith, I argue institutional changes in Congress after Watergate and after the Republican takeover in 1994 make investigations partisan, and the key to understanding this is to illuminate the inner workings of an investigation.[147]

I base my three hypotheses on the following assumptions: (1) in a majority party position, both Republican and Democratic parties act in the same way; (2) majority party leaders view executive branch foreign policy decisions in a rational choice manner, capitalizing on failures by launching investigations; and (3) U.S. presidents are concerned with political costs.

With party leaders viewing congressional elections as national elections, those leaders will have strong incentives to maximize their advantage in the next election.[148] Moreover, individual members, tied to the party brand, also have the desire to win their own elections.[149]

Hypothesis 1: A committee investigation will correlate positively with focusing on the rival political candidate in the next national election.

Investigations offer the majority party an opportunity to increase the prestige of its partisan brand, and for individual members, especially committee chairs, investigations offer the opportunity for national recognition.[150]

Hypothesis 2: A member's role will correlate positively with attending high-profile committee events.

Party leaders base the selection of committee chairs on loyalty and committee chairs follow these criteria for staff selection.[151] I argue committee chairs view loyalty as critical to maintaining party cohesion and discipline.[152] Loyalty is determined through a vetting process of prior Capitol Hill experience.[153]

Hypothesis 3: A staff member with prior Capitol Hill experience will correlate positively with work assignments on the committee.

RESEARCH DESIGN

This research employs a case study method. Case studies, defined as "an intensive study of a single unit for the purpose of understanding a larger class of (similar) units," have an important place in research when information is limited and for early theoretical development and testing.[154] I use the 2014–2017 Benghazi Committee investigation as the case study for testing my theory of partisan congressional investigations, as part of an evidence-oriented strategy that describes complex social phenomena.[155] This case study provides depth and accuracy, giving a "feel and flavor" of a congressional investigation.[156]

To conduct the test, I follow a process tracing methodology, in which I examine the factors explaining a partisan investigation.[157] Process tracing offers a "comparative advantage" over large-N studies in understanding and analyzing the decisions of individuals and groups.[158] It also has another benefit. As explained earlier in the chapter, Watergate was the critical antecedent of an aggressive Congress, and the 1995 reforms were the critical juncture of congressional investigations being placed under party control. Process tracing allows an identification (or even rejection) of the timing and impact of the path dependency of these 1995 reforms.[159]

CONCLUSION

This chapter explains the evolution of partisanship in congressional investigations. While oversight is a constitutional function of Congress, producing friction between the executive and legislative branches since 1792, investigations are increasingly aggressive, confrontational, and partisan. A critical antecedent to this shift was the Watergate investigation, while Speaker Newt Gingrich's reforms marked a critical juncture in the relationship between executive and legislative branches of government.

Previous research identifies this shift, but this study expands on the internal composition of the congressional investigation and explains the enforcement of party control and the execution of party strategy. The next chapter applies the partisan model to the Benghazi House Select Committee, focusing on the investigation and activities of the committee leadership and staff. I trace the focus of the investigation and analyze witness interviews, majority party reports, press releases, and document requests to assess the hypotheses.

NOTES

1. Bert A. Rockman, "Reinventing What for Whom?: President and Congress in the Making of Foreign Policy," *Presidential Studies Quarterly* 30, no. 1 (2000): 142.

2. Robert B. Zoellick, "Congress and the Making of US Foreign Policy," *Survival* 41, no. 4 (1999–2000): 20–21; Melvin R. Laird, "Iraq: Learning the Lessons of Vietnam," *Foreign Affairs* 84, no. 6 (2005): 22–43.

3. Richard E. Neustadt, *Presidential Power and the Modern Presidents: The Politics of Leadership from Roosevelt to Reagan* (New York: Free Press, 1990), 42–44.

4. Neustadt, *Presidential Power*, 44.

5. Notably, this does not apply to a president's use of force decision, which tends to be unilateral and based on international factors and power calculations. See Bradley F. Podliska, *Acting Alone: A Scientific Study of American Hegemony and Unilateral Use-of-Force Decision Making* (Lanham, MD: Lexington Books, 2010).

6. Dino P. Christenson and Douglas Kriner, "Mobilizing the Public Against the President: Congress and the Political Costs of Unilateral Action," *American Journal of Political Science* 61, no. 4 (2017): 783.

7. Christenson and Kriner, "Mobilizing the Public," 780.

8. Cheryl Johnson, *Rules of the House of Representatives: One Hundred Seventeenth Congress* (Washington, DC: Government Printing Office, 2021), 9.

9. Johnson, *Rules of the House of Representatives*, 9.

10. Amy Zegart, "The Domestic Politics of Irrational Intelligence Oversight," *Political Science Quarterly* 126, no. 1 (2011): 4; Lance Cole and Stanley Brand, *Congressional Investigations and Oversight: Case Studies and Analysis* (Durham, NC: Carolina Academic Press, 2011).

11. Kathleen Bawn, "Choosing Strategies to Control the Bureaucracy: Statutory Constraints, Oversight, and the Committee System," *Journal of Law, Economics, & Organization* 13, no. 1 (1997): 102.

12. Douglas Kriner and Eric Schickler, *Investigating the President: Congressional Checks on Presidential Power* (Princeton: Princeton University Press, 2016), 100.

13. Kriner and Schickler, *Investigating the President*, 81.

14. Kriner and Schickler, *Investigating the President*, 253.

15. Kriner and Schickler, *Investigating the President*, 245.

16. Melanie Marlowe, "Reclaiming Institutional Relevance through Congressional Oversight," in *Is Congress Broken? The Virtues and Defects of Partisanship, Polarization, and Gridlock*, edited by William Connelly, John Pitney, and Gary Schmitt (Washington, DC: Brookings Institution Press, 2017), 110–11.

17. Rahul Sagar, *Secrets and Leaks: The Dilemma of State Secrecy* (Princeton: Princeton University Press, 2013), 86; Norman J. Ornstein and Thomas E. Mann, "When Congress Checks Out," *Foreign Affairs* 85, no. 6 (2006): 67–82; Irving Younger, "Congressional Investigations and Executive Secrecy: A Study in the Separation of Powers," *University of Pittsburgh Law Review* 20 (1959): 755–84.

18. Zegart, "Domestic Politics," 17.

19. Marlowe, "Reclaiming Institutional Relevance," 112.

20. Sagar, *Secrets and Leaks*, 88.

21. Sagar, *Secrets and Leaks*, 89.

22. Douglas Kriner, "Can Enhanced Oversight Repair the Broken Branch," *Boston University Law Review* 89 (2009): 765–93; Marlowe, "Reclaiming Institutional Relevance," 112.

23. Younger, "Congressional Investigations," 756–58.

24. Kriner and Schickler, *Investigating the President*, 247.

25. Kriner, "Can Enhanced Oversight"; Cole and Brand, *Congressional Investigations and Oversight*; David Mayhew, "A Basic Profile of Member Roles," in *America's Congress: Actions in the Public Sphere, James Madison through Newt Gingrich* (New Haven, CT: Yale University Press, 2000).

26. Kriner, "Can Enhanced Oversight," 773.

27. Cole and Brand, *Congressional Investigations and Oversight*, 4.

28. Cole and Brand, *Congressional Investigations and Oversight*, 76.

29. Morgan was chairman of the House Foreign Affairs Committee from 1959 to 1977.

30. Morgan had a party unity score of 95.706 for the 90th Congress. The party unity score is when at least 50 percent of Democrats vote against at least 50 percent of Republicans. The score is taken from Keith T. Poole, "Party Unity Scores," May 31, 2015, https://legacy.voteview.com/Party_Unity.htm, accessed February 23, 2022.

31. "Foreign Assistance Act of 1968," Hearings before the Committee on Foreign Affairs House of Representatives, Ninetieth Congress Second Session on H.R. 15263, A Bill to Amend Further the Foreign Assistance Act of 1961, as Amended, and for Other Purposes, March 26, 27, 28, April 1, 2, 1968, Part IV (Washington, DC: Government Printing Office, 1968), 658.

32. "Foreign Assistance Act of 1968," Hearings before the Committee on Foreign Affairs House of Representatives, Ninetieth Congress Second Session on H.R. 15263, A Bill to Amend Further the Foreign Assistance Act of 1961, as Amended, and for Other Purposes, March 26, 27, 28, April 1, 2, 1968, Part IV (Washington, DC: Government Printing Office, 1968), 667.

33. John V. Tunney, *Measuring Hamlet Security in Vietnam: Report of a Special Study Mission of the Committee on Foreign Affairs* (Washington, DC: Government Printing Office, 1969), 8.

34. Lester L. Wolff, *Report of Special Study Mission to Asia* (Washington, DC: Government Printing Office, 1971), 23.

35. Linda L. Fowler, *Watchdogs on the Hill: The Decline of Congressional Oversight of U.S. Foreign Relations* (Princeton University Press, 2015), 61.

36. Paul C. Light, *Government by Investigation: Congress, Presidents, and the Search for Answers 1945–2012* (Washington, DC: Brookings Institution Press, 2014), 155.

37. Light, *Government by Investigation*, 156.

38. Fowler, *Watchdogs on the Hill*, 64.

39. Fowler, *Watchdogs on the Hill*, 47. Fulbright had a party unity score of 72.5 for the 89th Congress. Russell was chair of the Senate Armed Services Committee from 1955 to 1968. His low party unity score of 28.409 for the 89th Congress was due to his opposition to civil rights legislation. See U.S. Senate, "Richard Russell: A Featured Biography," *United States Senate*, n.d., https://www.senate.gov/senators/FeaturedBios/Featured_Bio_Russell.htm, accessed January 14, 2022. The party unity scores are taken from Keith T. Poole, "Party Unity Scores," May 31, 2015, https://legacy.voteview.com/Party_Unity.htm, accessed February 23, 2022.

40. Joseph A. Fry, *The American South and the Vietnam War: Belligerence, Protest, and Agony in Dixie* (Lexington, KY: University Press of Kentucky, 2015), 106.

41. Fry, *The American South and the Vietnam War*, 263.

42. Fry, *The American South and the Vietnam War*, 199.

43. See "Supplemental Defense Appropriations for Fiscal Year 1966," Hearings before the Committee on Appropriations and the Committee on Armed Services United States Senate, Eighty-Ninth Congress Second Session on H.R. 13546, Making Supplemental Appropriations for the Fiscal Year ending June 30, 1966, and for Other Purposes (Washington, DC: Government Printing Office, 1966); "Military

Procurement Authorizations for Fiscal Year 1967," Hearings before the Committee on Armed Services and the Subcommittee on Department of Defense of the Committee on Appropriations United States Senate, Eighty-Ninth Congress Second Session on S. 2950 Department of Defense Programs, and Authorization of Appropriations during Fiscal Year 1967 for Procurement of Aircraft, Missiles, Naval Vessels, and Tracked Combat Vehicles, and Research, Development, Test, and Evaluation for the Armed Forces, February 23, 25, 28, March 8, 9, 10, 24, 25, 29, 30, and 31, 1966; "Supplemental Military Procurement and Construction Authorizations, Fiscal Year 1967," Hearings before the Committee on Armed Services and the Subcommittee on Department of Defense of the Committee on Appropriations United States Senate, Ninetieth Congress First Session on S. 665 to Authorize Appropriations during Fiscal Year 1967 for Procurement of Aircraft, Missiles, Tracked Combat Vehicles, Research, Development, Test, Evaluation, and Military Construction for the Armed Forces, and for Other Purposes, January 23, 24, and 25, 1967.

44. Center for Legislative Archives, "A Brief History of the Committee: The Russell Era, 1955–1968," *National Archives*, n.d., https://www.archives.gov/legislative/finding-aids/reference/senate/armed-services/1955-1968.html, accessed January 13, 2022.

45. William G. Howell and Jon C. Pevehouse, *While Dangers Gather: Congressional Checks on Presidential War Powers* (Princeton, NJ: Princeton University Press, 2007), xv–xvi, 4–5.

46. For critical antecedents, see Dan Slater and Erica Simmons, "Informative Regress: Critical Antecedents in Comparative Politics," *Comparative Political Studies* 43, no. 7 (2010): 886–917.

47. Cole and Brand, *Congressional Investigations and Oversight*, 93–94.

48. The Church Committee was officially the Senate Select Committee to Study Governmental Operations with Respect to Intelligence Activities.

49. Frank John Smist, *Congress Oversees the United States Intelligence Community, 1947–1994* (Knoxville: University of Tennessee Press, 1994), 10.

50. Smist, *Congress Oversees*, 10.

51. Smist, *Congress Oversees*, 10–11.

52. Smist, *Congress Oversees*, 11. But, in the zero-sum game of jurisdictional politics within Congress, creating the SSCI meant taking intelligence oversight from the Foreign Relations, Armed Services, and Judiciary Committees. Members of these committees demanded compromise, and the result was a mixture of sole jurisdiction (e.g., CIA falls under SSCI, tactical intelligence falls under Armed Services) and shared jurisdiction (e.g., a foreign relations matter under both SSCI and Foreign Relations oversight). See Morton H. Halperin, Priscilla Clapp, and Arnold Kanter, *Bureaucratic Politics and Foreign Policy* (Washington, DC: Brookings Institution Press, 2006), 326–27. The result was congressional infighting and redundancy that has resulted in less effective oversight.

53. David Mayhew, *Divided We Govern: Party Control, Lawmaking, and Investigations, 1946–2002*, 2nd edition (New Haven, CT: Yale University Press, 2005), 28.

54. Brendan Nyhan, "Scandal Potential: How Political Context and News Congestion Affect the President's Vulnerability to Media Scandal," *British Journal of Political Science* 45, no. 2 (2015): 438–39.

55. John H. Aldrich and David W. Rohde, "The Transition to Republican Rule in the House: Implications for Theories of Congressional Parties," *Political Science Quarterly* 112, no. 4 (1997–1998): 541–67.

56. Barbara Sinclair, *Unorthodox Lawmaking: New Legislative Processes in the U.S. Congress*, 2nd edition (Washington, DC: CQ Press, 2000), 98–99.

57. For a definition of critical juncture, see Slater and Simmons, "Informative Regress," 887.

58. Ornstein and Mann, "When Congress Checks Out."

59. Sinclair, *Unorthodox Lawmaking*, 98–99.

60. Sinclair, *Unorthodox Lawmaking*, 97; Barbara Sinclair, *Party Wars: Polarization and the Politics of National Policy Making* (Norman: University of Oklahoma Press, 2006), 128; Julian Zelizer, *On Capitol Hill: The Struggle to Reform and Its Consequences, 1948–2000* (Cambridge: Cambridge University Press, 2004), 257. House leadership relies on an extended political network (EPN) of politically affiliated interest groups, think tanks, and activists for its policy proposals and analysis. See Zachary Albert and Raymond J. La Raja, "Political Parties and Policy Analysis," in *Policy Analysis in the United States*, edited by John A. Hird (Bristol. Policy Press, 2018).

61. Marlowe, "Reclaiming Institutional Relevance," 121.

62. Christopher J. Deering and Stephen S. Smith, *Committees in Congress*, 3rd edition (Washington, DC: CQ Press, 1997), 49.

63. Fowler, *Watchdogs on the Hill*, 51.

64. Fowler, *Watchdogs on the Hill*, 29–30, 51.

65. Committee on Governmental Affairs. *Final Report of the Committee on Governmental Affairs: United States Senate: Together with Additional and Minority Views: Investigation of Illegal or Improper Activities in Connection with 1996 Federal Election Campaigns* (105th Cong., 2d sess., 1998. Rept. 105-167), 3.

66. Paul C. Light, *Government by Investigation: Congress, Presidents, and the Search for Answers 1945–2012* (Washington, DC: Brookings Institution Press, 2014), 38.

67. Senator Thompson was chairman of the Senate Committee on Governmental Affairs from 1997 to 2001 and had a with a party unity score of 87.538 for the 105th Congress. The party unity score is taken from Keith T. Poole, "Party Unity Scores," May 31, 2015, https://legacy.voteview.com/Party_Unity.htm, accessed February 23, 2022.

68. Committee on Governmental Affairs. *Final Report of the Committee on Governmental Affairs: United States Senate: Together with Additional and Minority Views: Investigation of Illegal or Improper Activities in Connection with 1996 Federal Election Campaigns* (105th Cong., 2d sess., 1998. Rept. 105-167), 9–10.

69. Committee on Governmental Affairs. *Final Report of the Committee on Governmental Affairs: United States Senate: Together with Additional and Minority*

Views: Investigation of Illegal or Improper Activities in Connection with 1996 Federal Election Campaigns (105th Cong., 2d sess., 1998. Rept. 105-167), 3.

70. Jeff Gerth and David Johnston, "Evidence of Broad Plan by China to Buy Entrée to U.S. Technology," *New York Times*, December 15, 1998, https://www.nytimes.com/1998/12/15/us/evidence-of-broad-plan-by-china-to-buy-entree-to-us-technology.html, accessed January 13, 2022.

71. David E. Rosenbaum, "Campaign Finance: The Hearings; Anger Flares as Focus Shifts to Campaign remedies," *New York Times*, September 24, 1997, https://www.nytimes.com/1997/09/24/us/campaign-finance-the-hearings-anger-flares-as-focus-shifts-to-campaign-remedies.html, accessed January 13, 2022.

72. Committee on Governmental Affairs. *Final Report of the Committee on Governmental Affairs: United States Senate: Together with Additional and Minority Views: Investigation of Illegal or Improper Activities in Connection with 1996 Federal Election Campaigns* (105th Cong., 2d sess., 1998. Rept. 105-167), 4513.

73. Committee on Governmental Affairs. *Final Report of the Committee on Governmental Affairs: United States Senate: Together with Additional and Minority Views: Investigation of Illegal or Improper Activities in Connection with 1996 Federal Election Campaigns* (105th Cong., 2d sess., 1998. Rept. 105-167), 9531. The majority listed 68 listed staff members. See Committee on Governmental Affairs. *Final Report of the Committee on Governmental Affairs: United States Senate: Together with Additional and Minority Views: Investigation of Illegal or Improper Activities in Connection with 1996 Federal Election Campaigns* (105th Cong., 2d sess., 1998. Rept. 105-167), II–III.

74. Kriner and Schickler, *Investigating the President*, 217–22.

75. Kriner and Schickler, *Investigating the President*, 224.

76. Marlowe, "Reclaiming Institutional Relevance," 120.

77. Jacob R. Straus, "Congressional Commissions: Overview and Considerations for Congress," *CRS Report*, January 22, 2021, https://crsreports.congress.gov/product/pdf/R/R40076, accessed January 14, 2022.

78. The House Committee on Oversight and Governmental Reform and the Senate Committee on Homeland Security and Governmental Affairs are the primary oversight committees. See G. Edward DeSeve, *The Presidential Appointee's Handbook* (Washington, DC: Brookings Institution Press, 2017), 141.

79. Sinclair, *Party Wars*; Nolan McCarty, Keith T. Poole, and Howard Rosenthal, *Polarized America: The Dance of Ideology and Unequal Riches* (Boston: MIT Press, 2006); Gary C. Jacobson, "Partisan Polarization in American Politics: A Background Paper," *Presidential Studies Quarterly* 43, no. 4 (2013): 688–708; Gary C. Jacobson, "Polarization, Gridlock, and Presidential Campaign Politics in 2016," *The ANNALS of the American Academy of Political and Social Science* 667, no. 1 (2016): 226–46.

80. Light, *Government by Investigation*, 23, 42, 54.

81. Zelizer, *On Capitol Hill*, 177–78.

82. Congress picks its presidential target carefully, taking into consideration external factors. See David C.W. Parker and Matthew Dull, "Rooting Out Waste, Fraud, and Abuse: The Politics of House Committee Investigations, 1947 to 2004," *Political Research Quarterly* 66, no. 3 (2013): 630–44. If a president has a 60 percent

approval rating, he will face one-third fewer days of investigations than a president with a 50 percent approval rating. See Douglas Kriner and Liam Schwartz, "Divided Government and Congressional Investigations," *Legislative Studies Quarterly* 33, no. 2 (2008): 308.

83. Kriner and Schickler, *Investigating the President*, 90, 113, 244, 245.

84. Douglas Kriner and Eric Schickler, "Investigating the President: Committee Probes and Presidential Approval, 1953 – 2006," *The Journal of Politics* 76, no. 2 (2014): 526.

85. Kriner and Schickler, "Investigating the President"; Kriner and Schickler, *Investigating the President*; David C.W. Parker and Matthew Dull, "Divided We Quarrel: The Politics of Congressional Investigations, 1947–2004," *Legislative Studies Quarterly* 34, no. 3 (2009): 325.

86. Steven J. Balla and Christopher J. Deering, "Police Patrols and Fire Alarms: An Empirical Examination of the Legislative Preference for Oversight," *Congress & the Presidency* 40, no. 1 (2013): 29.

87. Eric M. Patashnik and Justin Peck, "Can Congress Do Policy Analysis? The Politics of Problem Solving on Capitol Hill," in *Does Policy Analysis Matter? Exploring Its Effectiveness in Theory and Practice*, edited by Lee S. Friedman (University of California Press, 2017), 88.

88. Marlowe, "Reclaiming Institutional Relevance," 112.

89. National Archives, "Federal Register: The Daily Journal of the United States Government," https://www.federalregister.gov/agencies, accessed October 25, 2021.

90. Balla and Deering, "Police Patrols and Fire Alarms."

91. Fowler, *Watchdogs on the Hill*, 40–41.

92. Mathew McCubbins and Thomas Schwartz, "Congressional Oversight Overlooked: Police Patrols versus Fire Alarms," *American Journal of Political Science* 28, no. 1 (1984): 165–79; Ornstein and Mann, "When Congress Checks Out"; Light, *Government by Investigation*, 41; Parker and Dull, "Rooting Out Waste," 631.

93. Balla and Deering, "Police Patrols and Fire Alarms," 29.

94. Fowler, *Watchdogs on the Hill*, 135.

95. Fowler, *Watchdogs on the Hill*, 137.

96. Light, *Government by Investigation*, 36. Both pre- and post-Watergate investigations can decrease public support for a president. See Kriner and Schickler, *Investigating the President*, 93.

97. Light, *Government by Investigation*, 42.

98. Parker and Dull, "Rooting Out Waste," 631.

99. Bryan W. Marshall and Bruce C. Wolpe, "From Presidential 'Shakedown' to Congressional Apology: The Politics of Committee Oversight of BP's Deepwater Horizon Crisis," in *The Committee: A Study of Policy, Power, Politics and Obama's Historic Legislative Agenda on Capitol Hill* (University of Michigan Press, 2018), 128, 131. The result was the passage of one bill, allowing Obama more flexibility in spending funds from the Oil Spill Liability Trust Fund. See Marshall and Wolpe, "From Presidential 'Shakedown,'" 131.

100. Jacobson, "Partisan Polarization," 697, 700, 703, 705.

101. Anthony Downs, *An Economic Theory of Democracy* (New York: Harper, 1957); Gary Cox and Mathew McCubbins, *Setting the Agenda: Responsible Party Government in the U.S. House of Representatives* (Cambridge: Cambridge University Press, 2005).

102. Douglas Kriner, *After the Rubicon: Congress, Presidents, and the Politics of Waging War* (Chicago: University of Chicago Press, 2010); Scott Sigmund Gartner and Gary M. Segura, "All Politics are Still Local: The Iraq War and the 2006 Midterm Elections," *PS: Political Science & Politics* 41, no. 1 (2008): 95–100; Howell and Pevehouse, *While Dangers Gather.*

103. John Aldrich, *Why Parties? The Origin and Transformation of Political Parties in America* (Chicago, IL: University of Chicago Press, 1995); Cox and McCubbins, *Setting the Agenda*; Kriner and Schickler, *Investigating the President.*

104. Neustadt, *Presidential Power*, 76.

105. George C. Edwards III, *At the Margins: Presidential Leadership of Congress* (New Haven, CT: Yale University Press, 1989), 206; Sarah A. Binder, "The Dynamics of Legislative Gridlock, 1947–96," *American Political Science Review* 93, no. 3 (1999): 527–28; Richard S. Conley, *The Presidency, Congress and Divided Government* (College Station, TX: Texas A&M University Press, 2003).

106. Kriner and Schickler, *Investigating the President*, 245.

107. Rockman, "Reinventing What for Whom?,"137.

108. Parker and Dull, "Divided We Quarrel"; Kriner and Schwartz, "Divided Government."

109. Fowler, *Watchdogs on the Hill*, 110. This applies to the Senate Armed Services and Foreign Relations Committees from 1947 to 2008.

110. Parker and Dull, "Divided We Quarrel," 333.

111. Parker and Dull, "Divided We Quarrel."

112. Kriner and Schwartz, "Divided Government."

113. Parker and Dull, "Divided We Quarrel," 331–32.

114. Parker and Dull, "Rooting Out Waste," 640.

115. Parker and Dull, "Rooting Out Waste," 639.

116. Norman J. Ornstein and Thomas E. Mann, "When Congress Checks Out," *Foreign Affairs* 85, no. 6 (2006): 71.

117. Kriner, "Can Enhanced Oversight," 778–79.

118. Douglas Kriner and Francis Shen, "Responding to War on Capitol Hill: Battlefield Casualties, Congressional Response, and Public Support for the War in Iraq," *American Journal of Political Science* 58, no. 1 (2014): 162.

119. Kriner and Schickler, *Investigating the President*, 212.

120. Kriner and Schwartz, "Divided Government," 314; Kriner and Schickler, *Investigating the President*, 92–93; Kriner, "Can Enhanced Oversight."

121. David P. Auerswald and Colton C. Campbell, "Congress and National Security," in *Congress and the Politics of National Security*, edited by David P. Auerswald and Colton C. Campbell (Cambridge: Cambridge University Press, 2012), 5; Louis Fisher, "War Powers," in *The Law of the Executive Branch: Presidential Power* (New York: Oxford University Press, 2014); Fowler, *Watchdogs on the Hill*; William G.

Howell and Jon C. Pevehouse, "Presidents, Congress, and the Use of Force," *International Organization* 59, no. 1 (2005): 211.

122. Fowler, *Watchdogs on the Hill*, 45.

123. Kriner and Schickler, *Investigating the President*, 89.

124. Nyhan, "Scandal Potential"; Miguel M. Pereira and Nicholas W. Waterbury, "Do Voters Discount Political Scandals over Time?," *Political Research Quarterly* 72, no. 3 (2019): 584–95.

125. Nyhan, "Scandal Potential," 457.

126. Kriner, "Can Enhanced Oversight," 766; Kriner and Shen, "Responding to War," 171.

127. Kriner and Schwartz, "Divided Government," 310.

128. Sinclair, *Party Wars*, 140.

129. Parker and Dull, "Divided We Quarrel," 325; Parker and Dull, "Rooting Out Waste," 633.

130. Smist, *Congress Oversees*, 19–24.

131. Deering and Smith, *Committees in Congress*, 146.

132. The other types of House committees are as follows: 1. Cartel (includes the Budget, Energy and Commerce, Ways and Means, and Appropriations Committees), 2. Distributive, and 3. Miscellaneous (includes the Agriculture, Interior, Merchant Marines, DC Committees). See Parker and Dull, "Rooting Out Waste," 634–35.

133. Parker and Dull, "Rooting Out Waste."

134. Light, *Government by Investigation*, 29. From Light's list of 100 investigations, I selected foreign policy investigations, if the investigation related to an executive branch foreign policy decision and included at least one of the following committees: (1) House or Senate Armed Services, (2) Senate Foreign Relations or Foreign Affairs or House Foreign Affairs or International Relations, (3) a select committee (e.g., Senate Select Committee on Intelligence, House Permanent Select Committee on Intelligence), (4) a subcommittee on foreign operations, or (5) a joint committee on a foreign policy issue. This gives a total of 26 investigations and a total of 78 committees. For the Cold War period (1945–1971), the investigations were as follows: (1) Pearl Harbor (1945), (2) Communists in government (1948), (3) Conduct of the Korean War (1951), (4) Air Force preparedness for the cold war (1956), (5) U.S. response to the Sputnik launch (1957), (6) Defense Department stockpiling (1962), (7) Lobbying by foreign governments (1962), (8) Military muzzling (1962), (9) Government information management (1963), (10) Conduct of the Vietnam War (1966), and (11) Vietnam prisoners of war (POWs) and missing in action (MIAs) (1969). For the end of Cold War consensus period (1972–1994), the investigations were as follows: (1) Energy shortages (1973), (2) Intelligence agency abuses (1975), (3) South Korean lobbying (1977), (4) Bombing of Beirut Marine barracks (1983), (5) Central America policy (1983), (6) Strategic missile forces (1983), (7) 1980 "October surprise" (1984), (8) White House Iran-Contra program (1987), (9) Vietnam POWs and MIAs (1991), (10) 1980 "October surprise" (1992), and (11) U.S. intelligence agencies in the post-cold war era (1994). For the Republican majority period (1995–2021), the investigations were as follows: (1) Secret arms shipments to Bosnia (1996), (2) Technology transfers to China (1997), (3) 9/11 terrorist attacks (2002), and (4)

Conduct of the Iraq War (2003). See Light, *Government by Investigation*, Appendix C. The Vietnam POWs and MIAs and 1980 "October surprise" investigations are traced back to their original investigation dates (1969 for Vietnam POWs and MIAs and 1984 for 1980 "October surprise") for the purpose of consistency, even though these original investigations were not identified in Light's list of 100 most significant investigations. To get the average party unity score for each period, I added the party unity score for each investigation committee chair and then divided by the number of investigations for the period. The party unity score is taken from Poole, "Party Unity Scores."

135. Deering and Smith, *Committees in Congress*, 162; David C. King, *Turf Wars: How Congressional Committees Claim Jurisdiction* (Chicago: University of Chicago Press, 1997), 111–12; William F. West, *Controlling the Bureaucracy: Institutional Constraints in Theory and Practice* (Armonk: M.E. Sharpe, 1995), 131.

136. Carol H. Weiss, "Congressional Committees as Users of Analysis," *Journal of Policy Analysis and Management* 8, no. 3 (1989): 411–31.

137. George C. Edwards III, Kenneth R. Mayer and Stephen J. Wayne, *Presidential Leadership: Politics and Policy Making*, 11th edition (Lanham, MD: Rowman & Littlefield, 2020), 338.

138. Deering and Smith, *Committees in Congress*, 163.

139. Deering and Smith, *Committees in Congress*, 166.

140. The organizations are as follows: (1) The Congressional Research Service reviews literature, collects and analyzes data to assist with program review. (2) The Office of Technology Assessment provides expertise for oversight tasks. (3) The Congressional Budget Office provides expertise for oversight tasks. (4) The General Accountability Office employs specialists in accounting, economics, and public management. See West, *Controlling the Bureaucracy*, 131.

141. Zegart, "Domestic Politics," 17.

142. Molly Reynolds, Norman J. Ornstein, Thomas E. Mann, and Michael J. Malbin, "Chapter 5: Congressional Staff and Operating Expenses," in *Vital Statistics on Congress* (Washington, DC; Brookings Institution, 2021).

143. King, *Turf Wars*, 111; Parker and Dull, "Rooting Out Waste," 639.

144. Nyhan, "Scandal Potential," 438.

145. Kriner and Schickler, "Investigating the President"; Cox and McCubbins, *Setting the Agenda*.

146. Pereira and Waterbury, "Do Voters Discount," 585. Pereira and Waterbury analyze House members and scandals, but they "have reasons to believe" their results "generalize to other offices." See Pereira and Waterbury, "Do Voters Discount," 592.

147. See Aldrich and Rohde, "Transition to Republican Rule"; Sinclair, *Unorthodox Lawmaking*; Sinclair, *Party Wars*; Deering and Smith, *Committees in Congress*.

148. Ornstein and Mann, "When Congress Checks Out"; Downs, *Economic Theory of Democracy*; Cox and McCubbins, *Setting the Agenda*.

149. Jacobson, "Partisan Polarization."

150. Parker and Dull, "Divided We Quarrel," 325; Parker and Dull, "Rooting Out Waste," 633; Kriner and Schickler, *Investigating the President*; James Campbell, "The Presidential Surge and Its Midterm Decline, 1868–1988," *Journal of Politics* 53,

no. 2 (1991): 477–87; Kriner and Schickler, "Investigating the President"; Aldrich, *Why Parties?*; Cox and McCubbins, *Setting the Agenda.*

151. See Sinclair, *Unorthodox Lawmaking*, 97–98; Ornstein and Mann, "When Congress Checks Out"; King, *Turf Wars*, 83, 111–12.

152. See Kriner and Schwartz, "Divided Government."

153. I believe staff develop a record of loyalty to the party and its congressional members, and this loyalty means staff do not have the ability to apply "counterpressure" to congressional members. Notably, staff do not have the protection of tenure or a merit system. See Neustadt, *Presidential Power*, 35; Edwards, Mayer and Wayne, *Presidential Leadership*, 338.

154. John Gerring, "What Is a Case Study and What Is It Good for?," *American Political Science Review* 98, no. 2 (2004): 342; Christopher H. Achen and Duncan Snidal, "Rational Deterrence Theory and Comparative Case Studies," *World Politics* 41, no. 2 (1989): 143–69; Gary King, Robert O. Keohane, and Sidney Verba, *Designing Social Inquiry: Scientific Inference in Qualitative Research* (Princeton, NJ: Princeton University Press, 1994); Barbara Geddes, "How the Cases You Choose Affect the Answers You Get: Selection Bias in Political Science," *Political Analysis* 2, no. 1 (1990): 131–50; Arend Lijphart, "Comparative Politics and the Comparative Method," *American Political Science Review* 65, no. 3 (1971): 692.

155. Stephen Van Evera, *Guide to Methods to Students of Political Science* (London: Cornell University Press, 1997), 29–30, 54–55. My unit of analysis, the Benghazi Committee investigation, is consistent with Kriner and Schickler's definition of investigation "as committee-led inquiries into allegations of abuse of power or misconduct by some official within the executive branch." See Kriner and Schickler, *Investigating the President*, 104.

156. Adam Przeworski and Henry Teune, *The Logic of Comparative Social Inquiry* (New York: Wiley-Interscience, 1970), 17; Bernard E. Brown, "The Case Method in Comparative Politics," in *Cases in Comparative Politics*, 3rd edition, edited by Bernard E. Brown and James B. Christoph (Boston, MA: Little, Brown, 1976), 3; Timothy McKeown, "Case Studies and the Statistical Worldview," *International Organization* 53, no. 1 (1999): 174; Gerardo L. Munck, "Canons of Research Design in Qualitative Analysis," *Studies in Comparative International Development* 33, no. 3 (1998): 35–36.

157. Christopher Layne, "Kant or Cant: The Myth of the Democratic Peace," *International Security* 19, no. 2 (1994): 13.

158. Jack S. Levy, "Case Studies: Types, Designs, and Logics of Inference," *Conflict Management and Peace Science* 25, no. 1 (2008): 11.

159. Levy, "Case Studies," 12; Slater and Simmons, "Informative Regress," 889.

Chapter 3

Benghazi Committee Investigation

INTRODUCTION

The official Benghazi Committee website projected an aura of completeness and objectivity. Members and staff had interviewed about 81 witnesses, obtained 75,000 new pages of documents, and wrote a final report that "reveal[ed] significant new information, [that] fundamentally change[d]" one's understanding of the terrorist attack.[1] Did this external projection match the internal dynamics of the investigation? This chapter reviews prior Benghazi congressional investigations and applies the partisan model to the Benghazi Committee investigation. Organizing the investigation into its partisan brand elements: leadership and staff and focus of the investigation, I test and assess my model using process tracing and logit regression analysis to find support for the hypotheses of members and staff activities being consistent with furthering party goals.

BENGHAZI CONGRESSIONAL INVESTIGATIONS, 2012–2014

In response to the Benghazi attack, the government conducted 12 investigations. The Federal Bureau of Investigation (FBI) initiated its investigation in September 2012, and the State Department Accountability Review Board (ARB) initiated its investigation in October 2012.[2] In terms of congressional investigations, six House committees, including the Select Committee on Benghazi, and four Senate committees conducted investigations.

House Committee on Oversight and Government Reform (OGR) Investigation

On October 5, 2012, the OGR Committee, chaired by Darrell Issa (R-CA), launched its investigation and held its first hearing, "The Security Failures of Benghazi," on October 10.[3] OGR Republicans took a two-track approach to the investigation: (1) Did the Obama administration mislead the public in its post-attack statements? (2) Had the Obama administration failed to provide adequate security for the Benghazi Mission compound?[4] The Democrats, led by Ranking Member Elijah Cummings (D-MD), immediately began accusing the Republicans of withholding documents and access to witnesses as part of a partisan investigation.[5]

On April 23, 2013, Issa, along with the Republican chairs of the Armed Services, Foreign Affairs, Intelligence, and Judiciary Committees, released a House Republican Conference interim progress report which blamed Clinton for a failure of security at the compound.[6] The report wrongly stated that Clinton's signature on an April 19, 2012, cable meant Clinton personally approved decreasing security in Libya, including that at the Benghazi compound.[7]

Labeled "whistleblowers," former deputy chief of Mission in Libya Gregory Hicks, former regional security officer in Libya Eric Nordstrom, and deputy coordinator for Operations Mark Thompson testified on May 8, 2013.[8] They believed the ARB panel "stopped short of interviewing people that . . . were involved in key decisions."[9] Hick's testimony on what was likely Stevens's last phone call was noteworthy with Hicks remembering that Stevens stated, "We're under attack."[10] The hearing, at times, included questions to witnesses which asked them to speculate on issues beyond their purview, such as the possibility of a military response or the crafting of the post-attack talking points.[11]

On September 16, 2013, the OGR Republican staff released an interim report, which questioned the "independence and integrity" of the ARB investigation.[12] Three days later, OGR held a third hearing with two panels. For the first panel, it focused on the ARB investigation and whether its report was a "whitewash" or "cover-up."[13] One of the allegations was that ARB co-chair Mullen interviewed Lamb and then notified Clinton confidante Mills that Lamb, who was scheduled to appear before the OGR, "could be a very difficult appearance for the State Department."[14] For the second panel, Patricia Smith, mother of Sean Smith, and Charles Woods, father of Tyrone Woods, testified about not receiving answers to what occurred in Benghazi.[15]

For its fourth and final hearing on May 1, 2014, OGR invited a panel of experts to discuss the Libyan security situation before, during, and after the attack.[16] The panel included Brigadier General Lovell, who was in the U.S. Africa Command JOC during the attack, who testified that he knew it was an al-Qaeda or al-Qaeda-affiliated (i.e., Ansar al-Sharia) attack "very, very soon, when we were still in the very early, early hours of this [attack]."[17]

Senate Committee on Homeland Security and Governmental Affairs Investigation

On October 12, 2012, the Homeland Security Committee announced that it would conduct an investigation on the Obama administration's post-attack statements. On December 30, 2012, Chair Joseph Lieberman (D-CT) and Ranking Member Susan Collins (R-ME) released a bipartisan report with 10 findings. Highlights included the following: (1) there was a lack of actionable intelligence prior to the attack; (2) the State Department did not increase security in Benghazi despite Intelligence Community (IC) reporting of a high-threat environment; (3) the military did not have "assets or personnel close enough" to respond to the attacks; and (4) the IC issued talking points before having "a high degree of confidence about what happened in Benghazi and in the midst of a national political campaign."[18]

House Permanent Select Committee on Intelligence (HPSCI) Investigation

HPSCI began its investigation "immediately after being notified of the attacks" and held 20 events and hearings.[19] On April 2, 2014, former acting director and deputy director of the CIA Michael Morell testified about the drafting of the HPSCI talking points. He stated that he and the CIA had "performed [their] duties in accordance with the highest standards of objectivity and nonpartisanship."[20]

On November 21, 2014, HPSCI released a report with 17 findings. The report highlights included the following: (1) the IC provided strategic warning and did not fail to provide tactical warning because there was no credible intelligence of an attack; (2) the CIA provided sufficient security at its annex; (3) the CIA was not shipping arms from Libya to Syria; (4) members of al-Qaeda in the lands of the Islamic Maghreb (AQIM), al-Qaeda in the Arabian Peninsula (AQAP), al-Qaeda in Iraq (AQI), the Muhammad Jamal Network (MJN), Ansar al-Sharia (AAS), Abu Abaydah Ibn Jarah Battalion (UJB), and Qadhafi loyalists participated in the attacks; (6) The chief of base in Benghazi did not issue a stand-down order to the annex Global Response Staff (GRS) team; (7) the CIA received all the military support that was available; (8) CIA's Office of Public Affairs and Morrell made significant changes to the HPSCI talking points; and (9) the CIA failed to challenge its initial assessment of a protest prior to the attack.[21]

Senate Committee on Foreign Relations Investigation

On January 23, 2013, Clinton testified for the first time before the Foreign Relations Committee and then before the House Foreign Affairs Committee.[22] Before the Foreign Relations Committee, Clinton, responding to Senator Ron Johnson's (R-WI) question about whether Rice had misled the public on the Sunday talk shows, made a statement that went viral: "Was it because of a protest or was it because of guys out for a walk one night who decided they would go kill some Americans? What difference, at this point, does it make?"[23]

House Foreign Affairs Committee Investigation

On the same day, January 23, 2013, Clinton also testified before the House Foreign Affairs Committee. Clinton's comments were less newsworthy, but according to Marlowe, the hearing was equally partisan. Democrats "used their time to praise the accomplishments" of Clinton and "express gratitude" for what she had done as secretary of state.[24] Republicans used "their time for making political statements about the failure of the administration" and asked questions "so quickly that Clinton was able to evade responding to many of them."[25] On February 7, 2014, the Republicans released a report calling the ARB investigation "seriously deficient" and used "to deflect criticism of its senior leadership."[26] It blamed the State Department for "[refusing] to meaningfully discipline any of the four employees that the ARB *did* fault."[27] It also examined the talking points and how Obama "promoted a flawed and deeply misleading public narrative."[28]

Senate Select Committee on Intelligence (SSCI) Investigation

SSCI began its investigation of the attack on September 13, 2012, and it held three hearings.[29] In a closed-door hearing on November 16, 2012, former CIA director Petraeus informed HPSCI and SSCI lawmakers that intelligence reports stated that al-Qaeda affiliate and AAS had conducted the attack, but the Obama administration did not publicly reveal that fact to avoid tipping off those extremist groups.[30]

On January 15, 2014, SSCI released a report with 14 findings. Highlights included the following: (1) the IC provided "ample strategic warning" that personnel in Benghazi were at risk; (2) the State Department should have increased its security posture in Benghazi given IC threat reporting; (3) there was no tactical intelligence warning of an attack; (4) the military was not in a position to respond "in short order" to the attack; and (5) IC analysts "inaccurately" reported a protest at the compound prior to the attack.[31] Notably, SSCI Democrats concluded the attack was "likely preventable," if the State Department had increased its security given the strategic warnings.[32] SSCI Republicans pointed out Lamb, Kennedy, Clinton, and Dempsey as "failures in leadership."[33] As detailed in the report appendix, SSCI met with the Office of the Director of National Intelligence (ODNI) General Counsel Robert Litt in three sessions to investigate the drafting of the HPSCI talking points. Litt briefed 11 (later 12) different drafts of the talking points that took place from Friday, September 14, 2012, to Saturday, September 15, 2012. ODNI and CIA made 8 of the 12 changes, while Rhodes, Sullivan, and Vietor made the other 4 changes.[34]

House Armed Services Committee (HASC) Investigation

On September 19, 2013, HASC held a hearing with a focus on understanding post-Benghazi Defense Department posture changes. Representative Martha Roby (R-AL) affirmed in her opening statement that military forces were not "unduly held back, or told to stand down, or refused permission to enter the fight. Rather, [the military was] so badly postured, they could not have made a difference."[35]

On February 7, 2014, HASC Republicans released its report, making it clear that it was reaffirming the findings of the April 23, 2013, House Republican Conference interim progress report.[36] Other highlights included the following: (1) the White House "failed to comprehend or ignored the dramatically deteriorating security situation in Libya"; (2) the Americans in Benghazi were "woefully vulnerable" due to a lack of military posture, threat intelligence, and the State Department wanting a reduced Department of Defense presence; (3) Ham and "most" at U.S. Africa Command believed it was a terrorist attack, not a protest; (4) the military response was "severely degraded" due to the location of the attack and its posture of forces; (5) military leadership "did not take all possible steps" in preparation for potentially prolonged operations; and (6) there was no "stand-down" order issued to military personnel in Tripoli, seeking to go to Benghazi.[37] The report affirms that the military "performed well in responding to the attacks," including making the decision not to send F-16s to Benghazi.[38]

Senate Committee on Armed Services (SASC) Investigation

On September 14, 2012, former secretary of defense Leon Panetta and former chair, joint chiefs of Staff General Martin Dempsey briefed SASC about what was known about the attack.[39] They returned on February 2, 2013, for a hearing. Panetta testified, "Although we had forces deployed to the region, time, distance, the lack of an adequate warning, events that moved very quickly on the ground prevented a more immediate response."[40] Dempsey testified, "[The military] did what [its] posture and capabilities allowed."[41]

In response to Senator John McCain's (R-AZ) question about why the military was unprepared pre-September 11 to respond to a volatile situation in Libya, Dempsey stated, "[The military] never received a request for support from the State Department."[42]

House Judiciary Committee Investigation

The Judiciary Committee, under Chair Bob Goodlatte (R-VA), released its investigation findings as part of the April 23, 2013, House Republican Conference interim progress report.[43] It focused on the FBI investigation and detailed how the FBI did not arrive to investigate the scene until more than three weeks after the attack.[44]

HOUSE SELECT COMMITTEE ON BENGHAZI INVESTIGATION, 2014–2017

The Benghazi Committee was the 10th and final congressional investigation of the Benghazi attack.

Creation of the Select Committee on Benghazi

An outside group, Judicial Watch, triggered the sixth House committee fire alarm investigation of the Benghazi attack. On April 29, 2014, Judicial Watch announced it had obtained an email from Rhodes via a Freedom of Information Act (FOIA) request. In the email, Rhodes coordinated the White House talking points and advised Rice that she should emphasize the attacks were "rooted in an Internet video, and not a broader failure of policy."[45]

On May 2, 2014, House Speaker John Boehner (R-OH) proposed the creation of the Select Committee on Events Surrounding the 2012 Terrorist Attack in Benghazi, and on May 8, 2014, the House voted to establish it. It was tasked with investigating the following:

- all policies, decisions, and activities that contributed to the attack on United States facilities in Benghazi, Libya, on September 11, 2012, as well as those that affected the ability of the United States to prepare for the attacks;
- all policies, decisions, and activities to respond to and repel the attacks on United States facilities in Benghazi, Libya, on September 11, 2012, including efforts to rescue United States personnel;
- internal and public executive branch communications about the attacks on United States facilities in Benghazi, Libya, on September 11, 2012;

- accountability for policies and decisions related to the security of facilities in Benghazi, Libya, and the response to the attacks, including individuals and entities responsible for those policies and decisions;
- executive branch authorities' efforts to identify and bring to justice the perpetrators of the attacks on U.S. facilities in Benghazi, Libya, on September 11, 2012;
- executive branch activities and efforts to comply with Congressional inquiries into the attacks on United States facilities in Benghazi, Libya, on September 11, 2012;
- recommendations for improving executive branch cooperation and compliance with congressional oversight and investigations;
- information related to lessons learned from the attacks and executive branch activities and efforts to protect United States facilities and personnel abroad; and
- any other relevant issues relating to the attacks, the response to the attacks, or the investigation by the House of Representatives into the attacks.[46]

The Benghazi Committee began as a bipartisan effort. Committee Chair Trey Gowdy (R-SC) and Ranking Member Cummings released two joint statements on July 9 and July 31, 2014.[47] The first two hearings on September 17, 2014, and December 10, 2014, were equally a bipartisan effort with the committee focused on reviewing the ARB recommendations.[48] In the first hearing, Cummings secured an agreement from Gowdy to have the State Department provide an update on the status of implementing the final seven ARB recommendations, which served as the focus of the second hearing.[49]

By the third hearing on January 27, 2015, and with a focus on the state of compliance with State Department and CIA document requests, the cooperation had ended amid accusations of partisanship.[50] Cummings stated the committee had taken a "partisan path," and he was "concerned about the glacial path of [the Benghazi] committee's investigation."[51] Gowdy responded that the Democrats were just as guilty of partisanship, having created "an asked-and-answered Web site" before the investigation had concluded.[52] With the exception of Michael Pompeo (R-KS) and Lynn Westmoreland (R-GA), the committee members directed their questions to the State Department official, deputy assistant secretary for house affairs Joel Rubin.[53]

APPLYING THE PARTISAN MODEL TO THE BENGHAZI COMMITTEE INVESTIGATION

My partisan model is based on two elements: (1) committee leadership and staff and (2) the focus of the investigation. The main premise of applying the partisan model to the Benghazi investigation is to test Boehner and House Speaker Paul Ryan's (R-WI) stewardship of the Republican Party as it sought to win the national election. Boehner and then Ryan ran the investigation in terms of strategy and operations; the members and staff were vetted to ensure they worked in a manner consistent with the Speaker's directives.

Benghazi Committee Leadership and Staff

On May 5, 2014, Boehner named the Republican members of the Benghazi Committee.[54] The party unity scores of the Republican members are listed in Table 3.1.[55] All of the members voted consistently with the Republican Party more than Boehner. Roby was the least loyal Republican member but still voted with the party 93 percent of the time. Notably, Boehner was Speaker from January 5, 2011, to October 31, 2015, and was in charge of the Benghazi investigation for about 17 months. Ryan was Speaker from November 1, 2015, to January 3, 2019, and was in charge of the Benghazi investigation for about 14 months.

As shown in Table 3.2, 8 of the 15, or 53 percent, of the Republican staff members had Capitol Hill experience.[56]

Focus of Investigation

For the investigation focus, I examine three inputs: witness interviews, press releases, and document requests.

Witness Interviews

One way to understand the focus of the Benghazi investigation is to analyze the witness interviews.[57] Table 3.3 provides a summary of the leadership or high-profile interviews. The Benghazi Committee not only interviewed more

Table 3.1 Benghazi Committee Republican Member Party Unity Scores

Majority Party Leadership and Committee Members	*Party Unity Score*
Speaker John Boehner (R-OH)	90.476
Speaker Paul Ryan (R-WI)	97.041
Committee Chair Trey Gowdy (R-SC)	97.605
Member Susan Brooks (R-IN)	96.209
Member Jim Jordan (R-OH)	97.038
Member Michael Pompeo (R-KS)	98.597
Member Martha Roby (R-AL)	93.128
Member Peter Roskam (R-IL)	95.948
Member Lynn Westmoreland (R-GA)	96.633

Table 3.2 Benghazi Committee Republican Staff

Staff Member	*Capitol Hill Experience*	*Position*	*Term of Employment*
Phil Kiko	Yes	Staff Director	May 22, 2014–July 31, 2016
Christopher Donesa	Yes	Deputy Staff Director	June 16, 2014–January 2, 2017
Dana Chipman	No	Chief Counsel	July 21, 2014–January 18, 2016
Sharon Jackson	No	Deputy Chief Counsel	August 25, 2014–January 2, 2017
Craig Missakian	No	Deputy Chief Counsel	September 2, 2014–January 2, 2017
Mark Grider	No	Deputy General Counsel	July 23, 2014–September 18, 2016
J. Mac Tolar	Yes	Senior Counsel	July 14, 2014–November 30, 2016
Sheria Clarke	Yes	Counsel	July 14, 2014–January 2, 2017
Carlton Davis	Yes	Counsel	July 7, 2014–January 2, 2017
Kimberly Betz	Yes	Member Liaison and Counsel	January 19, 2015–December 2, 2016
Sara Barrineau	No	Investigator	September 1, 2014–December 15, 2015
Luke Burke[a]	Yes	Investigator	Summer 2014–Summer 2015
Bradley Podliska	No	Investigator	September 2, 2014–August 1, 2015; December 13, 2016–January 2, 2017
Sarah Adams	No	Senior Adviser	January 5, 2015–January 2, 2017
Brien Beattie	Yes	Professional Staff Member	July 1, 2014–September 4, 2015

[a]Detailee.

State Department officials than other executive branch officials, but it did so earlier in its investigation. The first State Department interview was conducted on February 10, 2015, in contrast to the first White House interview conducted on December 16, 2015.[58] The interview of Defense Department's Stephen Hedger is noteworthy in that it occurred after the committee had already released its report.

Table 3.4 reveals more details about the focus of the Benghazi Committee interviews. The committee conducted more interviews of State Department witnesses (including with its seven leadership and high-profile individuals), longer interviews in terms of transcript page counts, and had on average more member and staff attendance at the interviews.

Table 3.5 offers a second analysis, a logit regression, of the leadership and high-profile witnesses. For this regression, the Benghazi Committee investigation witness interview is the unit of analysis. I follow the methodology that David C. W. Parker and Matthew Dull use to define a cartel committee,

Table 3.3 Leadership or High-Profile Witness Interviews

Witness (Leadership or High-Profile)	*Interview Date*	*Number of Interview Pages*	*Republican Members Present*	*Republican Staff Members Present*
	Department of Defense			
Secretary Leon Panetta	January 8, 2016	268	6	8
General Martin Dempsey	No interview request	–	–	–
Admiral James Stavridis	No interview request	–	–	–
General Carter Ham	June 8, 2016	191	4	4
Stephen Hedger	July 14, 2016	160	0	5
	Department of State			
Secretary Hillary Clinton	October 22, 2015	426	7	12
Huma Abedin	October 16, 2015	222	2	7
Cheryl Mills	September 3, 2015	348	4	9
Jacob Sullivan	September 5, 2015	334	4	10
Bryan Pagliano	September 10, 2015	12	6	6
Ambassador Susan Rice	February 2, 2016	224	3	5
Sidney Blumenthal[a]	June 16, 2015	294	7	8
	Intelligence Community			
Michael Flynn	September 29, 2015	170	1	4
David Petraeus	January 6, 2016	152	7	6
David Petraeus	March 19, 2016	61	0	3
	White House			
Barack Obama	No interview	–	–	–
Joseph Biden	No interview request	–	–	–
Ben Rhodes	February 2, 2016	210	2	5

[a]Blumenthal was not a State Department employee, but he was a Clinton confidant.

which is identified as committees "used by parties to protect and enhance the party's reputation and brand" and for the partisan brand in 2016, wherein the majority party saw an opportunity to enhance its reputation at the expense of the State Department and Clinton's 2016 presidential campaign.[59]

I use two dichotomous dependent variables to test my three hypotheses, which repeated from chapter 2, are as follows:

Hypothesis 1: A committee investigation will correlate positively with focusing on the rival political candidate in the next national election.

Hypothesis 2: A member's role will correlate positively with attending high-profile committee events.

Hypothesis 3: A staff member with prior Capitol Hill experience will correlate positively with work assignments on the committee.

Table 3.4 Witness Interview Details

Agency	*Number of Total Witnesses*	*Average Page Count of Interview*	*Number of Leadership/High-Profile Interviews*	*Average Page Count of Leadership/High-Profile Interview*	*Average Number of Members Present for Leadership/High-Profile Interviews*	*Average Number of Staff Present for Leadership/High-Profile Interviews*
Defense	24	126	3	206	3.3	5.7
State	57	177	7	266	4.7	7.5
Intelligence Community[a]	23	172	3	128	2.7	4.3
White House	3	144	1	210	2	5

[a]The page counts are based on released interview details. In total, 23 intelligence community witnesses were interviewed. Details were released for 6 witnesses (3 leaders and 3 others).

Table 3.5 Focus of Investigation: Witness Interview Models

	Hypothesis 1: Focus on Rival Political Candidate	*Hypothesis 2: Members Attend High-Profile Events*	*Hypothesis 3: Assignments for Staff with Prior Capitol Hill Experience*
Unit of Analysis	Witness Interview	Witness Interview	Witness Interview
Dependent Variable	*Member attendance*	*Member attendance*	*Veteran majority*
Explanatory Variable(s)	*State high-profile*	*High-profile*	1. *high-profile*, 2. *state high-profile*, 3. *member attendance*

Table 3.5 offers a summary of the models used to test the hypotheses.

For the first and second hypotheses (Table 3.5), I use a *member attendance* dependent variable, which identifies each individual committee member, Gowdy, Brooks, Jordan, Pompeo, Roby, and Westmoreland, for attendance at witness interviews.[60] For each of the 107 interviews, I code a "1" if the member attended an interview and a "0" if the member did not attend. For example, Westmoreland was the only member to attend the interview of former Defense Intelligence Agency (DIA) director Michael Flynn on September 29, 2015, so I code a "1" for Westmoreland and each of the other members is coded "0."

For the first hypothesis—focusing on a rival candidate (i.e., Clinton), I first construct a control variable, *state*, in which I define State Department as a "1" and other agencies as "0." I then construct an explanatory variable, *high-profile state*, for the seven individuals in State Department leadership or high-profile positions. These individuals—Clinton, deputy chief of Staff for Operations Huma Abedin, Clinton confidant Sidney Blumenthal, Mills, Information Resource Management special adviser Bryan Pagliano, Rice, and Sullivan—are coded "1" and others are coded "0."

For the second hypothesis, members—given their personal interest in enhancing their own reputation—will attend interviews of high-profile individuals, I construct a *high-profile* variable. High-profile individuals, defined as either holding a leadership position based on being the most senior member in an agency or combatant command or as high-profile individuals generating extensive news coverage, are listed in Table 3.3. For these individuals, I code a "1" and a "0" for others for the variable, *high-profile*.

As shown in Table 3.6 and for the first hypothesis, the Gowdy, Jordan, and Pompeo *attendance* variables attain statistical significance and are in the expected direction. The Brooks and Westmoreland *attendance* variables are in the expected direction. Interestingly, Roby *attendance*, which not attaining statistically significant, is in the opposite direction—she was not focused on Clinton or Clinton's inner circle. For Gowdy, if it was a State high-profile interview, the probability of him attending increases by 61 percent (Table 3.7).

Table 3.6 Witness Interview Data Set: Individual Member Logit Estimates

	Benghazi Committee: Individual Member Attendance at Witness Interviews					
Committee Member	Gowdy	Brooks	Jordan	Pompeo	Roby	Westmoreland
State	1.333**	.993	−1.216**	−1.386	1.044	.519
	(.600)	(.823)	(.699)	(1.25)	(1.124)	(.590)
High-Profile	.924	2.197**	1.492**	1.569*	2.303**	1.723**
	(.868)	(1.061)	(.894)	(1.114)	(1.319)	(.912)
State High-Profile	2.838**	.211	2.720**	3.219**	−.416	.985
	(1.453)	(1.400)	(1.496)	(1.721)	(1.596)	(1.448)
Constant	−.636*	-2.485***	−1.204***	−2.485***	−3.219***	−1.435***
	(.412)	(.736)	(.465)	(.736)	(1.020)	(.498)
N	89	89	89	89	89	89
LR Chi-Square(df)	20.42(3)	13.52(3)	23.74(3)	21.94(3)	7.87(3)	12.96(3)
Log Likelihood	−42.639	−39.388	−35.551	−20.308	−29.355	−49.695
Pseudo R2	0.1932	0.1465	0.2503	0.3507	0.1182	0.1154
Prob > Chi-Square	0.0001	0.0036	0.0000	0.0001	0.0488	0.0047

Notes: (1) Numbers in parentheses are standard errors. *p < .10; **p < .05; ***p < .01 (one-tailed tests). (2) Roskam is not able to be analyzed, due to the fact he only attended four interviews: Blumenthal, Clinton, Panetta, and Petraeus.

Table 3.7 Marginal Effects of Independent Variables on Individual Member Attendance at Interviews

Witness Interview	*Gowdy*	*Brooks*	*Jordan*	*Pompeo*	*Roby*	*Westmoreland*
Variable			*Percentage Change*			
State	−26.6	13.7	−19.7	−8.8	8.4	10.9
High-Profile	19.6	45.1	28.7	13.4	35.8	40.3
State High-Profile	61	3.3	57.8	48.4	−3.2	23.5

Jordan and Pompeo were more likely to attend by 57.8 and 48.4 percent, respectively. Both Brooks and Roby, as noted, were less interested in Clinton. Brooks was only 3.3 percent more likely to attend an interview, and Roby was 3.2 percent less likely to attend.

For the second hypothesis, Brooks, Jordan, Pompeo, Roby, and Westmoreland *attendance* attain statistical significance and are in the expected direction in attendance at high-profile interviews. Gowdy *attendance* is in the expected direction. For Brooks, if it was a high-profile interview, the probability of her attending increases by 45.1 percent (Table 3.7). Westmoreland, Roby, Jordan, and Pompeo were more likely to attend by 40.3, 35.8, 28.7, and 13.4 percent, respectively.

For the third hypothesis—staff with prior Capitol Hill experience will correlate with selective work assignments (Table 3.8), I construct a dependent variable, *veteran majority*, which is coded "1" if the majority of Republican staff members attending an interview had prior Capitol Hill experience and a "0" if only a minority of Republican staff members with experience comprised the interviewing group.[61] For example, four of five Republican staff attending the interview of Rhodes on February 2, 2016, were veterans, so I code a "1" for *veteran majority*. For my explanatory variables, I use *high-profile*, *high-profile state*, and *member attendance*.[62] I use a control *state* variable. In using one model, I am estimating for effects while controlling for all of these variables simultaneously. This allows me to identify whether Republican veteran staff majority attendance was due to a high-profile State Department witness or from an individual member's attendance.

For the model (Table 3.8), the *veteran majority* variable attains statistical significance and is in the expected direction for the explanatory variable, *state high-profile*. It attains statistical significance but is in the opposite direction for the control variable, *state*. The fact that the majority of the staff with no prior Capitol Hill experience comprised the majority at State Department interviews is likely due to the sheer number of State Department individuals interviewed. If it was a State Department high-profile witness, the probability of a majority of Republican staff with Capitol Hill experience attending the interview increases by 36.9 percent (Table 3.9). If it was a high-profile witness, the probability decreased by 23.8 percent. This may be due to the fact that veteran staff had a personal interest and were given the responsibility

Table 3.8 Witness Interview Data Set: Veteran Staff Logit Estimates

Benghazi Committee: Veteran Staff Attendance at Witness Interviews	
Variable	*Veteran Majority*
State	−2.012***
	(.671)
High-Profile	−.998
	(1.226)
State High-Profile	3.158*
	(1.994)
Gowdy	.824
	(1.284)
Brooks	.239
	(1.179)
Jordan	3.204**
	(1.803)
Pompeo	−1.186
	(1.826)
Roby	−1.935
	(1.720)
Westmoreland	−.849
	(.745)
Constant	1.493***
	(.606)
N	89
LR Chi-Square(df)	31.42(9)
Log Likelihood	−45.027
Pseudo R2	0.2587
Prob > Chi-Square	0.0003

Note: Numbers in parentheses are standard errors. *p < .10; **p < .05; ***p < .01 (one-tailed tests).

for focusing on Clinton and her inner circle. Individuals from other agencies generated less interest.

In terms of member attendance, the *veteran majority* variable attains statistical significance and is in the expected direction, if Jordan attended the interview. It is in the expected direction for Gowdy and Brooks. Notably, the variable does not attain statistical significance but is in the opposite direction for Pompeo, Roby, and Westmoreland. If Roby attended an interview, the probability of a majority of veteran Republican staff attending the interview decreases by 44.9 percent. This is an interesting finding, as it likely means that veteran staff were attuned to prominent Republicans like Gowdy and Jordan and less so for lesser-known members.

Jordan, in particular, drew considerable interest. If he attended an interview, the probability of a majority veteran Republican staff attending the interview increases by 47.1 percent. With Gowdy, the probability increases by 17.2 percent. This distinction in staff interest between Gowdy and Jordan

Table 3.9 Marginal Effects of Independent Variables on Veteran Staff Attendance at Interviews

Witness Interview	*Veteran Majority*
Variable	*Percentage Change*
State	−39.3
High-Profile	−23.8
State High-Profile	36.9
Gowdy	17.2
Brooks	5.2
Jordan	47.1
Pompeo	−28.5
Roby	−44.9
Westmoreland	−19.6

may be due to Jordan's ongoing conflict with Boehner about the direction of the Republican Party. It is possible, even likely, Boehner directed veteran staff to monitor and report on Jordan's attendance at the interviews. This Boehner-Jordan feud constituted a battle in the Republican Party fracture, which is described in chapter 4.

In terms of further qualitative analysis of hypothesis 3, Staff Director Phil Kiko or Deputy Staff Director Christopher Donesa, as staff leaders, attended every leadership or high-profile interview. Counsel Carlton Davis attended 12 of 14 leadership or high-profile interviews, and he was the lead interviewer for the politically charged interviews of Blumenthal and Hedger.[63] Notably, Chief Counsel Dana Chipman, the former judge advocate general of the Army, and an individual with no Capitol Hill experience had resigned before 19 of 24 Defense Department interviews, including before two of three leadership or high-profile interviews.[64]

Table 3.10 is a frequency count of staff attendance at witness interviews. Counsel Sheria Clarke led veteran Capitol Hill staff with attendance at 61 of 90 witness interviews, while Deputy Chief Counsel Sharon Jackson attended 45 interviews to lead non-experienced staff. Three staff members, Investigator Luke Burke, Investigator Bradley Podliska, and Professional Staff Member Brien Beattie, left the committee by the time the interviews occurred in significant numbers. Removing these outliers, the staff that attended the least number of interviews were Donesa, a veteran, with 20 interviews and Senior Adviser Sarah Adams, non-experienced, with 5 interviews. This veteran-non-experienced gap is even more pronounced given that no other veterans attended less than 35 interviews while only one non-experienced staff member, Chipman, attended more than that number.

Table 3.11 reveals that veteran Benghazi Committee Republican staff members not only attended more interviews than Republican staff members with no Capitol Hill experience, but they also attended an average of three more leadership or high-profile interviews.

Table 3.10 Staff Attendance at Witness Interviews

Staff Member	*Capitol Hill Experience*	*Number of Interviews*	*Percentage of Total Number of Interviews (90) (%)*	*Number of Leadership or High-Profile Interviews (14)*	*Percentage of Total Number of Leadership or High-Profile Interviews (%)*
Phil Kiko	Yes	37	41.1	12	85.7
Christopher Donesa	Yes	20	22.2	11	78.6
Dana Chipman	No	39	43.3	9	64.3
Sharon Jackson	No	45	50	7	50
Craig Missakian	No	25	27.8	8	57.1
Mark Grider	No	15	16.7	2	14.3
J. Mac Tolar	Yes	38	42.2	10	71.4
Sheria Clarke	Yes	61	67.8	7	50
Carlton Davis	Yes	37	41.1	12	85.7
Kimberly Betz	Yes	35	38.9	6	42.9
Sara Barrineau	No	26	28.9	3	21.4
Luke Burke[a]	Yes	0	0	0	0
Bradley Podliska	No	0	0	0	0
Sarah Adams	No	5	5.6	3	21.4
Brien Beattie	Yes	5	5.6	2	14.3

[a]Detailee.

Table 3.11 Staff Attendance at Witness Interviews Comparison

Staff Member	*Average Number of Interviews*	*Average Percentage of Total Number of Interviews (%)*	*Average Number of Leadership or High-Profile Interviews*	*Average Percentage of Total Number of Leadership or High-Profile Interviews (%)*
Capitol Hill Experience	29.1	32.7	7.5	53.6
No Capitol Hill Experience	22.1	24.6	4.6	32.7

Press Releases

A second way to understand the focus of the Benghazi investigation is to analyze its press releases (Table 3.12). From May 5, 2014, to February 6, 2015, there were 16 total press releases: 0 of the press releases were about Clinton, 3 were about the State Department, and 3 were about the White House, Defense Department, or IC.[65]

From March 4 to October 22, 2015, there were 36 total press releases: 26 were about Clinton, 3 were about the State Department, and 0 were about the White House, Defense Department, or IC. The 26 press releases about Clinton occurred after a March 2, 2015, *New York Times* article reported that Clinton used a private email account as secretary of State.[66] In a significant development, the Benghazi Committee dropped the rest of its scheduled hearings with the exception of the Clinton hearing, after the *New York Times* article.[67]

A Benghazi Committee December 3, 2015, press release sheds light on its post-Clinton hearing focus. Notably, the investigation was under Ryan's control at the time. The Benghazi Committee reported it had interviewed four witnesses: one from the State Department, one from the Defense Department, and two from the "national security community."[68] From October 31, 2015, to July 8, 2016, there were 38 total press releases: 1 of the press releases was about Clinton, 4 were about the State Department, and 14 were about the White House, Defense Department, or IC.

Table 3.12 Benghazi Committee Press Releases

Time Period	*Press Releases*	*Clinton*	*State*	*White House, Defense, or Intelligence Community (IC)*
May 5, 2014, to February 6, 2015	16	0	3	3
March 4 to October 22, 2015	36	26	3	0
October 31, 2015, to July 8, 2016	38	1	4	14

Table 3.13 Benghazi Committee Interim Progress Report Frequency Count

	Clinton	*State*	*White House*	*Defense*	*Intelligence Community*
70-Paragraph Total Report Count	11	18	6	2	6
56-Paragraph Body of Report Count	9	18	5	2	6
Word Frequency Count	13	71	14	3	21

On May 8, 2015, the Benghazi Committee (majority staff) released its Interim Progress Update.[69] Table 3.13 is a frequency count of the focus of the report in terms of the specific focus of each paragraph in the 70-paragraph report and a word frequency count for "Clinton," "State Department," "White House, "Defense Department," and "IC." Clinton is specified in 11 of the report's 70 paragraphs, and the State Department is identified in 18 paragraphs. Both are mentioned a combined 84 times in the report. The White House, Defense Department, and IC, in contrast, are identified a combined total of 14 paragraphs. The Defense Department, in particular, is only identified in 2 paragraphs of the 56 paragraphs in the body of the report.

Document Requests

A third way to understand the focus of the Benghazi investigation is to analyze its document requests. Table 3.14 is a comprehensive list of the Benghazi Committee document requests.[70] On September 30, 2014, the Benghazi Committee made the first of its 15 State Department document requests. Five document requests were focused on Clinton. In total, the Benghazi Committee received 72,343 new State Department document pages. On November 19, 2014, the Committee made the first of its eight IC document requests, but these requests were in just two time periods. On December 29, 2014, the committee made the first of its three White House document requests and received 1,451 document pages. On April 8, 2015, the Benghazi Committee made its only Defense Department document request and received 787 document pages.

The Committee provided a select list of its document requests (Table 3.15), highlighting the delays that it found important.[71]

Press releases accompanying document requests reinforce Table 3.15 and a focus on the State Department. On January 27, 2015, Gowdy reported that the Benghazi Committee had 40,000 State Department documents.[72] After the March 2, 2015, *New York Times* report that Clinton used a private email account, the Benghazi Committee released a statement stating that the "American people have a right to a full accounting of all the former

Table 3.14 Benghazi Committee Document Requests

Agency	*Document Date Request*	*Date Documents Received*	*Number of Document Pages*
State[a]	–	August 11, 2014; December 9, 2014	40,000 (25,000 + 15,000)
State	September 30, 2014		–
State[b]	November 18, 2014	February 13, 2015; June 25, 2015	995 (847 + 43 + 105)
IC[c]	November 19, 2014	–	–
IC[d]	November 19, 2014		
IC[e]	November 19, 2014		
State[b]	December 2, 2014		
White House	December 29, 2014	February 27, 2015; May 11, 2015; June 19, 2015; July 17, 2015; August 28, 2015; October 5, 2015; October 27, 2015; November 12, 2015	1,451 (266 + 203 + 266 + 340 + 247 + 34 + 47 + 48)
State	January 28, 2015	February 13, 2015; April 15 and 24, 2015	4,285 (4 + 1,758 + 2,523)
ISP[b]	March 3, 2015		
State	March 4, 2015	May 22, 2015; June 30, 2015; July 28, 2015; August 21 and 28, 2015; September 3 and 18, 2015; October 5, 9, and 15, 2015; November 6 and 24, 2015; December 31, 2015; January 21, 2016; February 26, 2016; April 8, 2016	39,950 (1,199 + 3,636 + 8,254 + 7,452 + 4,703 + 110 + 1,090 + 193 + 3,456 + 122 + 812 + 2,789 + 2,448 + 886 + 1,650 + 1,150)
State[b]	March 4, 2015	June 10 and 25, 2015; September 25, 2015; May 5, 2016	2,410 (1 + 105 + 1,899 + 405)
Defense	April 8, 2015	May 21, 2015; January 7, 2016	787 (726 + 61)
IC[d]	April 23, 2015	May 8, 2015	–
IC[c]	April 28, 2015	–	–
IC[e]	April 28, 2015		
State	May 19, 2015	July 2, 2015	68
White House	May 19, 2015		
State[f]	May 29, 2015	June 12, 2015	179
State[g]	June 1, 2015	July 9, 2015	338
State	June 2, 2015	October 5, 9, 16, 20, and 21, 2015; November 6 and 24, 2015; April 8, 2016	9,114 (1,370 + 1,828 + 2,587 + 1,296 + 866 + 344 + 647 + 175)

(*continued*)

Table 3.14 (Continued)

Agency	*Document Date Request*	*Date Documents Received*	*Number of Document Pages*
State	June 9, 2015		
State	June 12, 2015	February 25, 2016	4
State	July 6, 2015	August 6, 2015	
State	July 8, 2015		
State[b]	September 22, 2015		
IC[e]	August 7, 2015		
IC[e]	November 4, 2015		
White House	March 16, 2016	April 28, 2016: "Response received"	

[a]This is in response to a Committee on Oversight and Government Reform request. 15,000 of the 40,000 documents were new material. See Select Committee on the Events Surrounding the 2012 Terrorist Attack in Benghazi, *Final Report of the Select Committee on the Events Surrounding the 2012 Terrorist Attack in Benghazi: House of Representatives; Together with Additional and Minority Views* (114th Cong., 2d sess., 2016. H. Rept. 114-848), 356–357.
[b]Focused on Clinton.
[c]Focused on NSA.
[d]Focused on DIA.
[e]Focused on CIA.
[f]Focused on Blumenthal.
[g]Focused on Abedin.

Table 3.15 Benghazi Committee Select List of Document Requests

Agency	*Document Date Request*	*Date Documents Received*	*Days Delayed*
State	November 18, 2014	September 18, 2015	304
State	November 18, 2014	September 25, 2015	311
State	November 18, 2014	October 5, 2015	321
State	November 18, 2014	October 9, 2015	325
State	November 18, 2014	October 15, 2015	331
State	June 2, 2015	October 16, 2015	136
State	June 2, 2015	October 20, 2015	140
State	June 2, 2015	October 21, 2015	141
State	November 18, 2014	November 6, 2015	353
State	November 18, 2014	November 24, 2015	371
IC[a]	April 28, 2015	November 30, 2015	216
State	November 18, 2014	December 31, 2015	408
Defense	April 8, 2015	January 7, 2016	274
State	November 18, 2014	January 21, 2016	429
State	November 18, 2014	February 26, 2016	465
State	November 18, 2014	April 8, 2016	507
State	November 18, 2014	May 5, 2016	534
IC[a]	April 28, 2015	May 6, 2016	374

[a]Focused on NSA.

Table 3.16 Focus of Investigation: Boehner-Ryan Comparison

	Boehner			*Ryan*		
Agency	*Witness Interviews*	*Press Releases*[a]	*Document Requests*	*Witness Interviews*	*Press Releases*[a]	*Document Requests*
Defense	3	5	1	21	14	0
State	41	32	15	16	5	0
IC	10	5	7	13	14	1
White House	0	5	2	3	14	1

[a]For both Boehner and Ryan, White House, Defense Department, and Intelligence Community press releases are a combined total.

Secretary's emails."[73] On April 30, 2015, the Benghazi Committee reported that the State Department had turned over 4,000 documents from its ARB investigation of the attacks.[74] On June 16, 2015, the Benghazi Committee deposed Sidney Blumenthal and released a press statement, noting that it had obtained 120 pages of emails between Blumenthal and Clinton.[75]

On December 3, 2015, and in its only non-State Department document request press release, the Benghazi Committee reported it had 100,000 document pages from "various departments and agencies."[76] On April 8, 2016, Gowdy reported that more than 1,100 pages from Clinton's top aides, Mills, Sullivan, Abedin, Rice, and Kennedy, were turned over to the Benghazi Committee. The Benghazi Committee had requested the records in November 2014 and issued subpoenas in March and August 2015. On the same day, Gowdy also reported that he had more than 1,600 pages of Clinton's records.[77]

The final test, and arguably the most important, is to determine if the focus of the investigation changed based on whom the Speaker was (Table 3.16). Boehner was clearly focused on the State Department: 41 of 54 interviews, 32 of 37 press releases, and 15 of 25 document requests. In contrast, Ryan was more focused on the Defense Department, IC, and White House: 37 of 53 interviews, 14 of 19 press releases, and 2 of 2 document requests were focused on those agencies.

ASSESSMENT

The Benghazi Committee released its report on June 28, 2016, 134 days before the 2016 presidential election, and the focus of Boehner on Clinton and the State Department is dramatic.[78] *Hypothesis 1 is supported.* In terms of witness interviews, 57 of 107 interviews and 7 of 14 leadership or high-profile interviews were of State Department officials. On average, nearly 5 of 7 Republican members and half of the staff attended the interviews of State Department leadership or high-profile interviews. The logit regression corroborates member and staff interest in State Department leadership interviews.

In terms of press releases, prior to Clinton's October 22, 2015, hearing, 32 of 52 press releases were about her or the State Department. With the Interim Progress Update, 27 of 56 paragraphs focused on her or the State Department. In terms of document requests, 15 of 27 requests were focused on the State Department, and 5 of its 6 document request press releases focused on the State Department. Of the 74,306 reported document pages received, 72,343 were from the State Department.

This State-centric focus is in sharp contrast to investigating the White House. Only 3 of 107 interviews and 1 of 14 leadership or high-profile interviews were of White House officials. On average, only two of seven Republican members and one-third of the staff attended the interviews of White House leadership or high-profile interviews.

Hypotheses 2 is supported. The logit regression confirms the statistical significance of five of seven members attending leadership or high-profile interviews. In terms of marginal effects, the probability of six of the seven members attending a high-profile interview increases by a minimum of 13 percent.

Hypothesis 3 is supported. Capitol Hill staff veterans held significant roles, with each veteran, on average, attending nearly a third of all interviews and more than half of leadership or high-profile interviews. Per the logit regression, if it was a high-profile State Department witness interview or a Republican member was present, the majority of the Republican staff in attendance would be veterans. Jordan's attendance, in particular, triggered an abundance of veteran interest.

In sum, the explanatory variables act in the hypothesized direction, and the results specify several interesting aspects of partisan congressional investigations. Previous research stresses how partisan congressional investigations have become, and the study in this chapter provides a taxonomy of partisan investigations, explaining how they form and how they appear.

CONCLUSION

There were nine congressional investigations prior to the Benghazi Committee. These committees generally found that the State Department failed to provide adequate security in Benghazi; the military was badly postured and unable to respond; the IC provided strategic but not tactical warning of an impending attack; and the administration and IC were wrong to issue reports linking the video to the attack. The Benghazi Committee was created to further examine these findings.

In applying my partisan model to the Benghazi Committee investigation, I find that Boehner did select party establishment loyalists for committee membership. The staff was more evenly divided between those who had and those who had not been vetted through Capitol Hill experience. But the vetted Republican staff members were given higher priority in terms of assignments, attending more witness interviews and more leadership or high-profile interviews. In examining the focus of the investigation, I find that members and staff were focused on the State Department, as measured in terms of press releases, Interim Progress Update paragraphs, and documents requests, particularly under the leadership of Boehner. Under Ryan, the committee was more balanced.

In the next chapter, I examine the political costs of the Benghazi Committee. This involves an analysis of the investigation's impact on Clinton and a discussion of how a Republican Party fracture imposed costs on the investigation and its ability to uncover facts about the attack and the Obama administration's response. Further analysis reveals the source of the failure on the night of the attack—groupthink at a critical interagency meeting.

NOTES

1. The official website was archived. See Select Committee on Benghazi, "Home," n.d., https://archives-benghazi-republicans-oversight.house.gov/, accessed Janaury16, 2022.

2. The Accountability Review Board released its report on December 18, 2012 and was critical of the State Department for failing to upgrade security in a deteriorating security environment. Clinton endorsed the report's 29 recommendations. See State Department, *Accountability Review Board Report*, December 18, 2012, https://2009-2017.state.gov/documents/organization/202446.pdf, accessed October 22, 2021, and Hillary Clinton, "Secretary Clinton's Response to the Accountability Review Board Report," https://2009-2017.state.gov/documents/organization/203244.pdf, accessed October 22, 2021. The FBI investigation is still ongoing. See Federal Bureau of Investigation, "Seeking Information on Benghazi Attacks," https://www.fbi.gov/wanted/seeking-info/seeking-information-on-attacks-in-benghazi, accessed February 21, 2022. The Department of Defense considered the ARB to be its "primary after-action review," although it did a joint force development (J-7) review of each unit's after action reports. See "The Defense Department's Posture for September 11, 2013: What are the Lessons of Benghazi?," Hearing before the Subcommittee on Oversight and Investigations of the Committee on Armed Services United States House of Representatives, September 19, 2013, H.A.S.C. No. 113–59, 19; Howard McKeon, *Majority Interim Report: Benghazi Investigation Update* (Washington, DC: House Armed Services Committee, 2014), 25; Charles Joseph Leidig, Jr, *Interviews of Witnesses Before the Select Committee on the Events Surrounding the 2012 Terrorist Attack in Benghazi: House of Representatives* (114th Cong., 2d sess., Volume 10, 2016), 560.

3. Douglas Kriner and Eric Schickler, *Investigating the President: Congressional Checks on Presidential Power* (Princeton: Princeton University Press, 2016), 234.

4. Kriner and Schickler, *Investigating the President*, 234–35.

5. "The Security Failures of Benghazi," Hearing before the Committee on Oversight and Government Reform House of Representatives, October 10, 2012, Serial No. 112–193, 5; Kriner and Schickler, *Investigating the President*, 235.

6. Howard McKeon, Ed Royce, Bob Goodlatte, Darrell Issa, and Mike Rogers, *Interim Progress Report for the Members of the House Republican Conference on the Events Surrounding the September 11, 2012 Terrorist Attacks in Benghazi, Libya* (Washington, DC: Government Printing Office, 2013); Kriner and Schickler, *Investigating the President*, 240.

7. McKeon, Royce, Goodlatte, Issa, and Rogers, *Interim Progress Report*, 8; Glenn Kessler, "Issa's Absurd Claim that Clinton's 'signature' Means She Personally Approved It," *Washington Post*, April 26, 2013, https://www.washingtonpost.com/blogs/fact-checker/post/issas-absurd-claim-that-clintons-signature-means-she-personally-approved-it/2013/04/25/58c2f5b4-adf8-11c2-a986-eec837b1888b_blog.html, accessed December 16, 2021.

8. "Benghazi: Exposing Failure and Recognizing Courage," Hearing before the Committee on Oversight and Government Reform House of Representatives, May 8, 2013, Serial No. 113 30, 3.

9. "Benghazi: Exposing Failure," Hearing before the Committee on Oversight and Government Reform, 49, 92–93.

10. "Benghazi: Exposing Failure," Hearing before the Committee on Oversight and Government Reform, 24, 32.

11. "Benghazi: Exposing Failure," Hearing before the Committee on Oversight and Government Reform, 30, 43, 86–87.

12. Committee on Oversight and Government Reform, *Benghazi Attacks: Investigative Update Interim Report on the Accountability Review Board: Staff Report* (Washington, DC: Committee on Oversight and Government Reform, September 16, 2013), 7.

13. "Review of the Benghazi Attacks and Unanswered Questions," Hearing before the Committee on Oversight and Government Reform House of Representatives, September 19, 2013, Serial No. 113–59, 8, 37.

14. Mullen stated that his intention was to convey his concern about Lambs's "level of experience." See "Review of the Benghazi Attacks," Hearing before the Committee on Oversight and Government Reform, 46, 49.

15. "Review of the Benghazi Attacks," Hearing before the Committee on Oversight and Government Reform, 107–10.

16. "Benghazi, Instability, and a New Government: Success and Failures of U.S. Intervention in Libya," Hearing before the Committee on Oversight and Government Reform House of Representatives, May 1, 2014, Serial No. 113–110, 2.

17. "Benghazi, Instability," Hearing before the Committee on Oversight and Government Reform, 53.

18. Joseph Lieberman and Susan Collins, *Flashing Red: A Special Report on the Terrorist Attack at Benghazi* (Washington, DC: U.S. Senate Committee on Homeland Security and Governmental Affairs, 2012), 5, 7, 20, 29.

19. Mike Rogers and C.A. Ruppersberger, *Investigative Report on the Terrorist Attacks on U.S. Facilities in Benghazi, Libya, September 11–12, 2012* (Washington, DC: U.S. House of Representatives Permanent Select Committee on Intelligence, 2014), 3.

20. Michael Morell, "Written Statement for the Record: Michael Morell: Former Acting Director and Deputy Director of the CIA: House Permanent Select Committee on Intelligence: 2 April 2014," April 2, 2014, https://republicans-intelligence.house.gov/sites/intelligence.house.gov/files/documents/morellsfr04022014.pdf, accessed December 21, 2021.

21. Rogers and Ruppersberger, *Investigative Report*, 12, 14, 16, 17, 20, 23, 28–29, 30.

22. Hillary Clinton, "Secretary of State Hillary Rodham Clinton: Senate Committee on Foreign Relations: Washington, DC," January 23, 2013, https://www.foreign.senate.gov/imo/media/doc/SECRETARY%20OF%20STATE%20HILLARY%20RODHAM%20CLINTON.pdf, accessed October 22, 2021.

23. "Benghazi: The Attacks and the Lessons Learned," Hearing before the Committee on Foreign Relations United States Senate, January 23, 2013, S. Hrg. 113– 184, 28.

24. Melanie Marlowe, "Reclaiming Institutional Relevance through Congressional Oversight," in *Is Congress Broken? The Virtues and Defects of Partisanship, Polarization, and Gridlock*, edited by William Connelly, John Pitney, and Gary Schmitt (Washington, DC: Brookings Institution Press, 2017), 121.

25. Marlowe, "Reclaiming Institutional Relevance," 121.

26. House Foreign Affairs Committee, *Benghazi: Where is the State Department Accountability?: Majority Staff Report* (Washington, DC: House Foreign Affairs Committee, 2014), 2, 3.

27. House Foreign Affairs Committee, *Benghazi: Where is the State Department*, 3.

28. House Foreign Affairs Committee, *Benghazi: Where is the State Department*, 1.

29. Senate Select Committee on Intelligence, *Report of the U.S. Senate Select Committee on Intelligence Review of the Terrorist Attacks on U.S. Facilities in Benghazi, Libya, September 11–12, 2012 together with Additional* Views, 113th Cong., 2d sess., 2014. S. Report. 113–134, 1–2.

30. Kriner and Schickler, *Investigating the President*, 236.

31. Senate Select Committee on Intelligence, *Report of the U.S. Senate Select Committee*, 9, 11–12, 22, 28, 32.

32. Senate Select Committee on Intelligence, *Report of the U.S. Senate Select Committee*, Additional Views 1.

33. Senate Select Committee on Intelligence, *Report of the U.S. Senate Select Committee*, Additional Views of Senators Chambliss, Burr, Risch, Coats, Rubio, and Coburn 8–12.

34. Senate Select Committee on Intelligence, *Report of the U.S. Senate Select Committee*, 43–52.

35. "Defense Department's Posture," Hearing before the Subcommittee on Oversight and Investigations of the Committee on Armed Services, 2.

36. Howard McKeon, *Majority Interim Report: Benghazi Investigation Update* (Washington, DC: House Armed Services Committee, 2014), 1.

37. McKeon, *Majority Interim Report*, 2, 15.
38. McKeon, *Majority Interim Report*, 17, 19–20, 21.
39. "Department of Defense's Response to the Attack on U.S. Facilities in Benghazi, Libya, and the Findings of its Internal Review following the Attack," Hearing before the Committee on Armed Services United States Senate, February 7, 2013, S. Hrg. 113–164, 11.
40. "Department of Defense's Response," Hearing before the Committee on Armed Services, 10.
41. "Department of Defense's Response," Hearing before the Committee on Armed Services, 20.
42. "Department of Defense's Response," Hearing before the Committee on Armed Services, 28.
43. McKeon, Royce, Goodlatte, Issa, and Rogers, *Interim Progress Report.*
44. McKeon, Royce, Goodlatte, Issa, and Rogers, *Interim Progress Report*, 23, 30, 33.
45. Judicial Watch, "Judicial Watch Statement on House Benghazi Report," *Judicial Watch*, June 28, 2016, https://www.judicialwatch.org/judicial-watch-statement-house-benghazi-report/, accessed January 15, 2022; Judicial Watch, "Judicial Watch: Benghazi Documents Point to White House on Misleading Talking Points," *Judicial Watch*, April 29, 2014, www.judicialwatch.org/press-room/press-releases/judicial-watch-benghazi-documents-point-white-house-misleading-talking-points/, accessed January 15, 2022.
46. Select Committee on the Events Surrounding the 2012 Terrorist Attack in Benghazi, *Final Report of the Select Committee on the Events Surrounding the 2012 Terrorist Attack in Benghazi: House of Representatives; Together with Additional and Minority Views* (114th Cong., 2d sess., 2016. H. Rept. 114-848), 454–55; Select Committee on Benghazi, "About," n.d., https://archives-benghazi-republicans-oversight.house.gov/about, accessed January 16, 2022.
47. They did not release any joint statements after July 31, 2014. See Select Committee on Benghazi, "Select Committee Joint Statement on Khattala Briefing," July 9, 2014. https://archives-benghazi-republicans-oversight.house.gov/news/press-releases/select-committee-joint-statement-on-khattala-briefing, accessed January 16, 2022; Select Committee on Benghazi, "Select Committee Joint Statement on FBI Briefing," July 31, 2014, https://archives-benghazi-republicans-oversight.house.gov/news/press-releases/select-committee-joint-statement-on-fbi-briefing, accessed January 16, 2022.
48. Gowdy thanked Representative Adam Schiff (D-CA) for suggesting the topic of the hearing and thanked Cummings for always being cooperative. See "Hearing 1," Hearing before the Select Committee on the Events Surrounding the 2012 Terrorist Attack in Benghazi House of Representatives, September 17, 2014, 3, 65. In the second hearing, Cummings stated that the September and December hearings "demonstrate[d] the continued commitment of both Democrats and Republicans to making our embassies safe." See "Hearing 2," Hearing before the Select Committee on the Events Surrounding the 2012 Terrorist Attack in Benghazi House of Representatives, December 10, 2014, 3.

49. "Hearing 1," Hearing before the Select Committee, 32–33, 64–65; "Hearing 2," Hearing before the Select Committee, 3. By the second hearing, three of the seven ARB recommendations had been closed. See "Hearing 2," Hearing before the Select Committee, 42.

50. "Hearing 3," Hearing before the Select Committee on the Events Surrounding the 2012 Terrorist Attack in Benghazi House of Representatives, January 27, 2015, 2.

51. "Hearing 3," Hearing before the Select Committee, 3, 5.

52. "Hearing 3," Hearing before the Select Committee, 18. Roby complained that the Committee was receiving documents from State Department in "paper format" and with "no order to the paper documents." See "Hearing 3," Hearing before the Select Committee, 25.

53. "Hearing 3," Hearing before the Select Committee, 39–40, 44.

54. Select Committee on Benghazi, "Speaker Boehner Names Republican Members," May 5, 2014, https://archives-benghazi-republicans-oversight.house.gov/news/press-releases/boehner-names-republican-members-of-select-committee, accessed January 16, 2022.

55. The party unity scores are taken from Keith T. Poole, "Party Unity Scores," May 31, 2015, https://legacy.voteview.com/Party_Unity.htm, accessed February 23, 2022.

56. The Capitol Hill experience of staff members can be found via a search of legistorm.com. The career experiences of Chipman, Kiko, Donesa, Grider, Barrineau, and Adams can be found in a newspaper article. See Rachel Bade and Isaac Arnsdorf, "Meet the well-paid pros behind the Benghazi panel," *Politico*, October 21, 2015, https://www.politico.com/story/2015/10/meet-the-well-paid-pros-behind-the-benghazi-panel-215023, accessed January 16, 2022.

57. Select Committee on the Events Surrounding the 2012 Terrorist Attack in Benghazi, *Interviews of Witnesses Before the Select Committee on the Events Surrounding the 2012 Terrorist Attack in Benghazi*, Volumes 1–11 (Washington, DC: Government Printing Office, 2016). The witness interviews are also available on the govinfo.gov website. See House Select Committee on the Events Surrounding the 2012 Terrorist Attack in Benghazi, "Congressional Publications," *govinfo.gov*, n.d., https://www.govinfo.gov/committee/house-benghazi?path=/browsecommittee/chamber/house/committee/benghazi/collection/OTHER-1, accessed January 20, 2022. There is a list of witnesses interviewed in Appendix I of the Benghazi Report. The appendix narrowly focuses on witnesses to the attacks and is not a comprehensive list of interviews. For example, the Committee interviewed Stephen Hedger on July 14, 2016, and his name does not appear in the appendix. See Select Committee, *Final Report*, Appendix I.

58. The Committee reported it would conclude State Department interviews in April 2015 (the last one was conducted on April 28, 2016) and start White House interviews that same month. See Select Committee on Benghazi, "Select Committee on Benghazi Announces Commencement of Interviews," February 6, 2015, https://archives-benghazi-republicans-oversight.house.gov/news/press-releases/select-committee-on-benghazi-announces-commencement-of-interviews, accessed January 16, 2022.

59. David C. W. Parker and Matthew Dull, "Rooting Out Waste, Fraud, and Abuse: The Politics of House Committee Investigations, 1947 to 2004," *Political Research Quarterly* 66, no. 3 (2013): 634.

60. Roskam is not able to be analyzed, due to the fact he only attended four interviews: Blumenthal, Clinton, Panetta, and Petraeus.

61. If the veteran and non-veteran staff was evenly split at 50 percent, I code a "0."

62. Roskam is not analyzed again, due to his attendance at only four interviews.

63. Sidney Blumenthal, *Interviews of Witnesses Before the Select Committee on the Events Surrounding the 2012 Terrorist Attack in Benghazi: House of Representatives* (114th Cong., 2d sess., Volume 4, 2016), 1023; Stephen Hedger, *Interviews of Witnesses Before the Select Committee on the Events Surrounding the 2012 Terrorist Attack in Benghazi: House of Representatives* (114th Cong., 2d sess., Volume 11, 2016), 337. The interest in Blumenthal is further heightened by the fact that Chairman Gowdy's questions of Clinton, during her hearing, were focused on Blumenthal. See "Hearing 4," Hearing before the Select Committee on the Events Surrounding the 2012 Terrorist Attack in Benghazi House of Representatives, October 22, 2015, 317–25, 329–35.

64. Select Committee, *Final Report*, 597–99.

65. Select Committee on Benghazi, "News," n.d., https://archives-benghazi-republicans-oversight.house.gov/news, accessed January 16, 2022.

66. Michael S. Schmidt, "Hillary Clinton Used Personal Email Account at State Dept., Possibly Breaking Rules," *New York Times*, March 2, 2015, https://www.nytimes.com/2015/03/03/us/politics/hillary-clintons-use-of-private-email-at-state-department-raises-flags.html?_r=0, accessed January 16, 2022.

67. "Hearing 4," Hearing before the Select Committee, 6, 10, 314.

68. Select Committee on Benghazi, "Select Committee on Benghazi Announces Scheduled Testimony of Additional Witnesses," December 3, 2015, https://archives-benghazi-republicans-oversight.house.gov/news/press-releases/select-committee-announces-scheduled-testimony-of-additional-witnesses, accessed January 16, 2022. The Department of Defense witness is likely the Defense Intelligence Agency Tripoli analyst, who is incorrectly listed as an "ODNI Analyst" in the "Table of Witnesses by Interview Date." Neither the Tripoli analyst nor the ODNI analyst is listed in the "Contents" of Volume 7 of the Interviews of Witnesses. See Select Committee, *Final Report*, 597; "Table of Witnesses by Interview Date," *Interviews of Witnesses Before the Select Committee on the Events Surrounding the 2012 Terrorist Attack in Benghazi: House of Representatives* (114th Cong., 2d sess., Volume 11, 2016), 1620; "Contents," *Interviews of Witnesses Before the Select Committee on the Events Surrounding the 2012 Terrorist Attack in Benghazi: House of Representatives* (114th Cong., 2d sess., Volume 7, 2016), III.

69. Select Committee on Benghazi, "Select Committee Releases Interim Progress Update," May 8, 2015, https://archives-benghazi-republicans-oversight.house.gov/news/press-releases/select-committee-releases-interim-progress-update, accessed January 16, 2022.

70. This information is taken from Appendix J of the Benghazi Report. See Select Committee, *Final Report*, Appendix J. Appendix J has inconsistencies and differs

from what the Benghazi Committee reported in terms of document pages. For example, the Benghazi Committee reported it received 1,075 State Department document pages on April 8, 2016, on page 604, but on page 369, it lists "approximately 1,150 pages" and on page 610, it lists 1,146 pages. See Select Committee, *Final Report*, 369, 604, 610. The Benghazi Committee reported the following: (1) State Department: 71,640 pages, (2) CIA: 300 pages, (3) White House: 1,450 pages, (4) FBI: 200 pages, (5) Defense Department: 900 pages, (6) NSA: 750 pages, and (7) Sidney Blumenthal: 179 pages. This is a total of 75,419 pages. Notably, the Benghazi Committee states 1,450 document pages were received from the White House. But, many of these documents are listed as "re-production" (i.e., less-redacted versions of the same documents) and many were "publically available press clippings." See Select Committee, *Final Report*, 358, 386, 614–15.

71. Select Committee on Benghazi, "More than 10,000 Days of Delays: Obama Admin's Delays of Benghazi Documents Equivalent to Over 27 Years," May 18, 2016, https://archives-benghazi-republicans-oversight.house.gov/news/press-releases/over-10000-days-of-delays-obama-administration-s-delays-on-benghazi-documents, accessed January 16, 2022.

72. Select Committee on Benghazi, "Select Committee on Benghazi Gowdy Opening Statement at Benghazi Select Committee Hearing," January 27, 2015, https://archives-benghazi-republicans-oversight.house.gov/news/press-releases/gowdy-opening-statement-at-benghazi-select-committee-hearing, accessed January 16, 2022.

73. Select Committee on Benghazi, "Statement from the Communications Director on Clinton Email Addresses," March 4, 2015, https://archives-benghazi-republicans-oversight.house.gov/news/press-releases/statement-from-the-communications-director-on-clinton-email-addresses, accessed January 16, 2022.

74. Select Committee on Benghazi, "Benghazi Committee Gains Historic State ARB Document Access," April 30, 2015, https://archives-benghazi-republicans-oversight.house.gov/news/press-releases/benghazi-committee-gains-historic-state-arb-document-access, accessed January 16, 2022.

75. Select Committee on Benghazi, "Select Committee Obtains New Blumenthal Emails Before Deposition," June 16, 2015, https://archives-benghazi-republicans-oversight.house.gov/news/press-releases/select-committee-obtains-new-blumenthal-emails-before-deposition, accessed January 16, 2022.

76. Select Committee on Benghazi, "Select Committee on Benghazi Announces Scheduled Testimony of Additional Witnesses."

77. Select Committee on Benghazi, "Over One Year Later, State Department Finally Turns Over Records; Committee Still Waiting for Others," April 8, 2016, https://archives-benghazi-republicans-oversight.house.gov/news/press-releases/over-one-year-later-state-department-finally-turns-over-records-committee-still, accessed January 16, 2022.

78. David M. Herszenhorn, "House Benghazi Report Finds No New Evidence of Wrongdoing by Hillary Clinton," *New York Times*, June 28, 2016, https://www.nytimes.com/2016/06/29/us/politics/hillary-clinton-benghazi.html, accessed January 30, 2022.

Chapter 4

Political Costs of the Benghazi Committee Investigation

INTRODUCTION

This chapter analyzes the long-term impact of a partisan investigation. Starting with the phases of the investigation, from a seemingly neutral start to a period of hyper-focus on Hillary Clinton to a final period of diminished interest in investigating the White House, Intelligence Community (IC), and Pentagon. The strategic turns of the committee investigation imposed political costs on both Clinton and the Republicans. Regarding the latter, Republicans were not able to pinpoint Obama's or Clinton's responsibility for the direction of Libya, not able to explain a White House-State Department agreement to use the IC as a shield from taking blame for a false narrative, and not able to determine that the Pentagon did not follow its own doctrine in conducting an operation based on an incorrect interpretation of presidential orders. The biggest cost was failing to understand how a false picture was created due to groupthink at a crucial interagency meeting in the early hours of the terrorist attack.

PHASES OF THE INVESTIGATION

As detailed in chapter 3, the focus of the Benghazi Committee investigation can be tracked by examining its witness interviews, press releases, and document requests. John Boehner was clearly focused on the State Department. In contrast, Paul Ryan was more focused on the White House, Defense Department, and IC. This focus can be examined in greater granularity and organized into three phases: (1) a neutral phase under Boehner from the committee's creation on May 8, 2014, to March 1, 2015; (2) a "Clinton hyper-focus" phase under Boehner from March 2 to October 22, 2015; and (3) an "other agency" phase under Ryan from October 23, 2015, to the release of the committee's report on June 28, 2016.

In terms of press releases, as detailed in chapter 3, the committee issued 0 of its 16 press releases about Clinton during its neutral phase, 26 of its 36 press releases were about Clinton during its Clinton hyper-focus phase, and 14 of its 38 press releases were about the White House, Defense Department, or IC during its other agency phase. Only one press release was about Clinton during this phase.

The document requests are also consistent with the phases: the committee requested documents from State Department on September 30, 2014, nearly two months before its first request to another agency; it made 15 total State Department document requests (5 of which focused on Clinton) and concluded its State Department document requests on September 22, 2015, at the end of its Clinton hyper-focus phase. The committee's final three document requests were of the IC and White House; one of those two months prior to the other agency phase and the last two within the phase.

For witness interviews during the neutral phase, the committee conducted five interviews; all of which were of State Department officials (see Appendix). During the Clinton hyper-focus phase, it conducted 49 interviews, 35 of which were of State Department officials.[1] During the other agency phase, it conducted 52 interviews, 36 of those interviews were of White House, IC, or Defense Department officials.[2]

The witness interviews can be organized into six topics based on the questions asked: (1) Benghazi security environment: questions asked about the Libyan or Benghazi environment prior to the attack; (2) attack: questions asked about the September 11–12 attack; (3) Clinton: questions asked about Clinton's leadership or her emails; (4) congressional cooperation: questions asked about cooperating with the Benghazi Committee investigation, including making documents and witnesses available; (5) military response: questions asked about the military's actions after President Barack Obama's orders; and (6) talking points: questions asked about the administration's post-attack narrative.

The organization of topics illustrates the level of effort, and the decline of member and staff attendance at witness interviews after the Clinton hearing on October 22, 2015. As illustrated in Table 4.1, during the Clinton hyper-focus phase on the topic of Benghazi security environment, there were 32 interviews in which the topic was addressed. For each interview, there was an average of 1.2 members and 5.3 staff members present. Similarly, there was a little member or staff interest in the talking points, as there were only 12 interviews covering the topic with an average of 1.6 members and 5.4 staff members present. In contrast, despite there only being 8 interviews during

Table 4.1 Benghazi Committee Witness Interview Attendance by Topic

Topic	*Interviews with Topic*	*Republican Members Present*[a]	*Republican Staff Members Present*[a]
	Neutral Phase		
Benghazi Security Environment	5	1.8	4.8
	Clinton Hyper-Focus		
Benghazi Security Environment	32	1.2	5.3
Attack	13	1.9	6.2
Clinton	8	3.8	7.8
Congressional Cooperation	8	3.8	7.8
Military Response	7	2.3	6
Talking Points	12	1.6	5.4
	Other Agency Phase		
Benghazi Security Environment	22	2	4.3
Attack	26	1.9	4.0
Clinton	2	2.5	5.5
Congressional Cooperation	5	2.6	5
Military Response	28	2.1	4.0
Talking Points	14	2.2	4.6

[a]Average.

this phase with Clinton herself as the topic, at each interview, there was an average of 3.8 members and 7.8 staff members present.

On the other hand, as the investigation shifted away from Clinton and the State Department and toward the White House, Defense Department, and IC in the other agency phase, there was a significant decline in effort. When the topic of the Susan Rice talking points was addressed, there were 14 interviews and an average of 2.2 members and 4.6 staff members present. When the topic of military response was addressed, there were 28 interviews and an average of 2.1 members and 4.0 staff members present.

Staff interest, overall, in all six topics decreased significantly after the Clinton hyper-focus phase. There was about one less staff member present at topics covering the Benghazi security environment and talking points. There were approximately two less staff members present when the topic was the attack, Clinton, congressional cooperation, and the military response. The attack and military response were frequent topics during the other agency phase, but there were only four staff members present on average—a nearly 50 percent decline in staff member attendance compared to the topic of Clinton during the Clinton hyper-focus phase. For the last three months of the investigation, staff interview attendance decreased to an average of 3.25 staff members.

Member interest also decreased significantly in the other agency phase. Peter Roskam did not ask questions of interviewees after Clinton's hearing on October 22, 2015, and he stopped attending interviews after Leon Panetta's interview on January 8, 2016. Martha Roby did not ask questions of interviewees after David Petraeus's interview on January 6, 2016, and she stopped attending interviews after James Winnefeld's interview on March 3, 2016. Michael Pompeo did not ask questions of interviewees after Patrick Kennedy's interview on February 3, 2016, and he stopped attending interviews after John Kelly's interview on March 23, 2016. Only Trey Gowdy, Susan Brooks, Jim Jordan, and Lynn Westmoreland attended interviews in the final three months of the investigation. Brooks's interest, notably, was minimal, as she attended only 2 of the final 19 interviews. Gowdy, Jordan, and Westmoreland all attended 6 of the final 19 interviews—far outpacing their four colleagues.

The lack of effort in the other agency phase, particularly when the topics were the Benghazi security environment, the talking points, and military response, had a detrimental effect on holding individuals accountable, and this accountability is addressed in detail in the "White House and State Department Accountability: The Libyan Strategy," "White House and State Department Accountability: The Talking Points," and "Pentagon Accountability: The Response" subsections of the "Political Costs on Republicans" section of this chapter.

POLITICAL COSTS ON DEMOCRATS

The Benghazi investigations had an interesting dynamic. They failed to impose political costs on Obama's 2012 reelection, but they did decrease the poll numbers for Clinton during her 2016 presidential run.[3]

An aggressive investigation negatively impacts presidential approval ratings.[4] This can be extended to presidential candidate Clinton. In a May–June 2014 Washington Post-ABC poll, about half the respondents wanted another congressional investigation, but only 37 percent approved of how Clinton had handled the attack.[5] In a July 2015 Quinnipiac Poll, 57 percent of voters believed Clinton was neither honest nor trustworthy.[6] By the time of Clinton's hearing on October 22, 2015, 54 percent of Americans believed "the way [she] handled her email while serving as Secretary of State [was] an important indicator of her character and ability to serve as president."[7] Two weeks after the hearing, 60 percent of voters did not believe Clinton was honest and trustworthy.[8] When the Benghazi Committee final report was released, Clinton's favorability rating was 37 percent, and Donald Trump was considered more honest and trustworthy than Clinton, 45–37 percent.[9] As detailed in Table 4.2, Clinton's voter poll percentage decline is correlated with major events in the Benghazi investigation, and she emerged from the Benghazi investigation in a worse position than when the investigation started.

Table 4.2 Benghazi Committee Timeline-Clinton Poll Comparison

	Clinton Voter Percentage (%)
House Vote to Establish Benghazi Committee (May 8, 2014)	47 (July 8, 2014)
First Benghazi Committee Hearing (September 17, 2014)	44 (November 26, 2014)
Clinton's Email and Server Revealed (March 4, 2015)	45 (March 5, 2015)
Clinton Testifies (October 22, 2015)	40 (November 4, 2015)
Benghazi Committee Final Report Released (June 28, 2016)	42 (June 29, 2016)

Source: Clinton voter poll numbers from Quinnipiac University Poll, https://poll.qu.edu.
Primary vote percentage against leading Republican contender. Clinton became the presumptive nominee on June 6, 2016.

POLITICAL COSTS ON REPUBLICANS

Benghazi was a topic that the American people wanted investigated. A May 2013 Gallup poll found that 69 percent of Americans believed Benghazi was "serious enough to warrant continuing investigation." This included 49 percent of Democrats polled stating a "need" for Benghazi to be investigated.[10] News coverage of a congressional investigation is a key factor in rallying the public against a political target.[11] The Republicans were successful in generating thousands of news stories on Benghazi. Fox News aired nearly 2,500 stories, CNN more than 3,000 stories, and even liberal MSNBC aired more than 750 stories.[12] The American people support congressional investigations, even knowing they are partisan.[13]

But news coverage reveals both Democrats and Republicans were unsatisfied with the Benghazi investigation and the committee's *Final Report*. The progressive Media Matters chided news outlets for falsely reporting new information from the Benghazi report, "when in fact all of the 'key findings' in the report had been previously reported."[14] Steve Benen, a producer for "The Rachel Maddow Show," gloated that the committee ended "with a whimper" unable to prove Republican "Benghazi conspiracy theories."[15] The conservative Judicial Watch, whose FOIA request was the impetus for the creation of the Benghazi Committee, stated the investigation had been "bungled."[16] Trump labeled Gowdy a "Benghazi loser" and tweeted that Gowdy "failed miserably on Benghazi."[17]

The Republican dissatisfaction was a consequence of a Republican Party fracture, and the Benghazi investigation reflected how that divide failed to provide a definitive accounting of the Benghazi attack in terms of the Libyan strategic environment and in two key areas: White House and State

Department accountability in terms of the post-attack narrative and Pentagon accountability in terms of a military response to the attack. Quite simply, due to Republican Benghazi Committee disinterest, as a consequence of Boehner's strategy and resignation, members and staff did not dedicate resources to fully exploring the talking points or military response. The result was a *Final Report* that failed to identify which individuals were not held accountable for failure on the night of the attack and in the week following the attack.

The Republican Fracture

The dissatisfaction brought into public view fighting which had been occurring within the Republican Party since the inception of the Benghazi Committee—who and what to focus on in the investigation. The strife dated back to 1994. As identified in chapter 2, Newt Gingrich, as an institutional change, made the Speaker's office the center of political party power. In doing so, he and his successors held the power to select and impose term limits on committee chairs, cut staffs, and created task forces to work on behalf of the Speaker.[18] The result was a nationalization of Congress; a member's loyalty to the party, not necessarily his or her district, became paramount. And for this, the Speaker needed to maintain tight discipline and order over party members.

Boehner took office in 1991 and began a populist campaign against the establishment in Congress, including with his own party. He worked to close the corrupt House bank, helped draft the Contract with America, and won the number four spot in House leadership in 1995. In that spot, he learned to resent Gingrich's power, and in 1997, he was accused of plotting to have Gingrich removed from the Speakership. But, by 2006, Boehner was the majority leader and had become an ally of Bush in passing legislation, such as the No Child Left Behind Act of 2001 and the 2008 federal bailout of financial institutions.[19]

Boehner was also a compromiser, which became incompatible with the ideological purity requirements of the Republican Tea Party movement in 2010.[20] Jordan, on the other hand, took the chair of the conservative Republican Study Committee in 2011. The two, Boehner and Jordan, soon found themselves in conflict about what to do about raising the debt ceiling.[21] Boehner wanted a compromise with Obama: every new dollar of debt would be offset by a spending cut. Jordan led conservatives on a more ambitious plan: Cut, Cap, and Balance. Not only would every new dollar of debt be offset by spending cuts, but there would be a cap on new spending and a balanced budget amendment. The Jordan-backed legislation passed the House, but Boehner worked with Obama and Senate Democrats to pass a compromise.[22]

Boehner continued to work with Obama on fiscal spending and revenue compromises, and in 2013, two dozen conservatives voted against him for Speaker. Boehner retaliated, removing conservatives from committee assignments.[23] Jordan and Boehner would meet in the Summer of 2013 and declare an end to intra-party conflict. But immigration and Obamacare soon divided the party, and in January 2015, Jordan with a new group, the House Freedom Caucus, led a series of efforts to remove Boehner as Speaker.[24] Boehner, acknowledging the Republican Party had become a populist party, had had enough and announced his resignation on September 25, 2015.[25]

The Republican populist-establishment divide is evident in the investigation. As noted in the "Phases of the Investigation" section, the majority of Republicans were not actively involved in the other agency phase. Like Boehner, they had abandoned the investigation. For example, Roskam, arguably the member most loyal to Boehner, effectively stopped participating in the investigation after the Clinton hearing.[26] Gowdy and the committee's two most conservative members, Jordan and Westmoreland, remained the stalwarts.[27] Gowdy attended 18 interviews, Jordan attended 16 interviews, and Westmoreland attended 11 interviews. Gowdy and Jordan were both interested in the talking points issue, each attending 20 interviews when it was a topic. However, only Jordan continued to attend interviews on the topic in the final three months of the investigation.

Jordan also extensively focused on the topic for the Clinton hearing and in his co-authored "Additional Views" section of the Benghazi *Final Report*. For the former, Jordan asked Clinton, "Where did the false narrative start? It started with you, Madame Secretary." The *New York Times* labeled Jordan's performance as "sharp questions" and listed it as one of the "key moments" in the hearing.[28] Gowdy acknowledged that Jordan's questioning was the only new information obtained at the hearing.[29] For the latter, 15 of 27 substantive pages were focused on the talking points, a topic that Jordan and Pompeo labeled as the most significant of the investigation.[30]

The Benghazi Committee, by focusing on the State Department, missed the opportunity to hold key White House, State, and Pentagon decision-makers accountable. To understand the discontent and to properly determine accountability, it is necessary to avoid historians' fallacy or outcome bias.[31] This involves not focusing on the result—a well-conducted, military-style assault which killed four Americans—but, instead on the decision-making process during the events of September 11–12, 2012. For the White House and State Department, it means determining what the U.S. goals were in Libya and how a terrorist assault was labeled a protest gone awry. For the Pentagon, it means determining why military assets did not arrive in Benghazi.

White House and State Department Accountability: The Libyan Strategy

As detailed in "The Security Environment in Libya" section of chapter 1, Congress concluded that the Benghazi attack was evidence of failure of Clinton's "smart power." More specifically, in "Part III. Events Leading to the Terrorist Attacks in Benghazi" of the Benghazi *Final Report*, the committee concludes, "Apart from 'no boots on the ground,' U.S. policy remained indefinite and undefined throughout [Christopher] Stevens' tenure in Benghazi."[32] The Obama administration was "determined to avoid an extended state-building engagement" and had knowingly placed Stevens in "an undefined diplomatic status" to "do a difficult job in a dangerous environment."[33] The report, which is based on witness interviews and hearings, then details U.S. goals, State Department operations, and the deteriorating security environment over the next 88 pages.

The report is consistent with the Republican line of questioning in the October 22, 2015, Clinton hearing. It is also consistent with the literature of chapter 2. Members used "gotcha" questions and statements in the hearing, hoping to pin the Benghazi attack on a Clinton-led foreign policy. For the decision to intervene militarily in Libya, Roskam informed Clinton of what he believed happened:

> You got the State Department on board [to support military intervention]. You convinced the President. You overcame the objections of Vice President Biden and Secretary of Defense [Robert] Gates, the National Security Council. And you had another obstacle then, and that was the United Nations. And you were able to persuade the Russians, of all things, to abstain.[34]

Clinton simply deflected the statement: "this [intervention decision] was at the behest of and the direction of the President once he was presented with the varying arguments."[35] Roskam, later in the hearing, pressed his case that Libyan policy was "Clinton doctrine" and an example of Clinton's "smart power."[36] Clinton responded, "The [military intervention] decision, as all decisions in any administration, was made by the President. So the President deserves the historic credit."[37]

Gowdy also made an attempt to place Libyan policy on Clinton, stating that Clinton was receiving political advice from Sidney Blumenthal, not Stevens: "So help us understand how Sidney Blumenthal had that kind of access to you, Madam Secretary, but the Ambassador [Stevens] did not."[38] Clinton rejected the argument: "But I have said before and I will repeat again: Sid Blumenthal was not my adviser, official or unofficial, about Libya."[39] Westmoreland asked an open-ended question of what Clinton was responsible for in Libya.[40] She replied, "I was responsible for working on the policy both before and after the end of the Qadhafi regime."[41] Roskam followed up on Westmoreland's question, but he asked Clinton what she was specifically responsible for in Benghazi. To which, Clinton responded that she was responsible for deciding whether to make the Benghazi Mission compound permanent.[42] The Republicans made no other attempts to parse out what U.S. policy in Libya was and who was responsible for it.

When given the opportunity to pinpoint responsibility for U.S. foreign policy, Benghazi Committee staff had access to key White House and State Department witnesses but failed as well. Rather than hoping to secure victory with a "gotcha" knockout question to Clinton, the Republicans could have built a case of evidence starting with those not in senior leadership or politically motivated roles. This case could have started with two witnesses that did not have the partisan incentive to deflect and obfuscate: National Security Staff Member Benjamin Fishman and Libyan expert Ethan Chorin. However, as demonstrated below, Republican members and staff did not take advantage

Fishman, as the National Security Council director for Libya, was in a position to provide details of U.S. strategic and policy goals in Libya.[43] Fishman, in his interview on January 12, 2016, was clear that Obama made the military intervention decision and was setting the policy in Libya in April 2011.[44] Then, under Democratic questioning, Fishman shifts the decision-making responsibility to the State Department beginning in the Fall of 2011, saying that decisions regarding U.S. operations, including establishing the Benghazi Mission compound and how to handle the deteriorating Spring and Summer 2012 security environment were State Department decisions.[45] Post-Qadhafi and post-conflict planning was an international and interagency affair, as Fishman states that the "Defense Department, State Department, and probably Treasury Department, U.S., [*sic*] U.N." were responsible for it.[46]

When given the opportunity to clarify U.S. strategic and policy goals, Benghazi Committee staff, rather than clarifying the decision-making responsibilities, only asked questions and received answers for two issues: State Department making the decision to open the U.S. embassy in Tripoli and the White House and State Department recognizing the Transitional National Council.[47] As their final question, Benghazi Committee staff asked Fishman to clarify what international and interagency decisions were handled through the National Security Council and with whom the decision responsibility rested, and Fishman responded that "sort of sub-deputies" were responsible for economic revitalization, humanitarian issues, and security stabilization decisions. The Republican staff did not follow up.[48]

Benghazi Committee staff also interviewed Ethan Chorin, an expert on the Middle East and Africa and author of three books on Libya.[49] In his interview on March 11, 2016, Benghazi staff identified that Chorin had a close working relationship with Stevens, and they asked Chorin for his and Stevens's insights on what the U.S. hoped to accomplish in Libya. However, the Benghazi staff did not attempt to identify who in the U.S. government was responsible for setting strategy and policy in Libya—much less ask about specific U.S. policies in Libya.[50] The Democratic staff, ironically, attempted to get an answer for this question of responsibility, asking Chorin, from whom Stevens was getting pressure in terms of "keeping a unified Libya, secure Libya, stabilized Libya, and ensuring that the U.S. Government and other entities work together on that front."[51] Chorin stated that the "various arms of the U.S. Government," including Congress, were putting pressure on Stevens.[52] The Republican staff did not attempt to clarify the responsibilities of each of the "various arms of the U.S. Government."[53]

In failing to investigate who was responsible for the policy in Libya, Republicans missed an opportunity to add to a robust debate on whether the United States should have been (and should be) engaged in liberal institutionalism.[54] Clinton, herself, opened up this debate, stating in her January 23, 2013, Senate Foreign Relations Committee hearing that administration policy was as follows:

> We can kill [terrorist] leaders, but until we help establish strong democratic institutions, until we do a better job communicating our values and building relationships, we are going to be faced with this level of instability [in the Middle East and North Africa.][55]

Clinton provided more details in her memoir, *Hard Choices*: "There were loose weapons to collect, elections to organize, and democratic institutions and processes to establish."[56] Libya, as Clinton pointed out, was to be a success story like Colombia and Somalia.[57]

In this regard and more specifically, the Republicans could have made a determination whether Libya was the showpiece of Clinton's "smart power" strategy, placing the liability on her, or whether Obama was responsible based on the 2010 National Security Strategy (NSS) and the so-called Obama Doctrine.[58] With regard to the NSS, Obama was clear that the United States would lead multilateral efforts ("we must focus American engagement on strengthening international institutions and galvanizing the collective action that can serve common interests") and that the diplomatic instrument of national power was on equal footing with the military instrument ("Diplomacy is as fundamental to our national security as our defense capability").[59] However, Obama took a realist approach to foreign policy—viewing the military as being used only to address direct threats to the United States and not for nation-building. In Obama's view, George W. Bush was wrong for forcing regime change in Iraq, and the lesson learned was "Don't do stupid shit."[60]

As Boehner and Jordan fought for control of the Republican Party's direction, Obama and Clinton fought for the direction of American foreign policy.

In one camp, Obama and Denis McDonough were opposed to using the military as a tool of intervention. Obama believed in retrenchment, prioritizing commitments, avoiding overreach, and shifting the burden to allies and partners.[61] In the opposite camp, Clinton, Rice, and National Security Council Senior Director for Multilateral Affairs and Human Rights Samantha Power advocated for liberal interventionism, using the U.S. military to assure a humanitarian outcome.[62]

The result of the divide was a Libyan foreign policy that was devoid of direction. Obama was reluctant to get involved and only did so, based on the hawkish activism of Clinton. Clinton acknowledged the divide within the Obama administration, "There was little appetite for direct U.S. intervention."[63] Obama, with Clinton advocating, made the decision to use air power as a multilateral effort with the Europeans under the March 17, 2011, UN Security Council Resolution 1973 to enforce a no-fly zone over Libya.[64] NATO not only enforced a no-fly zone, but it began to bomb Qadhafi's forces in order to prevent a "massacre" as Obama declared.[65] The mission quickly became regime change.[66] To say Obama was reluctant would be an understatement, as he did not want to create a power vacuum for extremist groups to move in and create bigger problems for the United States.[67]

Prior to the air campaign, Obama was opposed to getting drawn into a complex landscape, and he made it clear that United States' involvement in Libya would be minimal. The NSC had set up a working group to plan for a post-Qadhafi Libya, comprised of members from the CIA, and the Treasury, State, and Defense Departments, but without White House support, the working group disbanded after the death of Qadhafi in October 2011.[68] Obama insisted the Europeans take the lead on rebuilding Libya, and the Europeans insisted on UN support. The only United States-NATO-UN agreement reached was no ground troops.[69] The future of Libya was pinned on the hope that oil wealth, an intact infrastructure, and a lack of sectarian and ethnic violence meant that Libyans could rebuild the country themselves.[70]

Unlike in Iraq and Afghanistan, Obama then seems to have made the State Department the primary agency for helping Libya in its transition to a stable democracy. Stevens was on his own without resources to steer the ship of American strategy and policy, and he did his best to ensure and prove State Department leadership.[71] He declined Ham's offer to allow the SST team to stay past August 2012, after the Defense Department refused to place them under his authority. The SST team would not have diplomatic immunity, did not have a viable Libyan force to train, and had been the source of tension within Libya (e.g., a shooting to prevent a carjacking, a fight at a UN party).[72] A national election occurred on July 7, 2012; the new parliament was expected to form a transitional government to govern for 18 months to put in place a constitution and hold new elections. Obama and senior U.S. officials in Washington viewed the election as a "mission accomplished" moment and turned their attention to Syria.[73]

Stevens, still without resources and then without the attention of Washington officials, explicitly cabled to draw attention to the increasing violence, and those in the IC also issued numerous reports concerning the escalating violence. But, back in Washington, the violence was viewed as the product of transnational terrorism, not a burgeoning civil war.[74] With Washington's attention on the Middle East, Ahmed Abu Khattala, the Libyan leader of Ansar al-Sharia, planned an attack on the Benghazi Mission compound, likely at least 12 hours, if not days, weeks, or months in advance.[75] Abu Khattala not only drew membership from the group tasked with protecting the Americans, the February 17 Brigade, but he even obtained weapons, such as mortar shells and machine gun rounds, to use in the attack from a February 17 camp.[76] The anti-Islamic video and a false rumor that Benghazi Mission compound guards had shot at protestors were used to motivate individuals, just a few dozen, to join in for the initial attack wave. Looters then followed, motivated by opportunity and greed.[77] Abu Khattala reportedly told a fighter to "flatten" the Benghazi Mission compound, and then he told others that they must "cleanse [them]selves for another battle"—an improvised attack on the CIA Annex.[78]

The resulting tragedy forced Washington to take notice of Libya again, and Obama then took sole leadership of foreign policy (back from Clinton and the State Department) and tried to steer Libya in a direction without risk and in a manner consistent with his vision of multilateralism.[79] In March 2013, Obama met with Libyan prime minister Ali Zeidan and agreed to Zeidan's request to have the U.S. military train a new Libyan army. On the same day, Obama announced his appointment of Deborah Jones, as Stevens's successor.[80] Obama also continued a program to have the U.S. military train a battalion of 800 Libyan special operations forces at Camp 27, outside of Tripoli. Both the programs were a disaster and were discontinued; subsequently, in July 2014, as Libya descended into civil war compounded by the arrival of Islamic State militants, Ambassador Jones closed the embassy.[81] Libya was a failed state.[82]

Without a thorough investigation of Libyan policy, the Republicans, as noted, were left to taking windmill swings at Clinton in her hearing. Roskam, without the evidence to support his claim and based on the nothingness of assumption, asked Clinton to respond to his "theory" of Libyan policy: "That you [Clinton] initiated a policy to put the United States into Libya as the Secretary of State and you overcame a number of obstacles within the administration to advocate for military action, and you were successful in doing that."[83] Clinton easily retorted, "From the very beginning you got it wrong, Congressman [Roskam]."[84]

An effective investigation would have started with members and staff interviewing Fishman and Chorin early in the process, and then proceeding up the chain of seniority. Fishman was forthcoming in listing individuals familiar with the Middle East and North Africa strategy:

1. He listed his supervisor, Senior Director for the Middle East Dan Shapiro and his successor, Steven Simon.
2. He worked with Senior Director for Strategic Planning Derek Chollett on post-conflict planning.
3. His primary State Department contact was the Maghreb Affairs Office with Senior Libyan desk officer Alyce Abdalla, deputy director Evyenia Sidereas, and director Bill Roebuck.
4. His primary interagency contact was principal deputy assistant secretary of State for Near Eastern Affairs Elizabeth Dibble.[85]

The Benghazi Committee interviewed Abdalla and Sidereas, notably before Fishman's interview, and only asked a total of five background-type questions about their relationship with Fishman and the interagency process.[86] The committee did not interview Shapiro, Simon, Chollett, Roebuck, or Dibble.[87] Power, as detailed, had a very prominent role in Libya, but she also was not interviewed.

White House and State Department Accountability: The Talking Points

As demonstrated in Tables 1.2 and 1.3 of chapter 1, the talking points that Rice used on the September 16 Sunday talk shows can be traced back from Rhodes's September 14 email to Clinton's September 13 Moroccan statement to Clinton's September 12 State Department remarks to Obama's September 12 Rose Garden remarks, and, finally, to the original 10:08 p.m. Clinton statement on September 11. Table 4.3 shows the linear flow of these statements.

The original author of the talking points can be identified with process tracing, a popular qualitative method for performing within-case analysis. Process tracing evaluates causal links and describes a phenomenon (e.g., talking points issued in response to a crisis) in a sequential manner.[88] One such process tracing test is the hoop test. For a hoop test, a fact must be able to "jump through a hoop" to be considered true. The hoop, in this case, is one of the original 10:08 p.m. September 11 talking points, as identified in the first column of Table 4.3:

1. "Some have sought to justify this vicious behavior as a response to inflammatory material posted on the Internet."
2. "The United States deplores any intentional effort to denigrate the religious beliefs of others."
3. "There is never any justification for violent acts of this kind."

Table 4.3 Administration Statements, September 11–16

10:08 p.m. September 11 State Department Statement	*September 12 Obama Rose Garden Remarks*	*September 12 Clinton State Department Remarks*	*September 13 Clinton Moroccan Statement*	*September 14 Rhodes Email*	*September 16 Rice Talk Show Statements*
Some have sought to justify this vicious behavior as a response to inflammatory material posted on the Internet.	–	Some have sought to justify this vicious behavior, along with the protest that took place at our Embassy in Cairo yesterday, as a response to inflammatory material posted on the Internet.	I also want to take a moment to address the video circulating on the Internet that has led to these protests in a number of countries.	To underscore that these protests are rooted in an Internet video, and not a broader failure of policy.	That what happened initially [in Benghazi] was that it was a spontaneous reaction to what had just transpired in Cairo as a consequence of the video (*FOX News Sunday*).
The United States deplores any intentional effort to denigrate the religious beliefs of others.	We reject all efforts to denigrate the religious beliefs of others.	–	Let me state very clearly—and I hope it is obvious—that the U.S. government had absolutely nothing to do with this video. We absolutely reject its content and message.	Third, we've made our view on this video crystal clear. The U.S. government had nothing to do with it. We reject its message and its contents.	What happened this week in Cairo, in Benghazi, in many other parts of the region . . . was a direct result—a direct result of a heinous and offensive video that was widely disseminated, that the U.S. government had nothing to do with, which we made clear is reprehensible and disgusting (ABC's *This Week*).

There is never any justification for violent acts of this kind.	But there is absolutely no justification to this type of senseless violence. None.	But let me be clear—there is no justification for this, none.	To us, to me personally, this video is disgusting and reprehensible. It appears to have a deeply cynical purpose: to denigrate a great religion and to provoke rage. But as I said yesterday, there is no justification, none at all, for responding to this video with violence.	We find it disgusting and reprehensible. But there is absolutely no justification at all for responding this movie with violence.	This is a response to a hateful and offensive video that was widely disseminated throughout the Arab and Muslim world. Obviously, our view is that there is absolutely no excuse for violence and that what has happened is condemnable (NBC's *Meet the Press*).

An author is eliminated as being at fault for conflating the Benghazi terrorist attack with the anti-Islamic video, if it is a fact that the author did not draft or was not in a position to draft one of the 10:08 September statements.[89]

The process starts after the 7:30 p.m. interagency conference call. Prior to the interagency conference call, as identified in chapter 1, the State Department position was the 6:09 p.m. (EDT) statement drafted by State Spokesperson Victoria Nuland: "We have no information regarding a connection between [the Cairo protests and Benghazi attack]."[90] Ben Rhodes and Jacob Sullivan spoke on the phone to confirm and approve the statement.[91]

At 9:32 p.m., Sullivan circulated a draft to Rhodes, Deputy Spokesperson for the National Security Council Bernadette Meehan, and State Department officials, which contained the following statements:

1. "Some have sought to justify this vicious behavior as a response to inflammatory material originating in the United States."
2. "The United States deplores any intentional effort to denigrate the religious beliefs of others."
3. "There is never any justification for wanton acts of this kind."[92]

The phrase, "originating in the United States" (bullet 1) would be removed, and the word, "wanton" (bullet 3) would be changed to "violent" in a 10:03 p.m. coordination email. In that coordination email, Rhodes, Sullivan, Nuland, Cheryl Mills, under secretary for political affairs Wendy Sherman, deputy assistant secretary for public affairs Philippe Reines, and deputy secretary of state for Management and Resources Thomas Nides were listed as having approved the statement for release.[93]

In total, nine individuals were asked about their possible participation in the drafting of the 10:08 p.m. statement. For the State Department, the senior adviser for strategic communications, Near Eastern Affairs Bureau stated, "I don't recall working on [any formal statements or press releases on September 11] or having responsibility for that."[94] Nides, when asked if he was "involved in putting that statement together," responded, "I was not."[95] Speechwriter Megan Rooney gave a firm "No," when she was asked about participating in the drafting of the statement.[96] She added, "[Speechwriters] usually, for the most part, usually [*sic*] didn't write written statements."[97] Speechwriter Dan Schwerin testified, "I saw [the statement] when it came out, so around 10 o'clock."[98] Deputy chief of staff for operations Huma Abedin testified that she did not draft statements, "Sometimes I read them, sometimes I didn't, but it, you know, really wasn't my job to edit them or finalize them."[99]

As for possible White House officials, Meehan, when asked if she had drafted or reviewed the statement, responded, "I was involved in reviewing it."[100] Rhodes acknowledged that he spoke to Sullivan, but did not draft the statement. He stated, "I remember speaking to [Sullivan] on the 11th about the [10:08 pm] statement that they were preparing to go out from Secretary Clinton, so that was the principal focus of our conversations, and that's what I remember talking about."[101] Rhodes was very specific:

> Well, this is a statement from the Secretary of State, originating from the State Department, so first of all, they would be principally responsible for putting together the statement. I would play a coordinating function from the White House. In terms of the information, in this case, you know, I would be relying principally on the State Department, not only because it's their statement but because it's referencing their awareness of the loss that we had suffered and the steps that Secretary Clinton had taken, including speaking to the President of Libya.[102]

Rhodes specified that he only spoke on the phone to Sullivan that night.[103] Based on the fact that the senior adviser for strategic communications, Near Eastern Affairs Bureau; Nides; Rooney; Schwerin; Abedin; Meehan; and Rhodes testified that they did not draft or were not in a position to draft the statement, they are eliminated as authors.

Nuland and Sullivan are the remaining individuals who were asked about the statement. Nuland, at first, implied that she had helped draft the 10:08 p.m. statement. She stated,

> So I participated in discussion about whether we should issue a statement that night, whether we could. And the drafting of that first statement the Secretary issued, I think about 10:30 and, then obviously I did, you know, I was responsible for the physical execution of that statement, pushing out to the press, answering follow-up inquiries, that kind of thing.[104]

However, later in her interview, she clarified,

> I can't recall who the original drafter was, whether it came from the NEA Bureau, or whether it was written by a combination of people. I may have been part of the drafting of it. I can't recall, but a number of people would have been involved in the clearance of it, including myself.[105]

Sullivan testified that he either wrote the statement alone or together with Nuland. Sullivan stated, "It would have been me and [Nuland that drafted the statement], and I'm just not sure if I did it or if [Nuland] and I did it together or—but it would have been the two of us."[106] Sullivan later in his testimony took credit for the statement, "What I was thinking about in writing this statement that night."[107]

So, based on this, Nuland and Sullivan pass the hoop test as the potential authors. Nuland, in her interview, fully supported the statement:

> So this was an effort to get in the Secretary's name a clear paragraph out there for the entire region to see that we condemn, you know, we considered the stuff on the Internet inflammatory; that we deplored any efforts to denigrate religion, so separating ourselves from the content of the film, reasserting America's response to respect for tolerance, but also beginning this trope that you see in all of the public statements for the following week that nonetheless, it's not a justification for violence.[108]

Further analysis confirms how the statement was likely drafted. As further detailed in the "Source of the Groupthink" subsection, Sullivan attended a 7:30 p.m. interagency conference call. After the meeting, he likely had a phone conversation with Rhodes, who had also attended the conference call. Rhodes stated, "I remember speaking to [Sullivan] on the 11th about the [10:08 pm] statement that they were preparing to go out from Secretary Clinton, so that was the principal focus of our conversations, and that what's I remember talking about."[109] Sullivan then met with Nuland, brainstormed phrases with her, and drafted the statement.

Sullivan's specific statements support this path. He testified, "I believe that it was my idea to include [the 'Some have sought' sentence]."[110] He justified its inclusion: "And I really thought it was important for the Secretary [Clinton] to get on record on this issue [about preventing further violence]."[111] Sullivan held the view as late as his testimony in September 2015 that the video "played a role in the Benghazi attacks."[112] Sullivan later in his testimony took credit for the other two sentences,

> The Secretary continued to make this point in the days that followed trying to stress two things. First, that we don't denigrate any religion and don't condone the denigration of any religion, but second, that that could never justify the kind of violence that we went on to see over those days in September of 2012. So—sitting here today, I'm glad I put this in.[113]

Pentagon Accountability: The Response

As detailed in chapter 1, an analysis of the testimony of Secretary Leon Panetta, Chief of Staff Jeremy Bash, Chair Martin Dempsey, Vice Chair James Winnefeld, General John Kelly, General Carter Ham, Admiral Charles Leidig, Admiral Richard Landolt, Admiral Brian Losey, General Michael Repass, General Robert Lovell, Joint Chiefs of Staff director of Operations Admiral Kurt Tidd, and commander of U.S. Air Forces in

Europe general Philip Breedlove offers the following findings of fact (all times EDT):

1. At a 5 pm White House meeting on September 11, Obama ordered the military to "use all of the resources at [the military's] disposal to try to make sure [the military] did everything possible to try to save lives there."[114]
2. At 6 pm, Panetta convened a single meeting with Dempsey, Ham, Winnefeld, Bash, and Kelly and then selected the units, as a result of that meeting.[115]
3. At 7 pm, Panetta ordered two FAST platoons, the CIF, and a U.S.-based SOF unit to respond.[116] Other than the U.S.-based SOF unit, military officials focused on U.S. European Command assets.[117] Officials ruled out F-16s at Aviano and other aircraft assets at Souda Bay.[118] Assets in or around Djibouti, on the Horn of Africa, were not considered.[119]
4. In a 7:30 pm conference call, White House, Pentagon, and State Department officials concluded the attack in Benghazi was over and a response was needed for unrest in the region.[120] The Pentagon shifted the mission from one of an attack on the Benghazi compound to one of rescuing Ambassador Stevens, who was assumed to be a hostage.[121]
5. By 9 pm, the Pentagon issued orders to send the CIF and U.S.-based SOF forces to a staging based in Sigonella.[122] One FAST platoon was to move to Tripoli and the other would eventually deploy to Souda Bay.[123] After these deployment decisions, Pentagon officials did not make any further decisions.[124]
6. By 1 am on September 12, the CIF was the first unit ready to deploy, but it did not deploy at that time (it deployed at 11:00 am).[125]
7. At 8:15 am, a C-17 was the first military asset to move towards Libya.[126]
8. At 2:56 pm, the FAST platoon was the first combat unit to arrive in Libya.[127]

In sum, Pentagon officials assumed the attack in Benghazi had been a singular event, resulting in Stevens being taken hostage. Officials confined their search for military units to U.S. European Command apart from a United States-based SOF unit. Other than diverting forces away from Benghazi, officials did not make or alter any orders after the initial set of deployment orders.

These findings can be used to understand the decisions made, or as Admiral Mullen stated about the purpose of the ARB, to focus on "operational accountability at the level of operational responsibility."[128] When planning the Benghazi operation, key Pentagon decision-makers introduced bias, based on prior experience; they assumed that they were facing another hostage rescue operation, such as the April 12, 2009, *Maersk Alabama* Captain Richard Phillips rescue or the January 25, 2012, operation that rescued Jessica Buchanan and Poul Hagen Thisted.[129] Landolt summed it up:

> What was going through my mind was 1979 and a hostage situation similar to Iran, and so—and I think that's probably what was going on in the minds of people back in the Pentagon because those forces were deployed without [U.S. Africa Command] ordering them.[130]

To counter this bias, the military has a joint doctrine, which is defined as "the fundamental principles that guide the employment of US military forces in coordinated action toward a common objective."[131] Doctrine is intended for situations such as Benghazi, and every officer, at a minimum, is expected to consider it when making decisions. More specifically, whether it is a campaign plan like Operation Overlord or a crisis response like the Buchanan and Thisted rescue, commanders should have followed the joint operation planning process, as promulgated at the time in the August 2011 *Joint Operation Planning* (JP 5-0) document.[132] The joint planning process, which achieves objectives by determining how to use military capabilities "in time and space," is iterative.[133] Planners may need to repeat steps or even start over as the environment changes or new information is learned. Table 4.4 lists the seven steps of the joint planning process.[134]

By using the findings of fact and tracing the Benghazi military response through the steps of the joint planning process, it is possible to determine whether the joint planning doctrine was followed.[135] As evident in Table 4.5, Pentagon officials implemented a contingency plan and issued orders for the operation, Jukebox Lotus, but they engaged in a disjointed decision process.[136] Bash specified the lack of a process, "This night [of the attack] nothing was normal. There were no protocols. There was no standard procedures for how to make deployment decisions on the fly in a crisis."[137] They did not go through the planning process and did not take actions consistent with the doctrine for four of the seven steps: mission analysis, course of action development, course of action analysis and wargaming, and course of action comparison. To put it bluntly, because officials did not use this process, they failed to understand that their actions and orders on the night of September 11 never had a chance to succeed.

As doctrine is just a guide and not a prescription, military commanders are not required to use a process or structure. But when they fail to follow guidance, they are imposing a mandate on their subordinates. Jeffrey Reilly, author of an influential book on operational design, notes that "intellectual discussions founder and critical thinking disintegrates."[138] Ryan White, a

Table 4.4 Joint Planning Process

Step		*Actions to be Taken*
1	Planning Initiation	– When the president, secretary of defense, or chair, Joint Chief of Staff directs a commander to commence planning in response to a potential or actual crisis. – The commander will develop an operational approach, which is a translation of strategy and current conditions into specific missions and tasks to arrive at a desired condition. The operational approach includes both operational art (a commander's skill, experience, and judgment) and operational design (a visual framework showing the ends, ways, means, and risk of an operation).
2	Mission Analysis	– The development of a mission statement that lists the tasks and identifies the forces needed to accomplish the mission.
3	Course of Action Development	– The design of multiple potential ways (or methods) to accomplish the mission.
4	Course of Action Analysis and Wargaming	– The process of identifying the advantages and disadvantages of each proposed course of action. – Wargaming is a representation of the potential conflict to evaluate each proposed course of action.
5	Course of Action Comparison	– The process of evaluating each COA independently based on a set of criteria to determine which COA has the highest probability of accomplishing the mission.
6	Course of Action Approval	– The decision of the commander whether to accept the recommendation of the staff as to the best course of action. – The commander may approve the recommended course of action, approve the course of action with modifications, select a different course of action from the staff recommendation, direct a course of action not considered, or defer the decision to consult with staff or commanders.
7	Plan or Order Development	– The use of the approved course of action to create a plan or order.

former Joint Warfighting course instructor, states why doctrine is important, "Joint Doctrine integrates the services planning efforts and provides a common lexicon, operating picture, and understanding of what command structures, forces, and timing will be."[139] The result of failing to follow doctrine is often impaired decisions, which do not "judiciously assess the environment, identify the problem requiring resolution, [or] develop an operational approach."[140] This impairment can be illustrated by creating a cognitive map of the military's non-doctrinal operational approach (Figure 4.1). The

Table 4.5 Pentagon Decision Process

Step		*Action to be Taken*	*Action Taken?*	*Actions Officials Took*
1	Planning Initiation	Commence planning?	Yes	Pentagon officials, after being ordered by Obama to protect Americans, commenced planning.
		Develop an operational approach?	No	The testimony of Pentagon officials supports the idea that they engaged in operational art, but there is no evidence that operational design was done.
2	Mission Analysis	Mission statement that lists the tasks and forces needed?	No	The operation order would have contained a mission statement, but the initial order was verbal and witnesses did not specify any details about a mission statement. Moreover, there is no evidence that officials engaged in an iterative process, as new facts became available (e.g., the mission was a response to conventional military-style attack). If this step had been taken, officials would have discovered that the units selected would not be able to respond in a time-relevant fashion. They then would have been expected to examine (or reexamine) using the F-16s or locating non-U.S. European Command units.
3	Course of Action Development	Multiple courses of action developed?	No	There is no evidence that officials followed a doctrinal process to develop multiple ways to respond to the attack. Officials proposed a course of action to achieve the wrong objective of a hostage rescue. Alternative courses, such as a response using F-16s or other assets, if considered, were quickly ruled out through informal discussion.

(*continued*)

Table 4.5 (Continued)

Step		Action to be Taken	Action Taken?	Actions Officials Took
4	Course of Action Analysis and Wargaming	Course of action analysis and wargame?	No	There is no evidence that officials attempted to analyze or wargame the one proposed course of action for a hostage rescue mission.
5	Course of Action Comparison	Compare courses of action?	No	There is no evidence a comparison was done, especially given there was only one proposed course of action.
6	Course of Action Approval	Course of action approval?	Yes	Officials approved a course of action, but they did not receive staff inputs nor select from multiple courses of action.
7	Plan or Order Development	Orders developed?	Yes	At 8:39 and 8:53 p.m., NMCC drafted orders for forces to prepare to deploy.

cognitive map contains operational design elements, which are taken from the August 2011 *Joint Operation Planning (*JP 5-0) document. The elements are interdependent and collectively combine to demonstrate how a commander intends to achieve operational success from start to finish. The elements are defined as follows:

1. Termination—ending military operation and ensure outcome endures;
2. Military end state—a point in which the military is no longer needed to achieve the objective;
3. Objectives—a goal toward which the operation is directed;
4. Decisive points—a geographic point, event, or factor that allows a commander to achieve an advantage;
5. Lines of Operation (LOO)—actions executed in sequence that achieve an objective;
6. Lines of Effort (LOE)—multiple tasks and missions involving nonmilitary factors that achieve an objective;
7. Anticipation—using indicators to forecast events;
8. Operational reach—the distance and duration that a joint force can employ capabilities; and
9. Arranging operations—the best combination of forces to accomplish the mission.[141]

For termination, Panetta and the Pentagon officials incorrectly interpreted Obama's order of saving Americans to mean saving American hostages and preventing further violence in the region. This mistranslation meant the Pentagon embarked on a different mission than the one assigned, and, indeed, Pentagon officials with Operation Jukebox Lotus kept military forces in Libya for an indefinite time period.[142] For military end state, the Jukebox Lotus orders stated that the end state was securing American facilities and interests in Tripoli and posturing forces for follow-on missions in Libya.[143] In addition to the termination and military end state being incorrect, the objective of using U.S. European Command and United States-based special operation forces to prepare to save American lives was also incorrect, as these assets would not arrive in time to save lives. All operations and efforts, as dictated by doctrine, are directed at achieving the termination, military end state, and objective, and the misidentification of these three elements had a cascading negative effect on the rest of the operation.

For the lines of operation, Pentagon officials directed the CIF, FAST, and SOF forces to move to Benghazi, Tripoli, and Sigonella. The line of effort was a State Department-led task to gain local militia support and country clearance. The decisive points were designated locations the military believed were needed in order to achieve the objective. Initially, these decisive points were Benghazi, Tripoli, and Sigonella before shifting to Tripoli and then primarily to Sigonella. As stated by the commanders in their testimony, Sigonella, as an intermediate base, was an ideal location for a staging area for a hostage rescue operation. Bash stated,

> The order was: [the forces are] going into Libya because we have a potential situation where we have an Ambassador potentially being held hostage, and we might have to stage a hostage rescue. The planning for that included them landing at an intermediate staging base, so that I believe they could unload and stage the assault force that might be necessary.[144]

It was also a location for a response to anticipated violence in North Africa.

As illustrated in Figure 4.1, the executed operational approach, if it had been constructed according to doctrine, would have provided the Pentagon officials an understanding their operation would fail. To put it simply, the selected course of action could not accomplish Obama's order of doing everything possible to save American lives. This was due to the fact that the CIF and United States-based SOF forces were aligned with the wrong objective: going to a staging base to prepare to save lives is not doing everything possible to save American lives. The line of effort of relying on local militias was properly aligned with Obama's order, but it had a low probability of success. Selecting the FAST platoons, which were based in Spain but had air transportation in Germany violated the operational reach and arranging

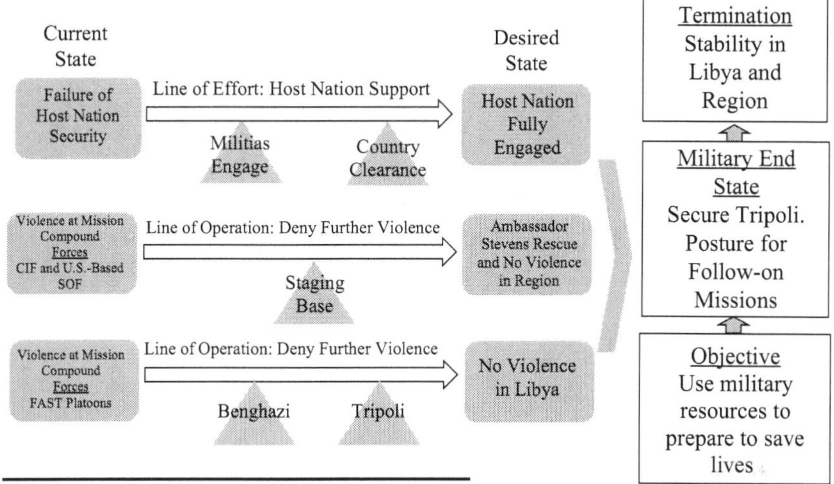

- Anticipation: Forecast Benghazi violence had ended. Anticipated future violence in Libya and region.
- Operational reach: CIF and FAST Platoons did not have co-located transportation.
- Arranging Operations: FAST Platoons to secure facilities; CIF and SOF perform hostage rescue.

Figure 4.1 Benghazi Non-Doctrinal Operational Approach. *Source*: Figure created by author.

operations elements. Most importantly, in terms of anticipation, military leaders did not continue to search for indicators to help guide them. They believed there would be no further violence in Benghazi due to misinformation received at two critical points (detailed in the "Source of the Groupthink" subsection). Commanders believed time was not as critical as a factor, which meant they failed to anticipate the urgency of the situation in Benghazi. The result was improperly selected units, lines of operation connected to the wrong objective, and an end state and termination point that went beyond the president's orders.

Had officials engaged in even an abbreviated crisis action version of the joint planning process and realized that the course of action which they selected would not save lives, at the very least they would have had the opportunity to revise their operational approach. They likely would have assumed more risk in attempting to achieve a more narrowly focused termination point of safely evacuating Americans from Libya (as opposed to stabilizing the region) and an objective of using all military resources to save American lives. With this objective, at a minimum, they would have had to consider a new line of operation of showing force by launching the F-16s. This line of operation would have meshed with a correctly crafted objective, and it could have corrected the operational reach and arranging operations elements of the non-doctrinal operational approach. With any counterfactual, there is no way to determine if this approach would have saved the lives of Doherty and Woods, but it would have served as undeniable evidence of a government expending every effort to bring its citizens home safely.

Source of the Groupthink

So, why did White House and State Department officials claim from 10:08 p.m. on September 11 to Rice's appearance on September 16 that the Benghazi attack had been a protest due to an anti-Islamic video? Why did the military conclude that forces should deploy to a staging base instead of to Benghazi? The answer rests with Irving Janis's groupthink:

> A mode of thinking that people engage in when they are deeply involved in a cohesive ingroup, when the members' strivings for unanimity override their motivation to realistically appraise alternative courses of action.[145]

In other words, participants align their opinions with a perceived consensus. Critical thinking and dissent are lost as participants collectively make a decision, which each individual might have rejected in the absence of peer pressure. A crisis, in particular, with its uncertainty pressures participants to unify and form a consensus in order to maintain group cohesion and preserve individual well-being. Consensus is reached to eliminate uncertainty but at the expense of accurate appraisals and policy options.[146]

With the Benghazi attack, leaders at the White House, State, and Pentagon reached a conclusion, a politically advantageous conclusion, that protestors had angrily stormed the Benghazi compound, taken the ambassador hostage, and that the military needed to organize a rescue as it had done with the January 25, 2012, Buchanan and Thisted rescue. This narrative was crafted based on supposition, and alternatives to this narrative, if even considered, were rejected.

Bash stated that at Panetta's 6 p.m. meeting, a hostage narrative took hold. He was very clear that it dominated the group's thinking:

> With regard to Benghazi specifically, my recollection is that the characterization of what the situation was, was that it was a potential hostage rescue situation, where the Ambassador potentially was being held by terrorists, and that the question on the table, as it kind of was laid out over that next little while, was how would we, how could we respond to the situation if we found ourselves, heaven forbid, in the situation in which the Ambassador was being held hostage.[147]

Bash further added that "the first and primary concern was obviously the whereabouts of the Ambassador and his wellbeing."[148]

The source of this groupthink, in which decision-makers relied on falsely formed consensus, can be traced to the 7:30 p.m. (EDT) on September 11 interagency conference call (or SVTC), in which Clinton and McDonough were the senior officials. As detailed in chapter 1, the participants in the 7:30 p.m. (EDT) White House conference call included McDonough, Clinton, Rhodes, Bash, Kelly, Mills, Sullivan, Kennedy, Fishman, and Matthew Olsen.[149] Participants faced uncertainty about the cause of violence at the Benghazi compound, other than receiving information from Hicks that Ansar al-Sharia had taken credit for what was described as an "attack" and "a running battle."[150]

Clinton spoke on behalf of the State Department at the conference call, and given the operational-level nature of SVTCs, her participation was labeled as "unusual."[151] As the senior official, Clinton, by default, was the leader of the group.

Kennedy stated that the purpose of the meeting was "simply a conforming of information" and to "[m]ake sure everybody had the same understanding."[152] At the meeting, a White House official relayed Obama's order to "do whatever needed to be done."[153] They translated those orders, based on two assumptions: they were dealing with Ambassador Stevens, being taken hostage, and they were dealing with potential violence in Libya and the region.

For the first assumption about the ambassador, Clinton was passed a message during the call, and Bash testified that

> [Clinton] kind of told folks what the substance of the message was, and it was that a blond-haired individual had been found at the hospital. And I remember her saying, and I think others saying, well, that must be Ambassador Stevens, you know.[154]

Clinton, by her seniority and in reading the message, had implicitly adopted a closed leadership style and imparted a concurrence-seeking atmosphere without deference to divergent options. Her announcement ended the discussion to other alternatives.[155] This is supported by the fact that Leidig made it clear that from 6 to 11 p.m. (12 a.m. to 5 a.m. EET), U.S. Africa Command was focused on locating the ambassador.[156]

The participants then began collectively crafting a narrative, and that narrative, according to the individuals in attendance was that the anti-Islamic video was the cause of the violence.[157] Olsen testified,

> I recall linking the [Cairo video protest and the Benghazi attack], you know, that this—we were thinking about what had happened in Cairo, we were thinking, okay, now this seems to be happening in Benghazi, and we're worried about other, obviously, other diplomatic posts in the Middle East and North Africa.[158]

Ironically and unbeknownst to the participants at the time, some of the attackers told a Libyan journalist, who had arrived as the Benghazi Mission compound as it was being attacked, that they were motivated by the video (as well as a false rumor that Benghazi compound guards had fired on a protestor).[159]

Five of the ten action items referenced the video.[160] The result of the conference call was to believe, despite a lack of evidence, that the Benghazi violence was a one-time event and, thus, a shift away from responding to the Benghazi attack and more toward responding to Tripoli and unrest in the region.[161] Military assets, in particular, were "diverted to a staging location."[162] Ham called Landolt to tell him the source of violence was the anti-Islamic video.[163]

About four hours later, an email and interagency conference call confirmed this focus on Stevens and the anti-Islamic video. At 11:45 p.m., McDonough emailed White House, State, and Defense officials to inform them that Smith was confirmed dead and that Stevens remained "unaccounted for."[164] He also detailed efforts to "take down" anti-Islamic videos, including Panetta calling Pastor Terry Jones and reaching out to YouTube.[165] Soon thereafter, at a second interagency conference call around 12 a.m., participants again believed that Stevens might have been located. Kelly testified,

> It was pretty close to midnight, I think, on a [State Department-led video teleconference] where the word was, hey, we got [Stevens]. . . . But the rumors were rampant about—they found him, he was okay, we didn't know what that meant.[166]

CONCLUSION

As organized by topics and level of effort, member and staff participation in the investigation declined under Ryan in the other agency phase. Nonetheless, the negative impact on Clinton, measured with voter polls, is consistent with academic literature. The diminished Republican effort in the other agency phase, particularly when the topics were Libyan strategy, the talking points, and military response, as well as the Republican Party fracture resulted in an incomplete investigation and the failure to identify key White House, State, and Defense individuals for their roles in setting the direction for Libya, responding to the attack, and in communicating earnestly with the American people. Investigators identified the crucial interagency meeting, but they failed to explain how Clinton's leadership style resulted in groupthink and led others to wrongly believe an anti-Islamic video had caused a hostage situation.

In the next chapter, I start by summarizing the findings of this study on the Benghazi Committee. This includes an explanation of the partisan model and its application to the committee and its investigation. Then, next steps in research are offered, including the possibility that partisan investigations may be key for exposing and preventing wrongdoing. The chapter ends with a return to solving the puzzle of partisan congressional investigations and why the Benghazi tragedy continues to divide us.

NOTES

1. The Benghazi Report's "Table of Witnesses by Interview Date" lists 47 interviews, but Clinton's hearing is treated as an interview. See "Table of Witnesses by Interview Date," *Interviews of Witnesses Before the Select Committee on the Events Surrounding the 2012 Terrorist Attack in Benghazi: House of Representatives* (114th Cong., 2d sess., Volume 11, 2016), 1619–21.

2. Petraeus was interviewed twice: January 6, 2016, and March 19, 2016.

3. Douglas Kriner and Eric Schickler, *Investigating the President: Congressional Checks on Presidential Power* (Princeton: Princeton University Press, 2016), 227, 236.

4. Kriner and Schickler, *Investigating the President*, 106.

5. Washington Post-ABC poll, May 29–June 1, 2014, https://www.politico.com/story/2014/06/benghazi-poll-51-percent-support-panel-hillary-clinton-107362, accessed October 22, 2021.

6. Quinnipiac Poll, July 30, 2015, https://poll.qu.edu/Poll-Release-Legacy?releaseid=2264, accessed February 15, 2022.

7. CNN/ORC Poll, October 14–17, 2015, http://i2.cdn.turner.com/cnn/2015/images/10/21/rel11e.-.benghazi.pdf, accessed October 21, 2021.

8. Quinnipiac Poll, November 4, 2015, https://poll.qu.edu/Poll-Release-Legacy?releaseid=2299, accessed February 15, 2022.

9. Quinnipiac Poll, June 29, 2016, https://poll.qu.edu/Poll-Release-Legacy?releaseid=2363, accessed February 15, 2022.

10. Gallup Poll, May 14–15, 2013, https://news.gallup.com/poll/162584/americans-attention-irs-benghazi-stories-below-average.aspx, accessed October 22, 2021.

11. Kriner and Schickler, *Investigating the President*, 253.

12. Kriner and Schickler, *Investigating the President*, 256–57.

13. Kriner and Schickler, *Investigating the President*, 81–82.

14. Tyler Cherry, "Media Fell for Bogus 'New Information' Spin In GOP Benghazi Report," *Media Matters*, June 29, 2016, https://www.mediamatters.org/washington-post/media-fell-bogus-new-information-spin-gop-benghazi-report, accessed February 17, 2022.

15. Steve Benen, "Republican Benghazi Committee Ends with a Whimper," *MSNBC*, June 28, 2016, https://www.msnbc.com/rachel-maddow-show/republican-benghazi-committee-ends-whimper-msna870586, accessed February 15, 2022.

16. Rudy Takala, "Conservative Group Says House Benghazi Panel 'Bungled' Investigation," *Washington Examiner*, March 24, 2016, https://www.washington-examiner.com/tag/hillary-clinton?source=%2Fconservative-group-says-house-beng-hazi-panel-bungled-investigation, accessed February 15, 2022.

17. Betsy Swan, "Scorned Trump Team Turns on Man They Once Loved," *Daily Beast*, December 28, 2015, https://www.thedailybeast.com/scorned-trump-team-turns-on-man-they-once-loved, accessed February 15, 2022.

18. Julian Zelizer, *On Capitol Hill: The Struggle to Reform and Its Consequences, 1948–2000* (Cambridge: Cambridge University Press, 2004), 256–57; Barbara Sinclair, *Party Wars: Polarization and the Politics of National Policy Making* (Norman: University of Oklahoma Press, 2006), 124–28; Barbara Sinclair, *Unorthodox Law-making: New Legislative Processes in the U.S. Congress*, 2nd edition (Washington, DC: CQ Press, 2000), 97–99.

19. Tim Alberta, "John Boehner Unchained," *Politico*, November/December 2017, https://www.politico.com/magazine/story/2017/10/29/john-boehner-trump-house-republican-party-retirement-profile-feature-215741/, accessed February 14, 2022.

20. Tim Dickinson, "Inside the Republican Suicide Machine," *Rolling Stone*, October 9, 2013, https://www.rollingstone.com/politics/politics-news/inside-the-republican-suicide-machine-122436/, accessed February 15, 2022.

21. Felicia Sonmez, "Jim Jordan: Boehner Plan Won't Pass House on Republican Support Alone," *Washington Post*, July 26, 2011, https://www.washingtonpost.com/blogs/2chambers/post/jim-jordan-boehner-plan-wont-pass-house-on-republican-sup-port-alone/2011/07/26/gIQAZqY1aI_blog.html, accessed February 15, 2022.

22. Alberta, "John Boehner Unchained."

23. Dickinson, "Inside the Republican."

24. Jessica Mendoza, "On impeachment, Jim Jordan goes for the takedown," *Christian Science Monitor*, November 19, 2019, https://www.csmonitor.com/USA/Politics/2019/1119/On-impeachment-Jim-Jordan-goes-for-the-takedown, accessed February 15, 2022.

25. Alberta, "John Boehner Unchained." Boehner is a not a fan of Jordan, calling him a "legislative terrorist." Jordan is dismissive of Boehner: "Oh, my goodness. I feel sorry for the guy if he's that bitter about a guy coming here and doing what he told the voters he was gonna do." See Alberta, "John Boehner Unchained."

26. Emma Dumain and Daniel Newhauser, "Boehner Satisfies Many Constituencies with Benghazi Panel Picks," *Roll Call*, May 9, 2014, https://rollcall.com/2014/05/09/boehner-satisfies-many-constituencies-with-benghazi-panel-picks-video/, accessed February 15, 2022.

27. CBS/AP, "The House GOP's Benghazi Investigation; Who's Who," *CBS News*, May 19, 2014, https://www.cbsnews.com/news/whos-who-on-the-gops-beng-hazi-investigation/, accessed February 15, 2022.

28. *New York Times*, "Highlights from Hillary Clinton's Day at the Benghazi Panel," *New York Times*, October 22, 2015, https://www.nytimes.com/interactive/projects/cp/congress/hillary-clinton-testimony-at-house-benghazi-panel/jim-jordan-sharp-questioning-about-night-of-attack, accessed February 15, 2022.

29. Maxwell Tani and Dan Turkel, "The Benghazi Chairman Couldn't Explain What He Learned after 10 Hours of Testimony from Hillary Clinton," *Business Insider*, October 22, 2015, https://www.businessinsider.com/trey-gowdy-hillary-clinton-testimony-gaffe-2015-10, accessed February 15, 2022.

30. Select Committee on the Events Surrounding the 2012 Terrorist Attack in Benghazi, *Final Report of the Select Committee on the Events Surrounding the 2012 Terrorist Attack in Benghazi: House of Representatives; Together with Additional and Minority Views* (114th Cong., 2d sess., 2016. H. Rept. 114-848), 420.

31. See David Hackett Fischer, *Historians' Fallacies: Toward a Logic of Historical Thought* (New York: Harper, 1970); Jonathan Baron and John C. Hershey, "Outcome Bias in Decision Evaluation," *Journal of Personality and Social Psychology* 54, no. 4 (1988): 569–79.

32. Select Committee, *Final Report*, 264.

33. Select Committee, *Final Report*, 264. The "no boots on the ground" policy meant no U.S. military presence.

34. "Hearing 4," Hearing before the Select Committee on the Events Surrounding the 2012 Terrorist Attack in Benghazi House of Representatives, October 22, 2015, 278.

35. "Hearing 4," Hearing before the Select Committee, 278.

36. "Hearing 4," Hearing before the Select Committee, 361.

37. "Hearing 4," Hearing before the Select Committee, 361.

38. "Hearing 4," Hearing before the Select Committee, 330.

39. "Hearing 4," Hearing before the Select Committee, 335.

40. "Hearing 4," Hearing before the Select Committee, 371–72.

41. "Hearing 4," Hearing before the Select Committee, 372.

42. "Hearing 4," Hearing before the Select Committee, 381.

43. In his professional biography, Fishman writes of his role: "As director for Libya, [Fishman] coordinated U.S. support for Libya's revolution." See Benjamin Fishman, "Experts: Ben Fishman," *The Washington Institute for Near East Policy*, n.d., https://www.washingtoninstitute.org/experts/ben-fishman, accessed July 11, 2022.

44. Benjamin Fishman, *Interviews of Witnesses Before the Select Committee on the Events Surrounding the 2012 Terrorist Attack in Benghazi: House of Representatives* (114th Cong., 2d sess., Volume 8, 2016), 575, 599.

45. Fishman, *Interviews of Witnesses*, 600–603.

46. Fishman, *Interviews of Witnesses*, 605.

47. Fishman, *Interviews of Witnesses*, 615–16.

48. Fishman, *Interviews of Witnesses*, 628.

49. Ethan Chorin, "About," *Forbes*, n.d., https://www.forbes.com/sites/ethanchorin/?sh=21c15f304bcd, accessed July 11, 2022. The third book, *Benghazi!: A New History of the Fiasco that Pushed America and its World to the Brink* (Hachette Books, 2022) was released in September 2022.

50. Ethan Chorin, *Interviews of Witnesses Before the Select Committee on the Events Surrounding the 2012 Terrorist Attack in Benghazi: House of Representatives* (114th Cong., 2d sess., Volume 9, 2016), 1062–64, 1066, 1080.

51. Chorin, *Interviews of Witnesses*, 1082.

52. Chorin, *Interviews of Witnesses*, 1082.

53. Chorin, *Interviews of Witnesses*, 1088.

54. See John Ikenberry, *After Victory: Institutions, Strategic Restraint, and the Rebuilding of Order after Major Wars* (Princeton: Princeton University Press, 2001) and Robert Keohane, *After Hegemony: Power and Discord in the World Political Economy* (Princeton: Princeton University Press, 1984).

55. "Benghazi: The Attacks and the Lessons Learned," Hearing before the Committee on Foreign Relations United States Senate, January 23, 2013, S. Hrg. 113–184, 17.

56. Hillary Clinton, *Hard Choices* (New York: Simon & Schuster, 2014), 388.

57. "Benghazi: The Attacks," Hearing before the Committee on Foreign Relations, 45.

58. White House, *The National Security Strategy of the United States of America* (Washington: President of the U.S., 2010).

59. White House, *National Security Strategy*, 3, 14.

60. Jeffrey Goldberg, "The Obama Doctrine," *The Atlantic*, April 2016, https://www.theatlantic.com/magazine/archive/2016/04/the-obama-doctrine/471525/, accessed July15, 2022. Clinton dismissed "Don't do stupid stuff [*sic*]" as "not an organizing principle," which made Obama "rip-shit angry." See Goldberg, "Obama Doctrine."

61. Goldberg, "Obama Doctrine."

62. Goldberg, "Obama Doctrine"; Clinton, *Hard Choices*, 370.

63. Clinton, *Hard Choices*, 366.

64. Frederic Wehrey, *The Burning Shores: Inside the Battle for the New Libya* (New York: Farrar, Straus and Giroux, 2018), 42–43; Alan J. Kuperman, "Obama's Libya Debacle: How a Well-Meaning Intervention Ended in Failure," *Foreign Affairs* 94, no. 2 (2015): 66; Clinton, *Hard Choices*, 370; for criticisms of multilateral uses of force, see Bradley F. Podliska, *Acting Alone: A Scientific Study of American Hegemony and Unilateral Use-of-Force Decision Making* (Lanham, MD: Lexington Books, 2010), 34–42.

65. Kuperman, "Obama's Libya Debacle," 66.

66. Kuperman, "Obama's Libya Debacle."

67. Wehrey, *Burning Shores*, 153. Obama later declared of the intervention, "It didn't work." See Goldberg, "Obama Doctrine."

68. Wehrey, *Burning Shores*, 66–68. Clinton, in a TV interview, mocked Qadhafi's death, saying, "We came, we saw, he died." See Wehrey, *Burning Shores*, 64.

69. Wehrey, *Burning Shores*, 68–69; Goldberg, "Obama Doctrine."

70. Wehrey, *Burning Shores*, 69.

71. Wehrey, *Burning Shores*, 76, 120–21.

72. Wehrey, *Burning Shores*, 120–21.

73. Wehrey, *Burning Shores*, 82. For the "mission accomplished" reference, see Catherine Lucey, "Bush Was Haunted by His Own 'Mission Accomplished,'" *Boston Globe*, April 14, 2018, https://www.bostonglobe.com/news/nation/2018/04

/14/bush-was-haunted-his-own-mission-accomplished/E73SdIkXxBfUGsbyXv7ISI/story.html, accessed July 13, 2022.

74. Wehrey, *Burning Shores*, 111–13.

75. David D. Kirkpatrick, "A Deadly Mix in Benghazi," *New York Times*, December 28, 2013, https://www.nytimes.com/projects/2013/benghazi/index.html#/?chapt=0, accessed July 18, 2022.

76. Wehrey, *Burning Shores*, 136.

77. Kirkpatrick, "Deadly Mix in Benghazi."

78. Kirkpatrick, "Deadly Mix in Benghazi."

79. Wehrey, *Burning Shores*, 146–47, 153. Jeffrey Goldberg declared August 30, 2013, as Obama's "liberation day," when Obama decided to defy the "Washington playbook" and not bomb Syria's chemical weapons arsenal. See Goldberg, "Obama Doctrine."

80. Wehrey, *Burning Shores*, 154–56.

81. Wehrey, *Burning Shores*, 157–59, 187, 190, 229.

82. Wehrey, *Burning Shores*, 239; Kuperman, "Obama's Libya Debacle."

83. "Hearing 4," Hearing before the Select Committee, 379.

84. "Hearing 4," Hearing before the Select Committee, 380.

85. Fishman, *Interviews of Witnesses*, 571–73.

86. Senior Libyan Desk Officer, Office of Maghreb Affairs, *Interviews of Witnesses Before the Select Committee on the Events Surrounding the 2012 Terrorist Attack in Benghazi: House of Representatives* (114th Cong., 2d sess., Volume 7, 2016), 449–50; Deputy Director, Office of Maghreb Affairs, *Interviews of Witnesses Before the Select Committee on the Events Surrounding the 2012 Terrorist Attack in Benghazi: House of Representatives* (114th Cong., 2d sess., Volume 7, 2016), 1028–29.

87. The OGR Committee interviewed Roebuck on August 5, 2013, and Dibble on July 10, 2013. The Benghazi Committee included those interviews in Volume 1 of its witness interviews. See *Interviews of Witnesses Before the Select Committee on the Events Surrounding the 2012 Terrorist Attack in Benghazi: House of Representatives* (114th Cong., 2d sess., Volume 1, 2016).

88. David Collier, "Understanding Process Tracing," *PS: Political Science and Politics* 44, no. 4 (2011): 823.

89. Collier, "Understanding Process Tracing," 826–27.

90. Jacob Sullivan, *Interviews of Witnesses Before the Select Committee on the Events Surrounding the 2012 Terrorist Attack in Benghazi: House of Representatives* (114th Cong., 2d sess., Volume 6, 2016), 722.

91. Ben Rhodes, *Interviews of Witnesses Before the Select Committee on the Events Surrounding the 2012 Terrorist Attack in Benghazi: House of Representatives* (114th Cong., 2d sess., Volume 8, 2016), 877.

92. Select Committee on the Events Surrounding the 2012 Terrorist Attack in Benghazi, *Documents Provided to the Select Committee on the Events Surrounding the 2012 Terrorist Attack in Benghazi: House of Representatives* (114th Cong., 2d sess., Volume 2, 2016), 557.

93. Sullivan, *Interviews of Witnesses*, 781.

94. Senior Adviser for Strategic Communications, Near Eastern Affairs Bureau, *Interviews of Witnesses Before the Select Committee on the Events Surrounding the 2012 Terrorist Attack in Benghazi: House of Representatives* (114th Cong., 2d sess., Volume 5, 2016), 356.

95. Thomas Nides, *Interviews of Witnesses Before the Select Committee on the Events Surrounding the 2012 Terrorist Attack in Benghazi: House of Representatives* (114th Cong., 2d sess., Volume 7, 2016), 777.

96. Megan Rooney, *Interviews of Witnesses Before the Select Committee on the Events Surrounding the 2012 Terrorist Attack in Benghazi: House of Representatives* (114th Cong., 2d sess., Volume 7, 2016), 51.

97. Rooney, *Interviews of Witnesses*, 19. Rooney, Schwerin, and Sullivan worked through the night of September 11 on Clinton's September 12 "Remarks on the Death of American Personnel in Benghazi, Libya." She and Schwerin started drafting the speech at Schwerin's apartment between 10 and 10:30 p.m., and Sullivan joined them after midnight. See Rooney, *Interviews of Witnesses*, 27–29, 36–37, 88; Dan Schwerin, *Interviews of Witnesses Before the Select Committee on the Events Surrounding the 2012 Terrorist Attack in Benghazi: House of Representatives* (114th Cong., 2d sess., Volume 7, 2016), 125, 133–34, 140.

98. Schwerin, *Interviews of Witnesses*, 145.

99. Huma Abedin, *Interviews of Witnesses Before the Select Committee on the Events Surrounding the 2012 Terrorist Attack in Benghazi: House of Representatives* (114th Cong., 2d sess., Volume 7, 2016), 293.

100. Bernadette Meehan, *Interviews of Witnesses Before the Select Committee on the Events Surrounding the 2012 Terrorist Attack in Benghazi: House of Representatives* (114th Cong., 2d sess., Volume 7, 2016), 916.

101. Rhodes, *Interviews of Witnesses*, 871.

102. Rhodes, *Interviews of Witnesses*, 887.

103. Rhodes, *Interviews of Witnesses*, 871, 873.

104. Victoria Nuland, *Interviews of Witnesses Before the Select Committee on the Events Surrounding the 2012 Terrorist Attack in Benghazi: House of Representatives* (114th Cong., 2d sess., Volume 2, 2016), 174.

105. Nuland, *Interviews of Witnesses*, 190. The Benghazi Committee did not interview Nuland. It used her transcript from her August 28, 2013, interview with the Oversight and Government Reform Committee.

106. Sullivan, *Interviews of Witnesses*, 672.

107. Sullivan, *Interviews of Witnesses*, 696.

108. Nuland, *Interviews of Witnesses*, 187.

109. Rhodes, *Interviews of Witnesses*, 871.

110. Sullivan, *Interviews of Witnesses*, 674. Rhodes went to considerable lengths to defend the statement in his testimony, while not taking credit for drafting it. See Rhodes, *Interviews of Witnesses*, 885–87, 913–16.

111. Sullivan, *Interviews of Witnesses*, 676.

112. Sullivan, *Interviews of Witnesses*, 678.

113. Sullivan, *Interviews of Witnesses*, 697.

114. Leon Panetta, *Interviews of Witnesses Before the Select Committee on the Events Surrounding the 2012 Terrorist Attack in Benghazi: House of Representatives* (114th Cong., 2d sess., Volume 8, 2016), 312.

115. Panetta, *Interviews of Witnesses*, 313, 316.

116. Select Committee, *Final Report*, 70–71.

117. Kurt Tidd, *Interviews of Witnesses Before the Select Committee on the Events Surrounding the 2012 Terrorist Attack in Benghazi: House of Representatives* (114th Cong., 2d sess., Volume 9, 2016), 1411.

118. Select Committee, *Final Report*, 60; Carter Ham, *Interviews of Witnesses Before the Select Committee on the Events Surrounding the 2012 Terrorist Attack in Benghazi: House of Representatives* (114th Cong., 2d sess., Volume 10, 2016), 1281; Charles Joseph Leidig, Jr., *Interviews of Witnesses Before the Select Committee on the Events Surrounding the 2012 Terrorist Attack in Benghazi: House of Representatives* (114th Cong., 2d sess., Volume 10, 2016), 609, 653; "Department of Defense's Response to the Attack on U.S. Facilities in Benghazi, Libya, and the Findings of its Internal Review following the Attack," Hearing before the Committee on Armed Services United States Senate, February 7, 2013, S. Hrg. 113–164, 29.

119. Leidig, *Interviews of Witnesses*, 631–32.

120. Select Committee, *Final Report*, 125; Select Committee, *Documents Provided*, 558.

121. Ham, *Interviews of Witnesses*, 1293, 1317, 1329.

122. Select Committee, *Final Report*, 100, 123, 574; Leidig, *Interviews of Witnesses*, 598–99.

123. Leidig, *Interviews of Witnesses*, 618, 623; Jeremy Bash, *Interviews of Witnesses Before the Select Committee on the Events Surrounding the 2012 Terrorist Attack in Benghazi: House of Representatives* (114th Cong., 2d sess., Volume 8, 2016), 653; "Department of Defense's Response," Hearing before the Committee on Armed Services, 91.

124. "Department of Defense's Response," Hearing before the Committee on Armed Services, 78, 95; Panetta, *Interviews of Witnesses*, 337, 403; Ham, *Interviews of Witnesses*, 1362–63; Richard Landolt, *Interviews of Witnesses Before the Select Committee on the Events Surrounding the 2012 Terrorist Attack in Benghazi: House of Representatives* (114th Cong., 2d sess., Volume 10, 2016), 941.

125. Michael Repass, *Interviews of Witnesses Before the Select Committee on the Events Surrounding the 2012 Terrorist Attack in Benghazi: House of Representatives* (114th Cong., 2d sess., Volume 10, 2016), 445; Select Committee, *Final Report*, 561.

126. Select Committee, *Final Report*, 561.

127. Select Committee, *Final Report*, 561.

128. "Review of the Benghazi Attacks and Unanswered Questions," Hearing before the Committee on Oversight and Government Reform House of Representatives, September 19, 2013, Serial No. 113–59, 21.

129. Stephanie McCrummen and Ann Scott Tyson, "Navy Kills 3 Pirates, Rescues Ship Captain off Somalia's Coast," *Washington Post*, April 13, 2009, https://www

.washingtonpost.com/wp-dyn/content/article/2009/04/12/AR2009041200467.html, accessed January 27, 2022; Abdi Sheikh, "U.S. Commandos Free Two Hostages in Daring Somalia Raid," *Reuters*, January 25, 2012, https://www.reuters.com/article/us-somalia-hostages-idUSTRE80O0I220120125, accessed January 27, 2022.

130. Landolt, *Interviews of Witnesses*, 926.

131. Joint Chiefs of Staff, *Doctrine for the Armed Forces of the United States* (JP 1), March 25, 2013, xxv. Officers, starting at the rank of major and as a condition of career progression, are required to become certified in the joint planning process as a part of Joint Professional Military Education (JPME). See Joint Chiefs of Staff, *Chairman of the Joint Chiefs of Staff Instruction: Officer Professional Military Education Policy (*CJCSI 1800.01F), May 15, 2020.

132. In September 2012, the officials would have used Joint Chiefs of Staff, *Joint Operation Planning (JP 5-0)*, August 11, 2011. In 2012, the process was called "joint operation planning process." It is currently called "joint planning process." The latter term is used for simplicity. Crisis planning goes through the same planning process as campaign or contingency planning, but it is typically driven by external events and is time-constrained. See Joint Chiefs of Staff, *Joint Operation Planning* (JP 5-0), II-28-II-35, IV-4. For an analysis of the German operational approach to defeating Operation Overlord, see Bradley Podliska, Karin Hecox, and Oliver Sagun, "Behind Enemy Plans: A Processing Tracing Analysis of Germany's Operational Approach to a Western Invasion," *Joint Force Quarterly* 100 (1st Quarter, January 2021): 107–15.

133. Joint Chiefs of Staff, *JP 5-0*, I-5, IV-2, IV-48.

134. For step 1 planning initiation, see Joint Chiefs of Staff, *JP 5-0*, III-1, III-6, IV-1-IV-4. For step 2 mission analysis, Joint Chiefs of Staff, *JP 5-0*, IV-4-IV-16. For step 3 course of action development, see Joint Chiefs of Staff, *JP 5-0*, IV-17-IV-27. For step 4 course of action analysis and wargaming, see Joint Chiefs of Staff, *JP 5-0*, IV-27-IV-36. For step 5 course of action comparison, see Joint Chiefs of Staff, *JP 5-0*, IV-36-IV-40. For step 6 course of action approval, see Joint Chiefs of Staff, *JP 5-0*, IV-40-IV-44. For step 7 plan or order development, see Joint Chiefs of Staff, *JP 5-0*, IV-44-IV-57.

135. Leidig stated that U.S. Africa Command staff started crisis action planning, but Leidig stated that Ham communicated to him the results of Pentagon decisions, including decisions made at the 6 p.m. meeting. The staff devised a course of action that included CIF and FAST deployment, as well as evacuation with medevac at Benghazi and Tripoli airfields. Ham and Landolt confirmed U.S. Africa Command was not involved in the decisions, including deploying the CIF and FAST units or deciding on Sigonella as a staging base. See Leidig, *Interviews of Witnesses*, 593, 596, 604, 606–608, 627, 650, 660; Ham, *Interviews of Witnesses*, 1284–86; Landolt, *Interviews of Witnesses*, 926, 930.

136. Ham testified that Panetta initially issued verbal orders. See Ham, *Interviews of Witnesses*, 1338. Losey stated that "0300 was implemented" with regard to the CIF supporting a redacted unit (likely the United States-based SOF) deploying to the intermediate staging base. Brigadier General Patrick Mordente, U.S. Transportation Command Deputy Director of Operations and Plans, also confirmed "0300" was initiated. They were referring to a contingency plan, JCS CONPLAN 0300, which is a

plan for special operation forces conducting a counterterrorism mission. Brian Losey, *Interviews of Witnesses Before the Select Committee on the Events Surrounding the 2012 Terrorist Attack in Benghazi: House of Representatives* (114th Cong., 2d sess., Volume 11, 2016), 214; Patrick Mordente, *Interviews of Witnesses Before the Select Committee on the Events Surrounding the 2012 Terrorist Attack in Benghazi: House of Representatives* (114th Cong., 2d sess., Volume 10, 2016), 830. However, the joint planning process would still apply. For another reference to JCS CONPLAN 0300, see Eric Schmitt, "Commandos See Duty on U.S. Soil In Role Redefined by Terror Fight," *New York Times*, January 23, 2005, https://www.nytimes.com/2005/01/23/washington/us/commandos-see-duty-on-us-soil-in-role-redefined-by-terror.html, accessed February 10, 2022. Orders for Operation Jukebox Lotus were issued, but Ham, in his testimony, was not familiar with the orders, much less the details of the orders. Ham, *Interviews of Witnesses*, 1355–61.

137. Bash, *Interviews of Witnesses*, 660.

138. Jeffrey M. Reilly, *Operational Design: Distilling Clarity from Complexity for Decisive Action* (Maxwell Air Force Base, AL: Air University Press, 2012), 1.

139. Ryan White, email message to the author, February 10, 2022.

140. Reilly, *Operational Design*, 1.

141. Joint Chiefs of Staff, *JP 5-0*, III-18-III-37. There are 13 elements of operational design, but not all 13 elements need to be used. See Joint Chiefs of Staff, *JP 5-0*, III-18.

142. Nick Turse and Sean D. Naylor, "Revealed: The U.S. Military's 36 Code-Named Operations in Africa," *Yahoo News*, April 17, 2019, https://www.yahoo.com/now/revealed-the-us-militarys-36-codenamed-operations-in-africa-090000841.html, accessed February 12, 2022.

143. Per questions posed to Ham, U.S. Africa Command Director of Operations Landolt issued orders for Operation Jukebox Lotus, but the orders were not released by the Benghazi Committee. The end state is taken from Ham's testimony. Ham, *Interviews of Witnesses*, 1355–61.

144. Bash, *Interviews of Witnesses*, 689.

145. Irving L. Janis, *Groupthink: Psychological Studies of Policy Decisions and Fiascoes*, second edition (Boston: Houghton Mifflin, 1983), 9.

146. Janis, *Groupthink*, 10–13, 37.

147. Bash, *Interviews of Witnesses*, 648–49.

148. Bash, *Interviews of Witnesses*, 649.

149. Fishman, *Interviews of Witnesses*, 622, 626; Bash, *Interviews of Witnesses*, 682–84; John Kelly, *Interviews of Witnesses Before the Select Committee on the Events Surrounding the 2012 Terrorist Attack in Benghazi: House of Representatives* (114th Cong., 2d sess., Volume 9, 2016), 1338; Cheryl Mills, *Interviews of Witnesses Before the Select Committee on the Events Surrounding the 2012 Terrorist Attack in Benghazi: House of Representatives* (114th Cong., 2d sess., Volume 6, 2016), 196; Matt Olsen, *Interviews of Witnesses Before the Select Committee on the Events Surrounding the 2012 Terrorist Attack in Benghazi: House of Representatives* (114th Cong., 2d sess., Volume 9, 2016), 187–88. Rhodes, Mills, Sullivan, and Fishman did not recall any specific details. See Rhodes, *Interviews of Witnesses*, 870; Mills,

Interviews of Witnesses, 154–55, 167–68, 196, 212, 213, 220–22, 224; Sullivan, *Interviews of Witnesses*, 665–71; Fishman, *Interviews of Witnesses*, 623–24.

150. Select Committee, *Documents Provided*, 513.

151. Mills, *Interviews of Witnesses*, 152, 204; Sullivan, *Interviews of Witnesses*, 530.

152. Patrick Kennedy, *Interviews of Witnesses Before the Select Committee on the Events Surrounding the 2012 Terrorist Attack in Benghazi: House of Representatives* (114th Cong., 2d sess., Volume 11, 2016), 1187.

153. Mills, *Interviews of Witnesses*, 200.

154. Bash, *Interviews of Witnesses*, 692.

155. Christopher P. Neck and Gregory Moorhead, "Groupthink Remodeled: The Importance of Leadership, Time Pressure, and Methodical Decision-Making Procedures," *Human Relations* 48, no. 5 (1995): 550–52; Janis, *Groupthink*, 262–63.

156. Leidig, *Interviews of Witnesses*, 590.

157. Select Committee, *Final Report*, 153–54. Participants even centered the blame on "Pastor Jones," an eccentric pastor in Florida that had no connection to the anti-Islamic video, "Innocence of Muslims." Panetta or Dempsey were listed as being responsible for calling him. See Select Committee, *Final Report*, 154.

158. Select Committee, *Final Report*, 153.

159. Kirkpatrick, "Deadly Mix in Benghazi."

160. Select Committee, *Final Report*, 154; Select Committee, *Documents Provided*, 558–59.

161. Select Committee, *Final Report*, 125, 154; Ham, *Interviews of Witnesses*, 1309–10.

162. Select Committee, *Documents Provided*, 620.

163. Landolt, *Interviews of Witnesses*, 941–42, 979.

164. Kelly, *Interviews of Witnesses*, 1391.

165. Kelly, *Interviews of Witnesses*, 1392.

166. Kelly, *Interviews of Witnesses*, 1276, 1279, 1339.

Conclusion

INTRODUCTION

This book began with political rivals Hillary Clinton and Donald Trump sharing similar views in October 2015 on the partisan nature of the Benghazi congressional investigation. Reflecting on this rare agreement among candidates and a large portion of the American public prompted me to investigate a central puzzle: *How did a terrorist attack become so partisan?* The explanation presented in preceding chapters does not inspire confidence, as elected members of Congress viewed a deadly terrorist attack that claimed the lives of four Americans through a lens of advancing party strategy. While disconcerting, such partisan motivations surrounding the Benghazi Committee are an extension of previous congressional actions. Following the Watergate scandal, 1975 reforms were a critical antecedent to the critical juncture of 1995 congressional reforms that consolidated party control over committee investigations. As such, any tragedy or mistake occurring at a time of divided legislative and executive control presents an occasion to mount political attacks on the opposition party to improve electoral prospects.

By examining the Benghazi Committee proceedings through the partisan model of congressional oversight, readers can better understand the motivations and short- and long-term consequences of such investigations. This chapter recounts the results from chapter 3 of applying this model and the secondary effects detailed in chapter 4. These findings present opportunities for future research in comparing Democratic partisan behavior, analyzing the role of public pressure, and examining partisanship as a legitimate form of oversight. This book concludes with reasons for optimism and recommendations to avoid partisanship, increase accountability of congressional members and staff, and implementation of executive-legislative tandem investigations.

FINDINGS

Fire Alarm illustrates that Congress, rather than responding to fire alarm crises and putting out the fire of disaster, can throw gasoline on it and further divide the American people. Representative Adam Schiff (D-CA) predicted the escalating partisan conflict, saying in the October 2015 Clinton hearing:

> I don't want four years from now or eight years from now or 12 years from now, another presidential election, for us to be in here, or for one side or the other, I don't want the Republicans to say, "Let's do Benghazi again, that really worked," or the Democrats to say, "They did it to us, let's do it to them."[1]

The House Select Committee to Investigate the January 6th Attack on the U.S. Capitol ("January 6th Committee") signifies a continuation of partisanship within the United States. In June 2021, 62 percent of Republicans called the January 6, 2021, incident a "riot" and 33 percent of Republicans called it an "insurrection." By the end of the June and July 2022, January 6th Committee hearings, only 45 percent of Republicans called it a "riot" and only 13 percent called it an "insurrection." Similarly, the percentage of Republicans that believed the January 6 incident was a "legitimate protest" rose from 47 percent in June 2021 to 61 percent in July 2022, as opposed to the Democrat percentage, which held steady at 14 percent viewing it as "legitimate protest."[2] The result is that Americans from across the political spectrum are losing faith in their system of government. In 2022, 36 percent of Americans responded that the system is sound, compared to 62 percent in 1980.[3]

The declining confidence can be understood to be a result of several partisan factors, including the House Speaker's selection of committee members based on loyalty, narratives surrounding tragedies adopting a partisan tone due to real or perceived electoral benefits, and the priming of congressional staff to ensure investigation findings support the party's narrative.

During the Benghazi investigations, Republicans focused on Clinton, prioritized high-profile investigation events, and ensured tight control of the investigation through vetted staff members. Republican members and staff not only conducted more interviews of State Department officials but were more likely to attend interviews of high-profile officials or those in leadership in greater numbers. Gowdy, Jordan, and Pompeo, based on the statistical analysis, were focused on Clinton and her inner circle. Brooks, Jordan, Pompeo, Roby, and Westmoreland focused on high-profile individuals, including those from the other agencies. More than 60 percent of the committee's press releases focused on Clinton, prior to her hearing, and more than 97 percent of its document pages were from the State Department. Capitol Hill veteran staff attended more than half of leadership or high-profile interviews, while non-Capitol Hill veterans attended less than a third of those interviews. At least one of the top two staff leaders, Kiko and Donesa, attended every leadership or high-profile interview. Veteran staff were most attuned to Clinton and her inner circle, comprising the majority of staff, in attendance for interviews.

The work of the Benghazi Committee is best understood in three phases: neutral, Clinton hyper-focus, and other agency phases. During the neutral and Clinton hyper-focus phases, more than 70 percent of the interviews were with State Department officials. During the other agency phase, nearly 70 percent of the interviews were with White House, Intelligence Community (IC), or Defense officials.

Similarly, the committee's work concerning witness interviews can be categorized into six topics. The committee focused on the topic of "Benghazi security environment," an issue applicable to Clinton, prior to her hearing. Also, more than half of the members and staff attended interviews, when the topic was "Clinton." However, when the investigation shifted to the other agency phase, less than one-third of members and one-third of staff attended interviews, when the topics were "talking points" or "military response." Member and staff interest dropped dramatically in the final three months as staff attendance decreased to approximately 20 percent, while three members did not attend a single interview.

The costs to Clinton were consistent with other accounts in that her voters dropped by 5 percent and her favorability decreased to 37 percent, while Trump was rated higher in terms of honesty and trustworthiness. The costs to the Republicans in terms of the investigation also became apparent, as a result of its hyper-focus on Clinton at the expense of effort in investigating the White House, Defense Department, and IC.

In particular, the strategic goals of the United States and who was responsible for setting and carrying out those goals was not identified. The evidence suggests an Obama-Clinton dynamic fraught with disconnect and conflict. Based on Clinton's urging, Obama intervened in Libya, turned the nation-building back to Clinton, and then directed U.S. policy after the Benghazi attack, removing Clinton from decision-making. Also, the impetus for the creation of the committee, to identify the author of the "blame the violence on a video" narrative, was never fully identified. The analysis demonstrates that Sullivan with Nuland's assistance authored a statement at 10:08 p.m. on the night of the attack, and this statement made its way into Rice's Sunday talk show talking points. Pentagon accountability was also not addressed. Pentagon officials did not use a doctrinally driven process, and, as a result, they misinterpreted Obama's orders to "do whatever you need to do to be able to protect our people there."[4] In short, they failed to understand how their actions and orders never had a chance to succeed. The genesis of this failure was groupthink occurring at the critical interagency meeting at 7:30 p.m. on the night of the attack.

The disconnect between what was being discussed in that meeting and what was occurring in Libya is dramatic. Gregory Hicks, in Libya, testified, "There was never a point that anyone [in Washington asked] me, 'Greg, is it over? Is everyone safe?'"[5] Carter Ham, in Washington, spoke of the groupthink mindset: "[The situation in Benghazi] was no longer immediate response to an ongoing attack; it was—it had shifted, in my mind, to potentially a hostage rescue situation."[6] He added further, "So, in my mind, the mission has shifted from response—Americans all now safe, minus one dead, one missing—shifting to a much more deliberate, intelligence-driven hostage rescue."[7]

The costs to the Republicans also became apparent through fractures between the Boehner and Jordan wings of the party. Jordan's attendance at witness interviews and his separate "Additional Views" section of the Benghazi *Final Report* indicates his intent to expand the investigation beyond Clinton and the State Department to Obama and the White House. Jordan's high-profile activity with the Benghazi Committee is consistent with the literature findings. Individual committee members can use investigations to enhance their own reputations.[8] Jordan became arguably Trump's most reliable ally in Congress.[9] Another Trump ally, Pompeo, went on to high-profile administration positions, including serving as Secretary of State.[10] Trump nominated Westmoreland for the Amtrak Board of Directors in 2017.[11]

Paul Ryan, understanding the new direction of the Republican Party, accepted the Speakership, only after winning House Freedom Caucus supermajority support.[12] He then "forged a relationship that was friendly" with Trump, before announcing his retirement in 2018.[13] Gowdy also developed a relationship with Trump, and in 2019, Trump attempted to hire Gowdy for his impeachment defense team.[14] Gowdy retired from Congress in 2019 and was hired in 2021 to host a *Fox News* show.[15] Brooks, Roby, and Roskam—all members that did not firmly align with the populism of Trump and the Republican Party—left Congress by 2021.[16]

DIRECTIONS FOR FUTURE RESEARCH

While this research contributes to understanding partisanship in congressional oversight, it also highlights areas for future research. The critical juncture identified in this study is relevant for the study of impeachment proceedings, as the frequency of introducing articles of impeachment against sitting presidents increased following the 1995 congressional reforms. Furthermore, a better understanding of how partisan investigations influence public opinion, and vice versa, as well as the benefits of such investigations for accountability and transparency will provide a more nuanced understanding of American politics.

Republicans in Congress introduced two impeachment resolutions against President Bill Clinton.[17] Democrats, in turn, introduced three impeachment resolutions against George W. Bush.[18] Following the Republican-led Benghazi investigation, Democrats took the opportunity to investigate, impeach, and attempt to remove Donald Trump from office. While the circumstances that prompted each of these proceedings vary, the frequency and partisan nature may presage a future of continuous interbranch strife.[19]

The number of congressional proceedings, ongoing as of 2022, surrounding the Trump presidency underscores the highly partisan nature of American politics. In July 2017, months after assuming office, two representatives from the Democratic minority filed articles of impeachment for obstruction of justice against President Trump, but minority party leadership did not support the articles.[20] On December 6, 2017, an impeachment resolution failed by a vote of 364-58.[21] In March 2019, as the majority party, Speaker Nancy Pelosi (D-CA) and Representative Jerrold Nadler (D-NY), chair of the House Judiciary Committee, announced an all-encompassing investigation of Trump's businesses and possible connections to Russia. Nadler stated that the investigation would be independent of Special Counsel Robert Mueller III's Russia investigation, and he implied impeachment would result.[22] Mueller released his investigative report in April 2019 and testified before the House Judiciary and Intelligence Committees in July 2019.[23] His report found no evidence of collusion between the Trump campaign and Russia, but it did not exonerate Trump from allegations of obstruction.[24]

In a phone call on July 25, 2019, with Ukrainian president Volodymyr Zelensky, Trump asked Zelensky to "look into" the activities of Democratic presidential candidate Joe Biden and his son, Hunter Biden. A whistleblower complaint filed in August 2019 alleged Trump of "using the power of his office to solicit interference from a foreign country in the 2020 election."[25] Following a leak of the complaint, Pelosi launched an impeachment inquiry on September 24, 2019, led by the HPSCI, OGR, and Foreign Affairs Committees. The Judiciary Committee passed articles of impeachment on a party-line vote, 23-17, accusing Trump of abusing the power of the office and of obstruction of Congress.[26] On December 16, the House approved the abuse of power article by a vote of 230-197 and the article for obstruction of Congress by a vote of 229-198. All Republicans voted against both articles.[27] The Republican Senate majority first voted against allowing subpoenas, and then voted to acquit Trump on February 5, 2020, as it did not reach the two-thirds threshold. All 53 Republican senators voted "not guilty" on the obstruction charge, while 52 Republicans voted "not guilty" on abuse of power, with only Senator Mitt Romney (R-UT) voting with Senate Democrats.[28]

Following January 6, 2021, attack on the Capitol, the House voted 232-197 to impeach Trump a second time on an article for "incitement of insurrection," with ten Republicans voting in favor. The Senate acquitted the former president 57-43, with seven Republicans voting "guilty."[29] The House subsequently voted to form the January 6th Committee on June 30, 2021, and the next day, Pelosi nominated seven Democrats and one Republican, Representative Liz Cheney (R-WY), to serve.[30] Minority Leader Kevin McCarthy then appointed five Republicans including Jordan and Representative Jim Banks (R-IN).[31] Pelosi, acknowledging her unprecedented action, removed Jordan and Banks. McCarthy later withdrew his five Republican appointments, and Pelosi responded by adding Representative Adam Kinzinger (R-IL) to the investigative committee.[32]

The Democrats, consistent with the literature described in the "Partisan Brand: Leadership and Focus of Investigation" subsection of chapter 2, ensured high-publicity news coverage for the January 6th investigation. The committee took the unusual step of hiring James Goldston, the former president of *ABC News*, to produce coverage for distribution across major networks as prime-time "thematic episodes" and a "must-watch mini-series."[33] Committee members read from a script, and Committee Chair Representative Bennie Thompson (D-MS) acknowledged making difficult choices about what testimony to leave "on the cutting room floor."[34] In turn, Republicans vowed to investigate the January 6th Committee, if they become the House majority party in 2023.[35]

As evident in Table 5.1, Trump's approval rating fell from 36 percent at his inauguration to 34 percent upon leaving office, but future studies may better determine what factors can be attributed to the congressional investigations.[36]

Table 5.1 Congressional Investigation Timeline-Trump Poll Comparison

	Trump Job Approval Rating
Impeachment Resolution Vote (December 6, 2017)	37% (December 12, 2017)
Trump Business and Russia Investigation Announced (March 4, 2019)	38% (March 5, 2019)
Mueller Hearings (July 24, 2019)	40% (July 29, 2019)
Ukrainian Impeachment Inquiry Commenced (September 24, 2019)	41% (September 30, 2019)
Trump Impeached (December 18, 2019)	43% (January 28, 2020)
Impeachment Articles Introduced (January 7, 2021)	33% (January 11, 2021)
Trump Impeached for Second Time (January 13, 2021)	34% (January 18, 2021)

Source: Trump approval rating numbers from Quinnipiac University Poll, https://poll.qu.edu.

Table 5.2 January 6th Committee Democratic Member Party Loyalty Scores

Majority Party Leadership and Committee Members	*Party Loyalty Score*
Speaker Nancy Pelosi (D-CA)	100%
Committee Chair Bennie Thompson (D-MS)	99%
Member Pete Aguilar (D-CA)	99%
Member Zoe Lofgren (D-CA)	99%
Member Elaine Luria (D-VA)	97%
Member Stephanie Murphy (D-FL)	97%
Member Jamie Raskin (D-MD)	99%
Member Adam Schiff (D-CA)	99%

Applying the Partisan Model

The partisan model, in its simple form, means selecting members and staff based on party loyalty to focus on damaging the opposing party's presidential candidate. The Benghazi Committee is one case study, but additional case studies can verify the veracity of the model. A cursory application of the model indicates that the form and function of the January 6th Committee are consistent with partisanship. Table 5.2 shows the party loyalty scores of Committee Democrats, all of whom voted with their party at least 97 percent of the time.[37] The January 6th Committee employed approximately 43 staff members, 26 of whom with prior Capitol Hill experience.[38] Future research, based on January 6th Committee proceeding reports and firsthand accounts, may reveal insights into the selection of specific Democratic members, selection of staff, and the role of the two Republican members on its committee

The divisive political environment in the United States also indicates a need to examine the causal mechanisms of public pressure on the legislative branch to investigate allegations of executive branch abuses. Public pressure on House Speaker Boehner prompted the 10th congressional investigation that may imply a causal loop: a congressional investigation, even a partisan one, exposes abuses, and the public forces the executive and legislative branches to make reforms.

Moreover, further studies may determine whether partisanship is an effective method of oversight. While the Republican investigation of the Benghazi attack reveals several mistakes, the committee was successful in revealing a political motive for the Obama administration's changing narrative on the night of the attack. At 6:09 p.m., the administration officials alleged no connection to the Cairo protest over an anti-Islamic video and the Benghazi attack, but in its 10:08 p.m. statement, officials conflated the Benghazi attack with the anti-Islamic video. Ben Rhodes, under oath, revealed the reasoning, "What we learned is that we had a fatality in Benghazi."[39] The investigation also exposed Clinton's exclusive use of private email. In revealing these findings to the American people, Republicans presented evidence for voters to consider in the upcoming election. While causing political problems for President Obama and Hillary Clinton, such investigations do support accountability and transparency that are fundamental to democracy.

SOLVING THE PUZZLE

Partisan investigations are not ideal for accountability and effective oversight can be accomplished in several ways. First, to avoid a continuation of the partisan turmoil following the reforms related to Watergate and enacted by the 104th Congress, the public must demand bipartisanship. Without bipartisanship, investigations lack legitimacy and are better understood as taxpayer-funded political attacks. The Senate may serve as a first test case. While the minority in the House may be sidelined with arbitrary rules, Senate minority committee members have more rights to demand bipartisan cooperation.[40]

The restoration of accountability at the individual member and staff level can reduce partisanship. An investigation requires an expert staff that can conduct research, collect evidence through hearings, document requests, question witnesses, and write a comprehensive, fact-based report.[41] As such, committee staff members should be vetted to ensure they are nonpartisan.[42] Voters must disincentivize the use of high-publicity investigations to bring down political opponents and demand legislation focusing on bureaucratic repair.[43]

Finally, congressional investigations should be launched in tandem with presidential commissions.[44] Blue-Ribbon Commissions such as the Roberts Commission investigation of the Pearl Harbor attack, the Warren Commission investigation of the assassination of President Kennedy, and the 9/11 Commission investigation of September 11, 2001, terrorist attacks are examples of successful nonpartisan inquires that produce actionable recommendations. Separate congressional investigations supplemented the work of the Roberts and Warren Commissions.[45]

CONCLUSION

Previous foreign policy disasters required the assurances of accountability. After a United States-backed invasion force was defeated in 2 days with more than 100 killed and nearly 1,100 taken prisoner out of a 1,400-man force, a reporter asked President Kennedy to tell the "real facts" behind the Bay of Pigs invasion.[46] He responded, "There's an old saying that victory has a hundred fathers and defeat is an orphan . . . Further statements, detailed discussions, are not to conceal responsibility because I am the responsible officer of the government."[47] The following week, Kennedy's approval rating was 83 percent and his approval rating for the invasion was 61 percent.[48]

The nation united after Kennedy's remarks, but the Benghazi tragedy has no such closure. It continues to divide the country, and the investigations only served to widen the American ideological divide. *Congressional investigations are little more than taxpayer-funded political attacks with minimal regard for finding the truth.* The Benghazi Committee serves as a reminder that Speakers are inclined to select party loyalists for an investigatory committee assignment, will target a rival political candidate seeking national office, and will ensure a loyal staff carries out the party strategy.

Upon entering the Benghazi compound, the terrorists triggered a fire alarm that went unanswered. In response to this unanswered fire alarm, the congressional "fire alarm" investigation failed to provide a full accounting of events that could inform comprehensive recommendations to address security shortfalls. Glen Doherty, Sean Smith, Christopher Stevens, Tyrone Woods, their families, and the American people deserve better.

NOTES

1. "Hearing 4," Hearing before the Select Committee on the Events Surrounding the 2012 Terrorist Attack in Benghazi House of Representatives, October 22, 2015, 374-75.

2. Monmouth University Polling Institute, July 7, 2022, https://www.monmouth.edu/polling-institute/reports/monmouthpoll_us_070722/, accessed July 17, 2022.

3. Monmouth University Polling Institute, July 7, 2022.

4. Department of Defense's Response to the Attack on U.S. Facilities in Benghazi, Libya, and the Findings of its Internal Review following the Attack," Hearing before the Committee on Armed Services United States Senate, February 7, 2013, S. Hrg. 113–164, 39.

5. Gregory Nathan Hicks, *Interviews of Witnesses Before the Select Committee on the Events Surrounding the 2012 Terrorist Attack in Benghazi: House of Representatives* (114th Cong., 2d sess., Volume 10, 2016), 261.

6. Carter Ham, *Interviews of Witnesses Before the Select Committee on the Events Surrounding the 2012 Terrorist Attack in Benghazi: House of Representatives* (114th Cong., 2d sess., Volume 10, 2016), 1294.

7. Ham, *Interviews of Witnesses*, 1317.

8. David C. W. Parker and Matthew Dull, "Divided We Quarrel: The Politics of Congressional Investigations, 1947–2004," *Legislative Studies Quarterly* 34, no. 3 (2009): 325; David C. W. Parker and Matthew Dull, "Rooting Out Waste, Fraud, and Abuse: The Politics of House Committee Investigations, 1947 to 2004," *Political Research Quarterly* 66, no. 3 (2013): 633.

9. Kyle Cheney, "Trump's GOP 'Warriors' Lead Charge Against Mueller," *Politico*, May 7, 2018, https://www.politico.com/story/2018/05/07/trump-mueller-republican-warriors-congress-571562, accessed July 5, 2022.

10. Gardiner Harris and Thomas Kaplan, "Senate Confirms C.I.A. Chief Mike Pompeo to Be Secretary of State," *New York Times*, April 26, 2018, https://www.nytimes.com/2018/04/26/us/politics/mike-pompeo-secretary-of-state.html, accessed July 5, 2022.

11. Tamar Hallerman, "Ex-Ga. Rep. Endures Nearly Two-Year Wait for Senate Confirmation," *Atlanta Journal-Constitution*, July, 31, 2019, https://www.ajc.com/news/state--regional-govt--politics/rep-endures-nearly-two-year-wait-for-senate-confirmation/TiU8RR7oKA0IcpairhSOSJ/, accessed July 5, 2022.

12. Mike DeBonis and Robert Costa, "'Supermajority' of House Freedom Caucus to back Paul Ryan's Speaker Bid," *Washington Post*, October 21, 2015, https://www.washingtonpost.com/politics/supermajority-of-house-freedom-caucus-to-back-paul-ryans-speaker-bid/2015/10/21/d7411964-781e-11e5-a958-d889faf561dc_story.html, accessed July 5, 2022.

13. Erica Werner, "Fiscal Hawk Ryan Leaves Behind Growing Deficits and a Changed GOP," *Washington Post*, April 11, 2018, https://www.washingtonpost.com/powerpost/fiscal-hawk-ryan-leaves-behind-growing-deficits-and-a-changed-gop/2018/04/11/827b68d4-3d93-11e8-a7d1-e4efec6389f0_story.html, accessed July 5, 2022.

14. Maggie Haberman and Annie Karni, "Inside Trump's Botched Attempt to Hire Trey Gowdy," *New York Times*, October 13, 2019, https://www.nytimes.com/2019/10/13/us/politics/trey-gowdy-trump-impeachment.html, accessed July 5, 2022.

15. Gabe Cavallaro, "Former U.S. Rep. Trey Gowdy to Host New Fox News Primetime Show Week of Feb. 1," *Greenville News*, January 29, 2021, https://www.greenvilleonline.com/story/news/politics/2021/01/29/trey-gowdy-host-fox-news-primetime-show-week-feb-1/4312289001/, accessed July 5, 2022.

16. Simone Pathé, "Susan Brooks Won't Seek a Fifth Term, Opening up Targeted Indiana Seat," *Roll Call*, June 14, 2019, https://rollcall.com/2019/06/14/susan-brooks-wont-seek-a-fifth-term-opening-up-targeted-indiana-seat/, accessed July 5, 2022; Juliegrace Brufke, "GOP Rep. Martha Roby to retire," *The Hill*, July 26, 2019, https://thehill.com/homenews/house/454934-gop-rep-martha-roby-to-retire/, accessed July 5, 2022; Rick Pearson, "Former U.S. Rep. Peter Roskam Joins Sidley Law Firm to Lobby, Consult," *Chicago Tribune*, July 16, 2019, https://www.chicagotribune.com/politics/ct-former-congressman-peter-roskam-joins-sidley-20190716-borrf6lkmfbjndwu6xoahkmqdi-story.html, accessed July 5, 2022.

17. Stephen W. Stathis and David C. Huckabee, "Congressional Resolutions on Presidential Impeachment: A Historical Overview," *CRS Report*, September 16, 1998, https://digital.library.unt.edu/ark:/67531/metadc819397/, accessed July 7, 2022.

18. Associated Press, "McKinney Introduces Bill to Impeach Bush," *NBC News*, December 8, 2006, https://www.nbcnews.com/id/wbna16116357, accessed July 7, 2022; Fox News, "Kucinich Brings Bush Impeachment Resolution to House Floor

Again," *Fox News*, January 13, 2015, https://www.foxnews.com/story/kucinich-brings-bush-impeachment-resolution-to-house-floor-again, accessed July 7, 2022.

19. House Republicans have stated they plan to impeach President Biden. See Mike Lillis, "House Conservatives Prep Plans to Impeach Biden," *The Hill*, August 30, 2022, https://thehill.com/homenews/house/3620081-house-conservatives-prep-plans-to-impeach-biden/, accessed September 2, 2022.

20. Brian Naylor, "Impeachment Timeline: From Early Calls to a Full House Vote," *NPR*, December 17, 2019, https://www.npr.org/2019/12/17/788397365/impeachment-timeline-from-early-calls-to-a-full-house-vote, accessed July 6, 2022.

21. Mike DeBonis, "House Votes to Kill Texas Lawmaker's Trump Impeachment Effort," *Washington Post*, December 6, 2017, https://www.washingtonpost.com/news/powerpost/wp/2017/12/06/house-democratic-leaders-oppose-texas-lawmakers-trump-impeachment-effort/, accessed July 8, 2022.

22. Nicholas Fandos, "With Sweeping Document Request, Democrats Launch Broad Trump Corruption Inquiry," *New York Times*, March 4, 2019, https://www.nytimes.com/2019/03/04/us/politics/trump-obstruction.html, accessed July 6, 2022.

23. Julie Hirschfeld Davis and Mark Mazzetti, "Highlights of Robert Mueller's Testimony to Congress," *New York Times*, July 24, 2019, https://www.nytimes.com/2019/07/24/us/politics/mueller-testimony.html, accessed July 8, 2022.

24. Naylor, "Impeachment Timeline."

25. Naylor, "Impeachment Timeline."

26. Naylor, "Impeachment Timeline."

27. Kathryn Watson, "How Members of Congress Voted on the Impeachment of President Trump," *CBS News*, December 19, 2019, https://www.cbsnews.com/news/impeachment-roll-call-vote-how-members-of-congress-voted-on-impeachment-of-president-trump-who-voted-for-against/, accessed July 6, 2022.

28. Philip Ewing, "'Not Guilty': Trump Acquitted On 2 Articles Of Impeachment As Historic Trial Closes," *NPR*, February 5, 2020, https://www.npr.org/2020/02/05/801429948/not-guilty-trump-acquitted-on-2-articles-of-impeachment-as-historic-trial-closes, accessed July 6, 2022.

29. Nicholas Fandos, "Trump Acquitted of Inciting Insurrection, Even as Bipartisan Majority Votes 'Guilty,'" *New York Times*, February 13, 2021, https://www.nytimes.com/2021/02/13/us/politics/trump-impeachment.html, accessed July 6, 2022.

30. Grace Segers, "House Votes to Create Select Committee to Investigate January 6 Attack," *CBS News*, June 30, 2021, https://www.cbsnews.com/news/january-6-select-committee-house-vote/, accessed February 24, 2022; Grace Segers, "Pelosi Names Members of January 6 Select Committee, Including Liz Cheney," *CBS News*, July 1, 2021, https://www.cbsnews.com/news/january-6-committee-liz-cheney-pelosi-members/, accessed February 24, 2022.

31. Annie Grayer and Melanie Zanona, "Jim Jordan Among 5 House Republicans Selected by McCarthy for January 6 Select Committee," *CNN*, July 20, 2021, https://www.cnn.com/2021/07/19/politics/house-republicans-chosen-for-january-6-committee/index.html, accessed February 24, 2022.

32. Hugo Lowell, "McCarthy Pulls Five Republicans from Capitol Attack Panel After Pelosi Rejects Two," *Guardian*, July 21, 2021, https://www.theguardian.com/us-news/2021/jul/21/nancy-pelosi-capitol-attack-committee-republicans, accessed February 24, 2022. The Republican National Committee censured Cheney and Kinzinger for their decision to join the January 6th Committee. See Gabby Orr, "In Censure of Cheney and Kinzinger, RNC Calls Events of January 6 'Legitimate Political Discourse,'" *CNN*, February 4, 2022, https://www.cnn.com/2022/02/04/politics/liz-cheney-adam-kinzinger-censure-rnc/index.html, accessed February 24, 2022.

33. Annie Karni, "The Committee Hired a TV Executive to Produce the Hearings for Maximum Impact," *New York Times*, June 9, 2022, https://www.nytimes.com/2022/06/09/us/the-committee-hired-a-tv-executive-to-produce-the-hearings-for-maximum-impact.html, accessed July 6, 2022.

34. Rebecca Beitsch and Mike Lillis, "Jan. 6 Panel Changed Script for Star Witness—at a Steep Cost," *The Hill*, July 14, 2022, https://thehill.com/homenews/house/3558249-jan-6-panel-changed-script-for-star-witness-at-a-steep-cost/, accessed July 14, 2022.

35. Alayna Treene and Jonathan Swan, "Republicans Plot Vengeance on Jan. 6 Committee," *Axios*, July 6, 2022, https://www.axios.com/2022/07/06/republicans-plot-vengeance-jan-6-committee, accessed July 6, 2022.

36. Quinnipiac Poll, January 26, 2017, https://poll.qu.edu/Poll-Release-Legacy?releaseid=2420, accessed July 11, 2022; Quinnipiac Poll, January 18, 2021, https://poll.qu.edu/Poll-Release?releaseid=3732, accessed July 11, 2022.

37. The Loyalty Scores Are Taken from the 117th Congress. See Jeffrey B. Lewis, Keith Poole, Howard Rosenthal, Adam Boche, Aaron Rudkin, and Luke Sonnet, *Voteview: Congressional Roll-Call Votes Database*, 2022. https://voteview.com/, accessed April 16, 2022.

38. Forty-one of the January 6th Committee staff members can be found via a LegiStorm search at https://www.legistorm.com/office/House_Select_Committee_to_Investigate_the_January_6th_Attack_on_the_U_S_Capitol/8821.html, accessed May 25, 2022. Hope Goins and Joe Maher are not listed as January 6th Committee staff members in LegiStorm, but they are listed as employees in January 6th Committee press releases. Goins has prior Capitol Hill experience and Maher does not. See Select Committee to Investigate the January 6th Attack on the United States Capitol, "Thompson Announces Senior Staff for Select Committee to Investigate the January 6th Attack on the U.S. Capitol," July 22, 2021, https://january6th.house.gov/news/press-releases/thompson-announces-senior-staff-select-committee-investigate-january-6th-attack, accessed May 25, 2022; Select Committee to Investigate the January 6th Attack on the United States Capitol, "Thompson Announces Additional Select Committee Senior Staff Members," August 6, 2021, https://january6th.house.gov/news/press-releases/thompson-announces-additional-select-committee-senior-staff-members, accessed May 25, 2022.

39. Ben Rhodes, *Interviews of Witnesses Before the Select Committee on the Events Surrounding the 2012 Terrorist Attack in Benghazi: House of Representatives* (114th Cong., 2d sess., Volume 8, 2016), 879.

40. Barbara Sinclair, "Partisan Polarization, Individualism, and Lawmaking in the Senate," In *Party Wars: Polarization and the Politics of National Policy Making* (Norman: University of Oklahoma Press, 2006).

41. See Christopher J. Deering and Stephen S. Smith, *Committees in Congress.* 3rd ed. (Washington, DC: CQ Press, 1997), 162–63.

42. National Commission on Terrorist Attacks upon the United States, Thomas H. Kean, and Lee Hamilton, *The 9/11 Commission report: final report of the National Commission on Terrorist Attacks upon the United States* (Washington, DC: National Commission on Terrorist Attacks upon the United States, 2004), 421.

43. See Paul C. Light, *Government by Investigation: Congress, Presidents, and the Search for Answers 1945-2012* (Washington, DC: Brookings Institution Press, 2014), 183, 184, 187.

44. See Light, *Government by Investigation*, 185, 187–89.

45. Lance Cole and Stanley Brand, *Congressional Investigations and Oversight: Case Studies and Analysis* (Durham, NC: Carolina Academic Press, 2011), 456, 490.

46. John F. Kennedy Presidential Library and Museum, "Bay of Pigs: Lessons Learned," *JFK Library*, n.d., https://www.jfklibrary.org/learn/education/teachers/curricular-resources/high-school-curricular-resources/bay-of-pigs-lessons-learned, accessed February 26, 2022.

47. John F. Kennedy, "News Conference 10, April 21, 1961," *JFK Library*, April 21, 1961, https://www.jfklibrary.org/archives/other-resources/john-f-kennedy-press-conferences/news-conference-10, accessed February 26, 2022.

48. Kennedy Presidential Library and Museum, "Bay of Pigs."

Appendix

Benghazi Committee Witness Interviews by Phase

Witness	Agency	Leadership or High-Profile	Interview Date	Topic(s)	Interview Pages	Republican Members Present	Republican Staff Members Present
Neutral Phase, May 8, 2014, to March 1, 2015							
Diplomatic Security Agent #6	State	No	February 10, 2015	Benghazi Security Environment	140	Brooks, Westmoreland (2). Both asked questions.	Donesa, Chipman, Jackson (Lead), Barrineau, Davis, Clarke (6)
Diplomatic Security Agent #9	State	No	February 12, 2015	Benghazi Security Environment	112	Brooks, Westmoreland (2). Westmoreland asked questions.	Chipman, Jackson (Lead), Barrineau, Tolar, Davis (5)
Diplomatic Security Agent #27	State	No	February 19, 2015	Benghazi Security Environment	38	None.	Chipman, Jackson (Lead), Barrineau, Clarke (4)
Diplomatic Security Agent #28	State	No	February 24, 2015	Benghazi Security Environment	194	Brooks, Westmoreland (2). Both asked questions.	Chipman, Jackson (Lead), Barrineau (3)
Diplomatic Security Agent #7	State	No	February 26, 2015	Benghazi Security Environment	182	Gowdy, Roby, Westmoreland (3). Westmoreland asked questions.	Chipman, Jackson (Lead), Barrineau, Tolar, Davis, Clarke (6)
Clinton Hyper-Focus Phase, March 2 to October 22, 2015							
Principal Officer #1	State	No	March 3, 2015	Benghazi Security Environment	107	None	Jackson (Lead), Barrineau, Clarke (3)
Diplomatic Security Agent #1	State	No	March 6, 2015	Benghazi Security Environment, Attack	196	None	Chipman, Jackson (Lead), Barrineau, Davis, Clarke (5)

Diplomatic Security Agent #15	State	No	March 12, 2015	Benghazi Security Environment	118	None	Chipman, Jackson (Lead), Grider, Clarke, Betz (5)
Principal Officer #2	State	No	March 13, 2015	Benghazi Security Environment	232	None	Chipman, Jackson, Grider, Davis, Clarke (Lead), Betz (6)
Diplomatic Security Agent #4	State	No	March 16, 2015	Benghazi Security Environment, Attack	212	Brooks, Westmoreland (2). Westmoreland asked questions.	Chipman, Jackson (Lead), Barrineau, Davis, Beattie, Clarke, Betz (7)
Diplomatic Security Agent #2	State	No	March 19, 2015	Benghazi Security Environment, Attack	188	Gowdy, Brooks, Roby, Westmoreland (4). Roby, Westmoreland asked questions.	Chipman, Grider, Barrineau, Davis (Lead), Clarke, Betz (6)
Diplomatic Security Agent #22	State	No	March 24, 2015	Benghazi Security Environment	170	Westmoreland (1). Asked questions.	Chipman, Jackson, Grider (Lead), Barrineau (4)
Principal Officer #3	State	No	March 26, 2015	Benghazi Security Environment	244	Westmoreland (1). Asked questions.	Jackson, Barrineau, Davis, Clarke (Lead) (4)
Diplomatic Security Agent #5	State	No	April 1, 2015	Benghazi Security Environment, Attack	168	Westmoreland (1). Asked questions.	Kiko, Jackson (Lead), Barrineau, Beattie, Clarke (5)
Diplomatic Security Agent #10	State	No	April 2, 2015	Benghazi Security Environment	194	None	Chipman, Missakian, Barrineau, Beattie, Clarke (Lead), Betz (6)

(continued)

Witness	*Agency*	*Leadership or High-Profile*	*Interview Date*	*Topic(s)*	*Interview Pages*	*Republican Members Present*	*Republican Staff Members Present*
Diplomatic Security Agent #12	State	No	April 9, 2015	Benghazi Security Environment	118	None	Chipman, Jackson, Barrineau (Lead), Davis, Clarke, Betz (6)
Diplomatic Security Agent #16	State	No	April 13, 2015	Benghazi Security Environment	170	None	Jackson, Grider (Lead), Barrineau, Clarke (4)
Diplomatic Security Agent #8	State	No	April 15, 2015	Benghazi Security Environment	270	None	Jackson, Missakian, Barrineau, Davis, Clarke, Betz (Lead) (6)
Principal Officer #4	State	No	May 8, 2015	Benghazi Security Environment, Attack	194	None	Chipman, Jackson, Davis, Clarke (Lead), Betz (5)
Diplomatic Security Agent #21	State	No	May 19, 2015	Benghazi Security Environment, Attack	178	Westmoreland (1). Asked questions.	Jackson, Barrineau, Clarke, Betz (Lead) (4)
Diplomatic Security Agent #13	State	No	May 21, 2015	Benghazi Security Environment	80	None	Chipman, Jackson, Grider (Lead), Barrineau, Betz (5)
GRS Agent #1	IC	No	May 22, 2015	Details not released.	–	Details not released.	Details not released.
GRS Agent #2	IC	No	May 22, 2015	Details not released.	–	Details not released.	Details not released.
GRS Agent #3	IC	No	May 29, 2015	Details not released.	–	Details not released.	Details not released.
CIA Official	IC	No	June 2, 2015	Details not released.	–	Details not released.	Details not released.

Deputy Chief of Base	IC	No	June 4, 2015	Details not released.	–	Details not released.	Details not released.
Sidney Blumenthal	State[a]	Yes	June 16, 2015	Benghazi Security Environment, Clinton, Congressional Cooperation	294	Gowdy, Brooks, Jordan, Pompeo, Roby, Roskam, Westmoreland (7). Gowdy, Brooks, Pompeo, Roby, Roskam, Westmoreland asked questions.	Kiko, Donesa, Chipman, Jackson, Missakian, Tolar, Davis (Lead), Beattie (8)
Communications Officer	IC	No	June 19, 2015	Details not released.	–	Details not released.	Details not released.
GRS Tripoli	IC	No	June 23, 2015	Details not released.	–	Details not released.	Details not released.
Director, Information Resource Management, Executive Secretariat	State	No	June 30, 2015	Clinton, Congressional Cooperation	102	None	Chipman, Jackson (Lead), Davis, Clarke, Betz (5)
Chief Records Officer	State	No	June 30, 2015	Clinton, Congressiona Cooperation	74	None	Chipman, Jackson (Lead), Davis, Clarke, Betz (5)
Chief of Station	IC	No	July 16, 2015	Details not released.	–	Details not released.	Details not released.
NEA Post Management Officer for Libya	State	No	July 23, 2015	Benghazi Security Environment	262	Westmoreland (1).	Chipman, Jackson (Lead), Barrineau, Clarke, Betz (5)
Senior Advisor for Strategic Communications, Near Eastern Affairs Bureau	State	No	July 29, 2015	Talking Points	184	None	Chipman, Jackson, Missakian, Grider (Lead), Barrineau (5)

(continued)

Witness	Agency	Leadership or High-Profile	Interview Date	Topic(s)	Interview Pages	Republican Members Present	Republican Staff Members Present
Ambassador Gene Cretz	State	No	July 31, 2015	Benghazi Security Environment	172	None	Chipman, Jackson, Clarke (Lead) (3)
Rosemary DiCarlo	State	No	August 11, 2015	Benghazi Security Environment, Talking Points	154	None	Missakian, Clarke (Lead), Betz (3)
Joan Polaschik	State	No	August 12, 2015	Benghazi Security Environment	282	None	Jackson (Lead), Clarke, Betz (3)
Diplomatic Security Agent #30	State	No	August 19, 2015	Benghazi Security Environment, Attack	122	None	Chipman, Grider (Lead), Davis, Barrineau, Clarke (5)
Diplomatic Security Agent #17	State	No	August 21, 2015	Benghazi Security Environment	50	None	Grider, Davis, Barrineau (Lead), Clarke (4)
Rexon Ryu	State	No	August 25, 2015	Benghazi Security Environment, Talking Points	168	None	Missakian, Clarke (Lead) (2)
CIF Commander	Defense	No	August 26, 2015	Military Response	118	None	Chipman (Lead), Tolar (2)
Contracting Official	State	No	August 27, 2015	Benghazi Security Environment, Attack	145	None	Missakian, Grider (Lead), Barrineau (3)
FAST Commander	Defense	No	September 2, 2015	Military Response	106	None	Chipman, Tolar (Lead) (2)

Cheryl Mills	State	Yes	September 3, 2015	Benghazi Security Environment, Attack, Clinton, Congressional Cooperation, Military Response, Talking Points	348	Gowdy, Brooks, Jordan, Westmoreland (4). All asked questions.	Kiko, Donesa, Chipman, Jackson (Lead), Missakian, Tolar, Barrineau, Davis, Betz (9)
Jacob Sullivan	State	Yes	September 5, 2015	Benghazi Security Environment, Attack, Clinton, Congressional Cooperation, Military Response, Talking Points	334	Gowdy, Brooks, Jordan, Westmoreland (4). All asked questions.	Kiko, Donesa, Chipman, Jackson, Missakian (Lead), Grider, Tolar, Davis, Beattie, Betz (10)
Bryan Pagliano	State	Yes	September 10, 2015	Clinton, Congressional Cooperation	12	Gowdy, Brooks, Jordan, Pompeo, Roby, Westmoreland (6).[b]	Kiko, Donesa, Chipman, Jackson (Lead), Davis, Betz (6)
DOD Special Operator	Defense	No	September 22, 2015	Benghazi Security Environment, Attack, Military Response	106	None	Chipman (Lead), Tolar, Adams (3)
Michael Morell	IC	No	September 28, 2015	Benghazi Security Environment, Talking Points	298	Brooks (1). Asked questions.	Kiko, Donesa, Chipman, Tolar, Davis (Lead), Clarke, Adams (7)

(*continued*)

Witness	Agency	Leadership or High-Profile	Interview Date	Topic(s)	Interview Pages	Republican Members Present	Republican Staff Members Present
Michael Flynn	IC	Yes	September 29, 2015	Benghazi Security Environment, Military Response, Talking Points	170	Westmoreland (1). Asked questions.	Donesa, Chipman, Tolar (Lead), Adams (4)
Spokesperson, Near Eastern Affairs Bureau	State	No	October 9, 2015	Talking Points	100	None	Missakian, Grider (Lead) (2)
Megan Rooney	State	No	October 9, 2015	Talking Points	110	None	Missakian (Lead), Grider (2)
Dan Schwerin	State	No	October 9, 2015	Talking Points	102	None	Chipman, Missakian (Lead) (2)
Huma Abedin	State	Yes	October 16, 2015	Benghazi Security Environment, Attack, Clinton, Congressional Cooperation, Talking Points,	222	Pompeo, Westmoreland (2). Both asked questions.	Kiko, Chipman, Jackson (Lead), Barrineau, Clarke, Davis, Betz (7)
Secretary Hillary Clinton[c]	State	Yes	October 22, 2015	Benghazi Security Environment, Attack, Clinton, Congressional Cooperation, Military Response, Talking Points	426	Gowdy, Brooks, Jordan, Pompeo, Roby, Roskam, Westmoreland (7). All asked questions.	Kiko, Donesa, Chipman, Jackson, Missakian, Grider, Tolar, Barrineau, Davis, Clarke, Adams, Betz (12)

Other Agency Phase, October 23, 2015, to June 28, 2016							
Tripoli Analyst	IC	No	November 10, 2015	Attack	–	No transcript provided.	No transcript provided.
Director, Office of Terrorism Analysis	IC	No	November 13, 2015	Details not released.	–	Details not released.	Details not released.
Senior Libyan Desk Officer, Office of Maghreb Affairs, Near Eastern Affairs Bureau	State	No	November 18, 2015	Benghazi Security Environment, Attack, Talking Points	112	None	Kiko, Jackson (Lead), Barrineau, Clarke, Betz (5)
Chief of Base	IC	No	November 19, 2015	Details not released.	–	Details not released.	Details not released.
Jeffrey Feltman	State	No	December 8, 2015	Benghazi Security Environment, Attack	180	Gowdy (1)	Jackson (Lead), Betz (2)
Chief of Operations, Near East Division	IC	No	December 10, 2015	Details not released.	–	Details not released.	Details not released.
Thomas Nides	State	No	December 16, 2015	Benghazi Security Environment, Attack, Military Response, Talking Points	132	Gowdy, Brooks, Jordan, Roby (4). Brooks and Jordan asked questions.	Chipman, Tolar, Clarke, Betz (Lead) (4)
Bernadette Meehan	White House	No	December 16, 2015	Talking Points	146	None	Chipman, Missakian (Lead), Clarke (3)
Deputy Director, Office of Maghreb Affairs, Near Eastern Affairs Bureau	State	No	December 17, 2015	Benghazi Security Environment, Attack, Talking Points	168	Westmoreland (1)	Missakian, Clarke (Lead) (2)

(continued)

Witness	Agency	Leadership or High-Profile	Interview Date	Topic(s)	Interview Pages	Republican Members Present	Republican Staff Members Present
David Petraeus	IC	Yes	January 6, 2016	Benghazi Security Environment, Attack, Military Response, Talking Points	152	Gowdy, Brooks, Jordan, Pompeo, Roby, Roskam, Westmoreland (7). Gowdy, Jordan, Pompeo, Roby, Westmoreland asked questions.	Kiko, Donesa, Chipman (Lead), Missakian, Davis, Adams (6)
Charlene Lamb	State	No	January 7, 2016	Benghazi Security Environment, Attack, Congressional Cooperation, Military Response	292	Gowdy, Brooks, Jordan, Roby, Westmoreland (5). Gowdy, Brooks, Jordan, Westmoreland asked questions.	Kiko, Jackson, Missakian, Davis, Clarke, Betz (Lead) (6)
Secretary Leon Panetta	Defense	Yes	January 8, 2016	Benghazi Security Environment, Military Response, Talking Points	268	Gowdy, Brooks, Jordan, Pompeo, Roby, Roskam, Westmoreland (7). Gowdy, Brooks, Jordan, Pompeo, Westmoreland asked questions.	Kiko, Donesa, Chipman (Lead), Missakian, Tolar, Davis, Clarke, Betz (8)
Benjamin Fishman	White House	No	January 12, 2016	Benghazi Security Environment, Attack, Military Response, Talking Points	76	Gowdy (1)	Kiko, Chipman, Jackson (Lead), Clarke, Betz (5)

Jeremy Bash	Defense	No	January 13, 2016	Attack, Military Response	222	Gowdy, Brooks, Jordan, Pompeo (4). Gowdy and Jordan asked questions.	Kiko, Donesa, Chipman (Lead), Davis, Clarke, Betz (6)
Ben Rhodes	White House	Yes	February 2, 2016	Attack, Talking Points	210	Gowdy, Jordan (2). Both asked questions.	Kiko, Missakian (Lead), Tolar, Davis, Clarke (5)
Ambassador Susan Rice	State	Yes	February 2, 2016	Attack, Talking Points	224	Gowdy, Jordan, Pompeo (3). All asked questions.	Kiko, Missakian (Lead), Tolar, Davis, Clarke (5)
Patrick Kennedy	State	No	February 3, 2016	Benghazi Security Environment, Attack, Clinton, Congressiona Cooperation, Military Response, Talking Points	436	Gowdy, Brooks, Jordan, Pompeo, Roby (5). Gowdy, Brooks, Jordan, and Pompeo asked questions.	Kiko, Donesa, Jackson (Lead), Missakian, Tolar, Davis, Clarke, Betz (8)
Erin Pelton	State	No	February 11, 2016	Attack, Talking Points	170	None	Missakian (Lead), Tolar, Grider (3)
Team Chief, Office of Terrorism Analysis	IC	No	February 16, 2016	Details not released.	–	Details not released.	Details not released.
Matt Olsen	IC	No	February 16, 2016	Benghazi, Security Environment, Attack, Military Response, Talking Points	256	None	Kiko, Donesa, Jackson, Tolar, Davis (Lead) (5)
Gentry Smith	State	No	February 25, 2016	Benghazi Security Environment	196	None	Kiko, Jackson, Betz (Lead) (3)

(continued)

Witness	*Agency*	*Leadership or High-Profile*	*Interview Date*	*Topic(s)*	*Interview Pages*	*Republican Members Present*	*Republican Staff Members Present*
GRS Agent #4	IC	No	March 1, 2016	Details not released.	–	Details not released.	Details not released.
Officer A	IC	No	March 2, 2016	Details not released.	–	Details not released.	Details not released.
James Winnefeld	Defense	No	March 3, 2016	Attack, Military Response	198	Gowdy, Roby (2). Gowdy asked questions.	Tolar, Clarke (Lead) (2)
Managing Director, Office of Management Policy, Rightsizing and Innovation	State	No	March 4, 2016	Congressional Cooperation	122	None	Jackson (Lead), Betz, Davis (3)
Raymond Maxwell	State	No	March 8, 2016	Clinton	108	None	Kiko, Jackson (Lead), Davis (3)
Ethan Chorin	State[d]	No	March 11, 2016	Benghazi Security Environment, Attack	34	None	Jackson (Lead), Clarke, Betz (3)
C-17 Pilot	Defense	No	March 16, 2016	Military Response	144	None	Kiko, Missakian, Tolar (Lead), Clarke (4)
David Petraeus	IC	Yes	March 19, 2016	Attack, Military Response, Talking Points	61	None	Kiko, Donesa, Davis (Lead) (3)
Locally Employed Staff (Libyan National)	–	No	March 22, 2016	Details not released.	–	Details not released.	Details not released.
John Kelly	Defense	No	March 23, 2016	Benghazi Security Environment, Military Response	162	Gowdy, Jordan, Pompeo, Westmoreland (4). Gowdy, Jordan asked questions.	Kiko, Donesa, Missakian, Tolar (Lead), Clarke (5)

Kurt Tidd	Defense	No	April 4, 2016	Military Response	88	None	Kiko, Tolar, Clarke (Lead) (3)
Physical Security Specialist	State	No	April 6, 2016	Benghazi Security Environment	208	None	Kiko, Jackson, Betz (Lead) (3)
Philip Breedlove	Defense	No	April 7, 2016	Military Response	112	None	Kiko, Tolar (Lead), Clarke (3)
Gregory Hicks	State	No	April 14, 2016	Benghazi Security Environment, Attack, Military Response	282	Brooks, Jordan, Westmoreland (3). All asked questions.	Kiko, Donesa, Jackson (Lead), Missakian, Tolar, Davis, Clarke, Betz (8)
Michael Repass	Defense	No	April 15, 2016	Attack, Military Response	158	Gowdy, Westmoreland (2). Both asked questions.	Kiko, Tolar (Lead), Clarke (3)
GRS-Team Lead	IC	No	April 19, 2016	Details not released.	–	Details not released.	Details not released.
Charles Leidig, Jr.	Defense	No	April 22, 2016	Benghazi Security Environment, Attack, Military Response	130	None	Kiko, Donesa, Tolar (Lead), Clarke (4)
Diplomatic Security Agent #29	State	No	April 28, 2016	Benghazi Security Environment	104	None	Kiko, Jackson (Lead), Betz (3)
Patrick Mordente	Defense	No	April 28, 2016	Military Response	108	None	Kiko, Tolar (Lead), Davis, Clarke (4)
ODNI Analyst	IC	No	April 29, 2016	Talking Points	92	Jordan (1). Asked questions.	Kiko, Donesa, Davis (Lead) (3)
Richard Landolt	Defense	No	May 5, 2016	Benghazi Security Environment, Attack, Military Response	106	None	Kiko, Tolar (Lead), Clarke (3)

(*continued*)

Witness	*Agency*	*Leadership or High-Profile*	*Interview Date*	*Topic(s)*	*Interview Pages*	*Republican Members Present*	*Republican Staff Members Present*
James Miller	Defense	No	May 10, 2016	Benghazi Security Environment, Military Response	130	None	Tolar (Lead), Clarke (2)
GRS Agent #5	IC	No	May 24, 2016	Details not released.	–	Details not released.	Details not released.
Drone Pilot #1	Defense	No	May 25, 2016	Attack, Military Response	74	Gowdy, Jordan (2). Both asked questions.	Kiko, Tolar (Lead), Clarke (3)
Drone Pilot #2	Defense	No	May 25, 2016	Attack, Military Response	34	Gowdy, Jordan (2). Jordan asked questions.	Tolar (Lead), Clarke (2)
General Carter Ham	Defense	Yes	June 8, 2016	Benghazi Security Environment, Military Response	191	Gowdy, Brooks, Jordan, Westmoreland (4). Gowdy, Jordan, and Westmoreland asked questions.	Kiko, Donesa, Tolar (Lead), Clarke (4)
Sensor Operator 1	Defense	No	June 9, 2016	Attack, Congressional Cooperation, Military Response	108	Gowdy, Jordan, Westmoreland (3). All asked questions.	Kiko, Tolar (Lead), Clarke (3)
Sensor Operator 2	Defense	No	June 9, 2016	Attack, Military Response	54	Westmoreland (1).	Tolar (Lead), Clarke (2)

Rear Admiral Brian Losey	Defense	No	June 16, 2016	Benghazi Security Environment, Military Response	86	Gowdy, Westmoreland (2). Both asked questions.	Tolar (Lead), Clarke (2)
Defense Attaché	Defense	No	June 17, 2016	Benghazi Security Environment, Attack, Military Response	86	None	Kiko, Tolar (Lead), Clarke (3)
F-16 Crew Chief	Defense	No	June 29, 2016	Military Response	78	None	Tolar (Lead), Clarke (2)
Stephen Hedger	Defense	Yes	July 14, 2016	Congressional Cooperation	160	None	Donesa, Jackson, Tolar, Davis (Lead), Clarke (5)

[a]Blumenthal was not a State Department employee, but he was a Clinton confidant.
[b]No committee members could ask Pagliano questions, as he exercised his Fifth Amendment rights.
[c]Conducted as a hearing.
[d]Chorin was a non-profit co-director and former State employee.

Bibliography

Achen, Christopher H., and Duncan Snidal. "Rational Deterrence Theory and Comparative Case Studies." *World Politics* 41, no. 2 (1989): 143–69.

Albert, Zachary, and Raymond J. La Raja. "Political Parties and Policy Analysis." In *Policy Analysis in the United States*, edited by John A. Hird. Bristol: Policy Press, 2018.

Alberta, Tim. "John Boehner Unchained." *Politico*, November/December 2017. https://www.politico.com/magazine/story/2017/10/29/john-boehner-trump-house-republican-party-retirement-profile-feature-215741/.

Aldrich, John H. *Why Parties? The Origin and Transformation of Political Parties in America*. Chicago, IL: University of Chicago Press, 1995.

Aldrich, John H., and David W. Rohde. "The Transition to Republican Rule in the House: Implications for Theories of Congressional Parties." *Political Science Quarterly* 112, no. 4 (1997–1998): 541–67.

Associated Press. "McKinney Introduces Bill to Impeach Bush." *NBC News*, December 8, 2006. https://www.nbcnews.com/id/wbna16116357.

Auerswald, David P., and Colton C. Campbell. "Congress and National Security." In *Congress and the Politics of National Security*, edited by David P. Auerswald and Colton C. Campbell. Cambridge: Cambridge University Press, 2012.

Bade, Rachel, and Isaac Arnsdorf. "Meet the Well-Paid Pros Behind the Benghazi Panel." *Politico*, October 21, 2015. https://www.politico.com/story/2015/10/meet-the-well-paid-pros-behind-the-benghazi-panel-215023.

Balla, Steven J., and Christopher J. Deering. "Police Patrols and Fire Alarms: An Empirical Examination of the Legislative Preference for Oversight." *Congress & the Presidency* 40, no. 1 (2013): 27–40.

Baron, Jonathan, and John C. Hershey. "Outcome Bias in Decision Evaluation." *Journal of Personality and Social Psychology* 54, no. 4 (1988): 569–79.

Bawn, Kathleen. "Choosing Strategies to Control the Bureaucracy: Statutory Constraints, Oversight, and the Committee System." *Journal of Law, Economics, & Organization* 13, no. 1 (1997): 101–26.

Beitsch, Rebecca, and Mike Lillis. "Jan. 6 Panel Changed Script for Star Witness – at a Steep Cost." *The Hill*, July 14, 2022. https://thehill.com/homenews/house/3558249-jan-6-panel-changed-script-for-star-witness-at-a-steep-cost/.

Benen, Steve. "Republican Benghazi Committee Ends with a Whimper." *MSNBC*, June 28, 2016. https://www.msnbc.com/rachel-maddow-show/republican-benghazi-committee-ends-whimper-msna870586.

Bennett, Andrew. "Processing Tracing and Causal Inference." In *Rethinking Social Inquiry: Diverse Tools, Shared Standards*, 2nd edition, edited by Henry E. Brady and David Collier. Lanham, MD: Rowman & Littlefield, 2010.

Binder, Sarah A. "The Dynamics of Legislative Gridlock, 1947–96." *American Political Science Review* 93, no. 3 (1999): 519–33.

Brown, Bernard E. "The Case Method in Comparative Politics." In *Cases in Comparative Politics*, 3rd edition, edited by Bernard E. Brown and James B. Christoph. Boston, MA: Little, Brown, 1976.

Brufke, Juliegrace. "GOP Rep. Martha Roby to Retire." *The Hill*, July 26, 2019. https://thehill.com/homenews/house/454934-gop-rep-martha-roby-to-retire/.

Campbell, James. "The Presidential Surge and Its Midterm Decline, 1868–1988." *Journal of Politics* 53, no. 2 (1991): 477–87.

Cavallaro, Gabe. "Former U.S. Rep. Trey Gowdy to Host New Fox News Primetime Show Week of Feb. 1." *Greenville News*, January 29, 2021. https://www.greenvilleonline.com/story/news/politics/2021/01/29/trey-gowdy-host-fox-news-primetime-show-week-feb-1/4312289001/.

CBS/AP. "The House GOP's Benghazi Investigation; Who's who." *CBS News*, May 19, 2014. https://www.cbsnews.com/news/whos-who-on-the-gops-benghazi-investigation/.

Center for Legislative Archives. "A Brief History of the Committee: The Russell Era, 1955–1968." *National Archives*, n.d. https://www.archives.gov/legislative/finding-aids/reference/senate/armed-services/1955-1968.html.

Cheney, Kyle. "Trump's GOP 'warriors' Lead Charge Against Mueller." *Politico*, May 7, 2018. https://www.politico.com/story/2018/05/07/trump-mueller-republican-warriors-congress-571562.

Cherry, Tyler. "Media Fell for Bogus 'New Information' Spin in GOP Benghazi Report." *Media Matters*, June 29, 2016. https://www.mediamatters.org/washington-post/media-fell-bogus-new-information-spin-gop-benghazi-report.

Chorin, Ethan. "About." *Forbes*, n.d. https://www.forbes.com/sites/ethanchorin/?sh=21c15f304bcd.

Christenson, Dino P., and Douglas Kriner. "Mobilizing the Public Against the President: Congress and the Political Costs of Unilateral Action." *American Journal of Political Science* 61, no. 4 (2017): 769–85.

Clinton, Hillary. *Hard Choices*. New York: Simon & Schuster, 2014.

———. "Secretary Clinton's Response to the Accountability Review Board Report." n.d. https://2009-2017.state.gov/documents/organization/203244.pdf.

———. "Secretary of State Hillary Rodham Clinton: Senate Committee on Foreign Relations: Washington, DC." January 23, 2013. https://www.foreign.senate.gov/imo/media/doc/SECRETARY%20OF%20STATE%20HILLARY%20RODHAM%20CLINTON.pdf.

CNN/ORC Poll. October 14–17, 2015. http://i2.cdn.turner.com/cnn/2015/images/10/21/rel11e.-.benghazi.pdf.

Cole, Lance, and Stanley Brand. *Congressional Investigations and Oversight: Case Studies and Analysis*. Durham, NC: Carolina Academic Press, 2011.

Collier, David. "Understanding Process Tracing," *PS: Political Science and Politics* 44, no. 4 (2011): 823–30.

Conley, Richard S. *The Presidency, Congress and Divided Government*. College Station, TX: Texas A&M University Press, 2003.

Cox, Gary W., and Mathew D. McCubbins. *Setting the Agenda: Responsible Party Government in the U.S. House of Representatives*. Cambridge: Cambridge University Press, 2005.

Davis, Julie Hirschfeld, and Mark Mazzetti. "Highlights of Robert Mueller's Testimony to Congress." *New York Times*, July 24, 2019. https://www.nytimes.com/2019/07/24/us/politics/mueller-testimony.html.

DeBonis, Mike. "House Votes to Kill Texas Lawmaker's Trump Impeachment Effort." *Washington Post*, December 6, 2017. https://www.washingtonpost.com/news/powerpost/wp/2017/12/06/house-democratic-leaders-oppose-texas-lawmakers-trump-impeachment-effort/.

DeBonis, Mike, and Robert Costa. "'Supermajority' of House Freedom Caucus to back Paul Ryan's speaker bid." *Washington Post*, October 21, 2015. https://www.washingtonpost.com/politics/supermajority-of-house-freedom-caucus-to-back-paul-ryans-speaker-bid/2015/10/21/d7411964-781e-11e5-a958-d889faf561dc_story.html.

Deering, Christopher J., and Stephen S. Smith. *Committees in Congress*, 3rd edition. Washington, DC: CQ Press, 1997.

DeSeve, G. Edward. *The Presidential Appointee's Handbook*. Washington, DC: Brookings Institution Press, 2017.

Dickinson, Tim. "Inside the Republican Suicide Machine." *Rolling Stone*, October 9, 2013. https://www.rollingstone.com/politics/politics-news/inside-the-republican-suicide-machine-122436/.

Downs, Anthony. *An Economic Theory of Democracy*. New York: Harper, 1957.

Dumain, Emma, and Daniel Newhauser. "Boehner Satisfies Many Constituencies with Benghazi Panel Picks." *Roll Call*, May 9, 2014. https://rollcall.com/2014/05/09/boehner-satisfies-many-constituencies-with-benghazi-panel-picks-video/.

Easley, Jonathan. "Republican; Benghazi Probe 'Designed to Go After' Hillary." *The Hill*, October 14, 2015. https://thehill.com/blogs/ballot-box/presidential-races/256982-gop-lawmaker-benghazi-probe-designed-to-go-after-hillary.

Edwards III, George C. *At the Margins: Presidential Leadership of Congress*. New Haven, CT: Yale University Press, 1989.

Edwards III, George C., Kenneth R. Mayer and Stephen J. Wayne. *Presidential Leadership: Politics and Policy Making*, 11th edition. Lanham, MD: Rowman & Littlefield, 2020.

Ewing, Philip. "'Not Guilty': Trump Acquitted On 2 Articles Of Impeachment As Historic Trial Closes." *NPR*, February 5, 2020. https://www.npr.org/2020/02/05/801429948/not-guilty-trump-acquitted-on-2-articles-of-impeachment-as-historic-trial-closes.

Fandos, Nicholas. "Trump Acquitted of Inciting Insurrection, Even as Bipartisan Majority Votes 'Guilty.'" *New York Times*, February 13, 2021. https://www.nytimes.com/2021/02/13/us/politics/trump-impeachment.html.

———. "With Sweeping Document Request, Democrats Launch Broad Trump Corruption Inquiry." *New York Times*, March 4, 2019. https://www.nytimes.com/2019/03/04/us/politics/trump-obstruction.html.

Federal Bureau of Investigation. "Seeking Information on Benghazi Attacks." n.d. https://www.fbi.gov/wanted/seeking-info/seeking-information-on-attacks-in-benghazi.

Fischer, David Hackett. *Historians' Fallacies: Toward a Logic of Historical Thought*. New York: Harper, 1970.

Fisher, Louis. "Military Operations in Libya: No War? No Hostilities?" *Presidential Studies Quarterly* 42, no. 1 (2012): 176–89.

———. "War Powers." In *The Law of the Executive Branch: Presidential Power*. New York: Oxford University Press, 2014.

Fishman, Benjamin. "Experts: Ben Fishman." *The Washington Institute for Near East Policy*, n.d. https://www.washingtoninstitute.org/experts/ben-fishman.

Fowler, Linda L. *Watchdogs on the Hill: The Decline of Congressional Oversight of U.S. Foreign Relations*. Princeton University Press, 2015.

Fox News. "Ex-White House Spokesman Downplays Controversy over Benghazi Talking Points." *Fox News*, May 2, 2014. https://www.foxnews.com/politics/ex-white-house-spokesman-downplays-controversy-over-benghazi-talking-points.

———. "Kucinich Brings Bush Impeachment Resolution to House Floor Again." *Fox News*, January 13, 2015. https://www.foxnews.com/story/kucinich-brings-bush-impeachment-resolution-to-house-floor-again.

Fry, Joseph A. *The American South and the Vietnam War: Belligerence, Protest, and Agony in Dixie*. Lexington, KY: University Press of Kentucky, 2015.

Gallup Poll. May 14–15, 2013. https://news.gallup.com/poll/162584/americans-attention-irs-benghazi-stories-below-average.aspx.

Gartner, Scott Sigmund, and Gary M. Segura. "All Politics are Still Local: The Iraq War and the 2006 Midterm Elections." *PS: Political Science & Politics* 41, no. 1 (2008): 95–100.

Geddes, Barbara. "How the Cases You Choose Affect the Answers You Get: Selection Bias in Political Science." *Political Analysis* 2, no. 1 (1990): 131–50.

George, Alexander, and Andrew Bennett. *Case Studies and Theory Development in the Social Sciences*. Cambridge, MA: MIT Press, 2004.

Gerring, John. "What Is a Case Study and What Is It Good for?." *American Political Science Review* 98, no. 2 (2004): 341–54.

Gerth, Jeff, and David Johnston. "Evidence of Broad Plan by China to Buy Entrée to U.S. Technology." *New York Times*, December 15, 1998. https://www.nytimes.com/1998/12/15/us/evidence-of-broad-plan-by-china-to-buy-entree-to-us-technology.html.

Goldberg, Jeffrey. "The Obama Doctrine." *The Atlantic*, April 2016. https://www.theatlantic.com/magazine/archive/2016/04/the-obama-doctrine/471525/.

Grayer, Annie, and Melanie Zanona. "Jim Jordan among 5 House Republicans Selected by McCarthy for January 6 Select Committee." *CNN*, July 20, 2021. https://www.cnn.com/2021/07/19/politics/house-republicans-chosen-for-january-6-committee/index.html.

Haberman, Maggie, and Annie Karni. "Inside Trump's Botched Attempt to Hire Trey Gowdy." *New York Times*, October 13, 2019. https://www.nytimes.com/2019/10/13/us/politics/trey-gowdy-trump-impeachment.html.

Hallerman, Tamar. "Ex-Ga. rep. Endures Nearly Two-Year Wait for Senate Confirmation." *Atlanta Journal-Constitution*, July, 31, 2019. https://www.ajc.com/news/state--regional-govt--politics/rep-endures-nearly-two-year-wait-for-senate-confirmation/TiU8RR7oKA0IcpairhSOSJ/.

Halperin, Morton H., Priscilla Clapp, and Arnold Kanter. *Bureaucratic Politics and Foreign Policy*. Washington, DC: Brookings Institution Press, 2006.

Harris, Gardiner, and Thomas Kaplan. "Senate Confirms C.I.A. Chief Mike Pompeo to Be Secretary of State." *New York Times*, April 26, 2018. https://www.nytimes.com/2018/04/26/us/politics/mike-pompeo-secretary-of-state.html.

Herszenhorn, David M. "House Benghazi Report Finds No New Evidence of Wrongdoing by Hillary Clinton." *New York Times*, June 28, 2016. https://www.nytimes.com/2016/06/29/us/politics/hillary-clinton-benghazi.html.

House Select Committee on the Events Surrounding the 2012 Terrorist Attack in Benghazi. "Congressional Publications." *govinfo.gov*, n.d. https://www.govinfo.gov/committee/house-benghazi?path=/browsecommittee/chamber/house/committee/benghazi/collection/OTHER-1.

Howell, William G., and Jon C. Pevehouse, "Presidents, Congress, and the Use of Force." *International Organization* 59, no. 1 (2005): 209–32.

———. *While Dangers Gather: Congressional Checks on Presidential War Powers*. Princeton, NJ: Princeton University Press, 2007.

Hughes, Dana. "Four State Department Officials Relieved of Duties After Benghazi Report." *ABC News*, December 19, 2012. https://abcnews.go.com/blogs/politics/2012/12/three-state-department-officials-resign-after-benghazi-report.

Ikenberry, John. *After Victory: Institutions, Strategic Restraint, and the Rebuilding of Order after Major Wars*. Princeton: Princeton University Press, 2001.

Jacobson, Gary C. "Partisan Polarization in American Politics: A Background Paper." *Presidential Studies Quarterly* 43, no. 4 (2013): 688–708.

———. "Polarization, Gridlock, and Presidential Campaign Politics in 2016." *The ANNALS of the American Academy of Political and Social Science* 667, no. 1 (2016): 226–46.

Janis, Irving L. *Groupthink: Psychological Studies of Policy Decisions and Fiascoes*, 2nd edition. Boston: Houghton Mifflin, 1982.

John F. Kennedy Presidential Library and Museum. "Bay of Pigs: Lessons Learned." *JFK Library*, n.d., https://www.jfklibrary.org/learn/education/teachers/curricular-resources/high-school-curricular-resources/bay-of-pigs-lessons-learned.

Johnson, Cheryl. *Rules of the House of Representatives: One Hundred Seventeenth Congress*. Washington, DC: Government Printing Office, 2021.

Joint Chiefs of Staff. *Chairman of the Joint Chiefs of Staff Instruction: Officer Professional Military Education Policy (CJCSI 1800.01F)*, 15 May 2020. https://www.jcs.mil/Portals/36/Documents/Doctrine/education/cjcsi_1800_01f.pdf?ver=2020-05-15-102430-580.

———. *Doctrine for the Armed Forces of the United States (JP 1)*, 25 March 2013. https://www.jcs.mil/Portals/36/Documents/Doctrine/pubs/jp1_ch1.pdf.

———. *Joint Operation Planning (JP 5-0)*, 11 August 2011.

Judicial Watch. "Judicial Watch: Benghazi Documents Point to White House on Misleading Talking Points." *Judicial Watch*, April 29, 2014. www.judicialwatch.org/press-room/press-releases/judicial-watch-benghazi-documents-point-white-house-misleading-talking-points/.

———. "Judicial Watch Statement on House Benghazi Report." *Judicial Watch*, June 28, 2016, https://www.judicialwatch.org/judicial-watch-statement-house-benghazi-report/.

Karni, Annie. "The Committee Hired a TV Executive to Produce the Hearings for Maximum Impact." *New York Times*, June 9, 2022. https://www.nytimes.com/2022/06/09/us/the-committee-hired-a-tv-executive-to-produce-the-hearings-for-maximum-impact.html.

Kennedy, John F. "News Conference 10, April 21, 1961." *JFK Library*, April 21, 1961. https://www.jfklibrary.org/archives/other-resources/john-f-kennedy-press-conferences/news-conference-10.

Keohane, Robert. *After Hegemony: Power and Discord in the World Political Economy*. Princeton: Princeton University Press, 1984.

Kessler, Glenn. "Fact Check: State Department Contradicts Biden." *Washington Post*, October 11, 2012. https://www.washingtonpost.com/news/post-politics/wp/2012/10/11/fact-check-state-department-contradicts-biden/.

———. "Issa's Absurd Claim that Clinton's 'Signature' Means She Personally Approved It." *Washington Post*, April 26, 2013. https://www.washingtonpost.com/blogs/fact-checker/post/issas-absurd-claim-that-clintons-signature-means-she-personally-approved-it/2013/04/25/58c2f5b4-adf8-11e2-a986-eec837b1888b_blog.html.

King, David C. *Turf Wars: How Congressional Committees Claim Jurisdiction*. Chicago: University of Chicago Press, 1997.

King, Gary, Robert O. Keohane, and Sidney Verba. *Designing Social Inquiry: Scientific Inference in Qualitative Research*. Princeton: Princeton University Press, 1994.

Kirkpatrick, David D. "A Deadly Mix in Benghazi." *New York Times*, December 28, 2013, https://www.nytimes.com/projects/2013/benghazi/index.html#/?chapt=0.

Kirkpatrick, David D., and Steven Lee Myers. "Libya Attack Brings Challenges for U.S." *New York Times*, September 13, 2012. https://www.nytimes.com/2012/09/13/world/middleeast/us-envoy-to-libya-is-reported-killed.html.

Kriner, Douglas. *After the Rubicon: Congress, Presidents, and the Politics of Waging War*. Chicago: University of Chicago Press, 2010.

———. "Can Enhanced Oversight Repair the Broken Branch." *Boston University Law Review* 89 (2009): 765–93.

Kriner, Douglas, and Eric Schickler. "Investigating the President: Committee Probes and Presidential Approval, 1953–2006." *The Journal of Politics* 76, no. 2 (2014): 521–34.

———. *Investigating the President: Congressional Checks on Presidential Power*. Princeton: Princeton University Press, 2016.

Kriner, Douglas, and Francis Shen. "Responding to War on Capitol Hill: Battlefield Casualties, Congressional Response, and Public Support for the War in Iraq." *American Journal of Political Science* 58, no. 1 (2014): 157–74.

Kriner, Douglas, and Liam Schwartz. "Divided Government and Congressional Investigations." *Legislative Studies Quarterly* 33, no. 2 (2008): 295–321.

Kuperman, Alan J. "Obama's Libya Debacle: How a Well-Meaning Intervention Ended in Failure." *Foreign Affairs* 94, no. 2 (2015): 66–77.

Kuzoian, Alex. "This 60-second animation shows how divided Congress has become since 1949." *Business Insider*, September 11, 2019. https://www.businessinsider.com/animation-rise-partisanship-congress-house-representatives-60-years-2016-4

Laird, Melvin R. "Iraq: Learning the Lessons of Vietnam." *Foreign Affairs* 84, no. 6 (2005): 22–43.

Layne, Christopher. "Kant or Cant: The Myth of the Democratic Peace." *International Security* 19, no. 2 (1994): 5–49.

LegiStorm. "House Select Committee on Benghazi—Staff Salaries." *LegiStorm*, n.d., https://www.legistorm.com/office/House_Select_Committee_on_Benghazi/2911.html.

———. "House Select Committee to Investigate the January 6th Attack on the U.S. Capitol – Staff Salaries." *LegiStorm*, n.d., https://www.legistorm.com/office/House_Select_Committee_to_Investigate_the_January_6th_Attack_on_the_U_S_Capitol/8821.html.

Levy, Jack S. "Case Studies: Types, Designs, and Logics of Inference." *Conflict Management and Peace Science* 25, no. 1 (2008): 1–18.

Lewis, Jeffrey B., Keith Poole, Howard Rosenthal, Adam Boche, Aaron Rudkin, and Luke Sonnet. *Voteview: Congressional Roll-Call Votes Database*, 2022. https://voteview.com/.

Lieberman, Joseph I., and Susan Collins. *Flashing Red: A Special Report on the Terrorist Attack at Benghazi*. Washington, DC: U.S. Senate Committee on Homeland Security and Governmental Affairs, 2012.

Light, Paul C. *Government by Investigation: Congress, Presidents, and the Search for Answers 1945–2012*. Washington, DC: Brookings Institution Press, 2014.

Lijphart, Arend. "Comparative Politics and the Comparative Method." *American Political Science Review* 65, no. 3 (1971): 682–93.

Lillis, Mike. "House Conservatives Prep Plans to Impeach Biden." *The Hill*, August 30, 2022. https://thehill.com/homenews/house/3620081-house-conservatives-prep-plans-to-impeach-biden/.

Lowell, Hugo. "McCarthy Pulls Five Republicans from Capitol Attack Panel after Pelosi Rejects Two." *Guardian*, July 21, 2021. https://www.theguardian.com/us-news/2021/jul/21/nancy-pelosi-capitol-attack-committee-republicans.

Lucey, Catherine. "Bush Was Haunted by His Own 'Mission Accomplished.'" *Boston Globe*, April 14, 2018. https://www.bostonglobe.com/news/nation/2018/04/14/bush-was-haunted-his-own-mission-accomplished/E73SdIkXxBfUGsbyXv7ISI/story.html.

Madison, Lucy. "Biden Beer Invitation: 'No Malarkey.'" *CBS News*, September 11, 2012. https://www.cbsnews.com/news/biden-beer-invitation-no-malarkey/.

Marlowe, Melanie. "Reclaiming Institutional Relevance through Congressional Oversight." In *Is Congress Broken? The Virtues and Defects of Partisanship, Polarization, and Gridlock*, edited by William Connelly, John Pitney, and Gary Schmitt. Washington, DC: Brookings Institution Press, 2017.

Marshall, Bryan W., and Bruce C. Wolpe. "From Presidential 'Shakedown' to Congressional Apology: The Politics of Committee Oversight of BP's Deepwater Horizon Crisis." In *The Committee: A Study of Policy, Power, Politics and Obama's Historic Legislative Agenda on Capitol Hill*. University of Michigan Press, 2018.

Mayhew, David. *America's Congress: Actions in the Public Sphere, James Madison through Newt Gingrich*. New Haven, CT: Yale University Press, 2000.

———. *Divided We Govern: Party Control, Lawmaking, and Investigations, 1946–2002*, 2nd edition. New Haven, CT: Yale University Press, 2005.

McCarty, Nolan, Keith T. Poole, and Howard Rosenthal. *Polarized America: The Dance of Ideology and Unequal Riches*. Boston: MIT Press, 2006.

McCrummen, Stephanie, and Ann Scott Tyson. "Navy Kills 3 Pirates, Rescues Ship Captain off Somalia's Coast." *Washington Post*, April 13, 2009. https://www.washingtonpost.com/wp-dyn/content/article/2009/04/12/AR2009041200467.html.

McCubbins, Mathew, and Thomas Schwartz. "Congressional Oversight Overlooked: Police Patrols versus Fire Alarms." *American Journal of Political Science* 28, no. 1 (1984): 165–79.

McKeon, Howard P. *Majority Interim Report: Benghazi Investigation Update*. Washington, DC: House Armed Services Committee, 2014.

McKeon, Howard P., Ed Royce, Bob Goodlatte, Darrell Issa, and Mike Rogers. *Interim Progress Report for the Members of the House Republican Conference on the Events Surrounding the September 11, 2012 Terrorist Attacks in Benghazi, Libya*. Washington, DC: Government Printing Office, 2013.

McKeown, Timothy. "Case Studies and the Statistical Worldview." *International Organization* 53, no. 1 (1999): 161–90.

Mendoza, Jessica. "On Impeachment, Jim Jordan Goes for the Takedown." *Christian Science Monitor*, November 19, 2019. https://www.csmonitor.com/USA/Politics/2019/1119/On-impeachment-Jim-Jordan-goes-for-the-takedown.

Miller, Zeke, and Alex Rogers. "Timeline: The Benghazi Emails: How the Obama Administration Created the Benghazi Talking Points." *Time*, May 16, 2013. https://swampland.time.com/2013/05/16/timeline-the-benghazi-emails/.

Monmouth University Polling Institute. July 7, 2022. https://www.monmouth.edu/polling-institute/reports/monmouthpoll_us_070722/.

Morell, Michael. "Written Statement for the Record: Michael Morell: Former Acting Director and Deputy Director of the CIA: House Permanent Select Committee on

Intelligence: 2 April 2014." April 2, 2014. https://republicans-intelligence.house.gov/sites/intelligence.house.gov/files/documents/morellsfr04022014.pdf.

Munck, Gerardo L. "Canons of Research Design in Qualitative Analysis." *Studies in Comparative International Development* 33, no. 3 (1998): 18–45.

National Archives. "Federal Register: The Daily Journal of the United States Government." https://www.federalregister.gov/agencies.

National Commission on Terrorist Attacks upon the United States, Thomas H. Kean, and Lee Hamilton. *The 9/11 Commission report: final report of the National Commission on Terrorist Attacks upon the United States*. Washington, DC: National Commission on Terrorist Attacks upon the United States, 2004.

Naylor, Brian. "Impeachment Timeline: From Early Calls to a Full House Vote." *NPR*, December 17, 2019. https://www.npr.org/2019/12/17/788397365/impeachment-timeline-from-early-calls-to-a-full-house-vote.

Neck, Christopher P., and Gregory Moorhead. "Groupthink Remodeled: The Importance of Leadership, Time Pressure, and Methodical Decision-Making Procedures." *Human Relations* 48, no. 5 (1995): 537–57.

Neustadt, Richard E. *Presidential Power and the Modern Presidents: The Politics of Leadership from Roosevelt to Reagan*. New York: Free Press, 1990.

New York Times. "Highlights from Hillary Clinton's Day at the Benghazi Panel." *New York Times*, October 22, 2015. https://www.nytimes.com/interactive/projects/cp/congress/hillary-clinton-testimony-at-house-benghazi-panel/jim-jordan-sharp-questioning-about-night-of-attack.

———. "What They Said Before and After the Attack in Libya." *New York Times*, September 12, 2012. https://archive.nytimes.com/www.nytimes.com/interactive/2012/09/12/us/politics/libya-statements.html.

Nyhan, Brendan. "Scandal Potential: How Political Context and News Congestion Affect the President's Vulnerability to Media Scandal." *British Journal of Political Science* 45, no. 2 (2015): 435–66.

Obama, Barack. "Remarks on the Attack on the U.S. Mission in Benghazi, Libya." September 12, 2012. https://www.govinfo.gov/content/pkg/DCPD-201200713/pdf/DCPD-201200713.pdf.

Ornstein, Norman J., and Thomas E. Mann. "When Congress Checks Out." *Foreign Affairs* 85, no. 6 (2006): 67–82.

Orr, Gabby. "In Censure of Cheney and Kinzinger, RNC Calls Events of January 6 'Legitimate Political Discourse." *CNN*, February 4, 2022. https://www.cnn.com/2022/02/04/politics/liz-cheney-adam-kinzinger-censure-rnc/index.html.

Parker, David C.W., and Matthew Dull. "Divided We Quarrel: The Politics of Congressional Investigations, 1947–2004." *Legislative Studies Quarterly* 34, no. 3 (2009): 319–45.

———. "Rooting Out Waste, Fraud, and Abuse: The Politics of House Committee Investigations, 1947 to 2004." *Political Research Quarterly* 66, no. 3 (2013): 630–44.

Patashnik, Eric M., and Justin Peck. "Can Congress Do Policy Analysis? The Politics of Problem Solving on Capitol Hill." In *Does Policy Analysis Matter? Exploring Its Effectiveness in Theory and Practice*, edited by Lee S. Friedman. University of California Press, 2017.

Pathé, Simone. “Susan Brooks Won’t Seek a Fifth Term, Opening up Targeted Indiana Seat.” *Roll Call*, June 14, 2019. https://rollcall.com/2019/06/14/susan-brooks-wont-seek-a-fifth-term-opening-up-targeted-indiana-seat/.

Pearson, Rick. “Former U.S. Rep. Peter Roskam Joins Sidley Law Firm to Lobby, Consult.” *Chicago Tribune*, July 16, 2019. https://www.chicagotribune.com/politics/ct-former-congressman-peter-roskam-joins-sidley-20190716-borrf6lkmfbjndwu6xoahkmqdi-story.html.

Pereira, Miguel M., and Nicholas W. Waterbury. “Do Voters Discount Political Scandals over Time?.” *Political Research Quarterly* 72, no. 3 (2019): 584–95.

Podliska, Bradley F. *Acting Alone: A Scientific Study of American Hegemony and Unilateral Use-of-Force Decision Making*. Lanham, MD: Lexington Books, 2010.

Podliska, Bradley, Karin Hecox, and Oliver Sagun. “Behind Enemy Plans: A Processing Tracing Analysis of Germany’s Operational Approach to a Western Invasion.” *Joint Force Quarterly* 100 (1st Quarter, January 2021): 107–15.

Poole, Keith T. “Party Unity Scores.” May 31, 2015. https://legacy.voteview.com/Party_Unity.htm.

Przeworski, Adam, and Henry Teune. *The Logic of Comparative Social Inquiry*. New York: Wiley-Interscience, 1970.

Quinnipiac Poll. July 8, 2014. https://poll.qu.edu/Poll-Release-Legacy?releaseid=2058.

———. November 26, 2014. https://poll.qu.edu/Poll-Release-Legacy?releaseid=2116.

———. March 5, 2015. https://poll.qu.edu/Poll-Release-Legacy?releaseid=2172.

———. July 30, 2015. https://poll.qu.edu/Poll-Release-Legacy?releaseid=2264.

———. November 4, 2015. https://poll.qu.edu/Poll-Release-Legacy?releaseid=2299.

———. June 29, 2016. https://poll.qu.edu/Poll-Release-Legacy?releaseid=2363.

———. January 26, 2017. https://poll.qu.edu/Poll-Release-Legacy?releaseid=2420.

———. December 12, 2017. https://poll.qu.edu/Poll-Release-Legacy?releaseid=2507.

———. March 5, 2019. https://poll.qu.edu/Poll-Release-Legacy?releaseid=2603.

———. July 29, 2019. https://poll.qu.edu/Poll-Release-Legacy?releaseid=3635.

———. September 30, 2019. https://poll.qu.edu/Poll-Release-Legacy?releaseid=3642.

———. January 28, 2020. https://poll.qu.edu/Poll-Release?releaseid=3762.

———. January 11, 2021. https://poll.qu.edu/Poll-Release?releaseid=3733.

———. January 18, 2021. https://poll.qu.edu/Poll-Release?releaseid=3732

Reilly, Jeffrey M. *Operational Design: Distilling Clarity from Complexity for Decisive Action*. Maxwell Air Force Base, AL: Air University Press, 2012.

Reynolds, Molly, Norman J. Ornstein, Thomas E. Mann, and Michael J. Malbin. *Vital Statistics on Congress*. Washington, DC: Brookings Institution, 2021.

Rockman, Bert A. “Reinventing What for Whom?: President and Congress in the Making of Foreign Policy.” *Presidential Studies Quarterly* 30, no. 1 (2000): 133–54.

Rogers, Mike, and C.A. Ruppersberger. *Investigative Report on the Terrorist Attacks on U.S. Facilities in Benghazi, Libya, September 11–12, 2012*. Washington, DC:

U.S. House of Representatives Permanent Select Committee on Intelligence, 2014.

Rosenbaum, David E. "Campaign Finance: The Hearings; Anger Flares as Focus Shifts to Campaign Remedies." *New York Times*, September 24, 1997. https://www.nytimes.com/1997/09/24/us/campaign-finance-the-hearings-anger-flares-as-focus-shifts-to-campaign-remedies.html.

Rucker, Philip. "Romney Repeats Sharp Criticism of Obama after Benghazi, Cairo Attacks." *Washington Post*, September 12, 2012. https://www.washingtonpost.com/politics/decision2012/romney-repeats-sharp-criticism-of-obama-on-libya-egypt-attacks/2012/09/12/31074af4-fcdf-11e1-b153-218509a954e1_story.html.

Sagar, Rahul. *Secrets and Leaks: The Dilemma of State Secrecy*. Princeton: Princeton University Press, 2013.

Schmidt, Michael S. "Hillary Clinton Used Personal Email Account at State Dept., Possibly Breaking Rules." *New York Times*, March 2, 2015. https://www.nytimes.com/2015/03/03/us/politics/hillary-clintons-use-of-private-email-at-state-department-raises-flags.html?_r=0.

Schmitt, Eric. "Commandos See Duty on U.S. Soil In Role Redefined by Terror Fight." *New York Times*, January 23, 2005. https://www.nytimes.com/2005/01/23/washington/us/commandos-see-duty-on-us-soil-in-role-redefined-by-terror.html.

Segers, Grace. "House Votes to Create Select Committee to Investigate January 6 Attack." *CBS News*, June 30, 2021. https://www.cbsnews.com/news/january-6-select-committee-house-vote/.

———. "Pelosi Names Members of January 6 Select Committee, Including Liz Cheney." *CBS News*, July 1, 2021. https://www.cbsnews.com/news/january-6-committee-liz-cheney-pelosi-members/.

Sheikh, Abdi. "U.S. Commandos Free Two Hostages in Daring Somalia Raid." *Reuters*, January 25, 2012. https://www.reuters.com/article/us-somalia-hostages-idUSTRE80O0I220120125.

Sinclair, Barbara. *Party Wars: Polarization and the Politics of National Policy Making*. Norman: University of Oklahoma Press, 2006.

———. *Unorthodox Lawmaking: New Legislative Processes in the U.S. Congress*, 2nd edition. Washington, DC: CQ Press, 2000.

Slack, Megan. "Marking the Eleventh Anniversary of 9/11." *Obama White House*, September 11, 2012. https://obamawhitehouse.archives.gov/blog/2012/09/11/marking-eleventh-anniversary-911.

Slater, Dan, and Erica Simmons. "Informative Regress: Critical Antecedents in Comparative Politics." *Comparative Political Studies* 43, no. 7 (2010): 886–917.

Smist, Frank John. *Congress Oversees the United States Intelligence Community, 1947–1994*. Knoxville: University of Tennessee Press, 1994.

Sonmez, Felicia. "Jim Jordan: Boehner Plan Won't Pass House on Republican Support Alone." *Washington Post*, July 26, 2011. https://www.washingtonpost.com/blogs/2chambers/post/jim-jordan-boehner-plan-wont-pass-house-on-republican-support-alone/2011/07/26/gIQAZqY1aI_blog.html.

State Department. *Accountability Review Board Report*. December 18, 2012. https://2009-2017.state.gov/documents/organization/202446.pdf.

Stathis, Stephen W., and David C. Huckabee. "Congressional Resolutions on Presidential Impeachment: A Historical Overview." *CRS Report*, September 16, 1998. https://digital.library.unt.edu/ark:/67531/metadc819397/.

Straus, Jacob R. "Congressional Commissions: Overview and Considerations for Congress." *CRS Report*, January 22, 2021. https://crsreports.congress.gov/product/pdf/R/R40076.

Swan, Betsy. "Scorned Trump Team Turns on Man They Once Loved." *Daily Beast*, December 28, 2015. https://www.thedailybeast.com/scorned-trump-team-turns-on-man-they-once-loved.

Sweet, Lynn. "President Obama Official Schedule and Guidance, Sept. 11, 2012. 9–11 Observance." *Chicago Sun-Times*, November 19, 2013. https://chicago.suntimes.com/politics/2013/11/19/18547803/president-obama-official-schedule-and-guidance-sept-11-2012-9-11-observance.

Takala, Rudy. "Conservative group says House Benghazi panel 'bungled' investigation." *Washington Examiner*, March 24, 2016. https://www.washingtonexaminer.com/tag/hillary-clinton?source=%2Fconservative-group-says-house-benghazi-panel-bungled-investigation.

Tani, Maxwell, and Dan Turkel. "The Benghazi Chairman Couldn't Explain What He Learned after 10 Hours of Testimony from Hillary Clinton." *Business Insider*, October 22, 2015. https://www.businessinsider.com/trey-gowdy-hillary-clinton-testimony-gaffe-2015-10.

Tapper, Jake. "Ambassador Susan Rice: Libya Attack Not Premeditated," *ABC News*, September 16, 2012, https://abcnews.go.com/blogs/politics/2012/09/ambassador-susan-rice-libya-attack-not-premeditated/.

———. "Father of Slain Former SEAL, New Report, Raise Questions About Response to Benghazi Attack." *ABC News*, October 26, 2012. https://abcnews.go.com/blogs/politics/2012/10/father-of-slain-former-seal-new-report-raise.

Treene, Alayna, and Jonathan Swan. "Republicans Plot Vengeance on Jan. 6 Committee." *Axios*, July 6, 2022. https://www.axios.com/2022/07/06/republicans-plot-vengeance-jan-6-committee.

Trump, Donald. "Donald Trump Calls Benghazi Committee 'Very Partisan.'" *CNN*, October 25, 2015. https://www.cnn.com/videos/politics/2015/10/25/donald-trump-benghazi-committee-partisan-sot-state-of-the-union.cnn.

Tunney, John V., *Measuring Hamlet Security in Vietnam: Report of a Special Study Mission of the Committee on* Foreign Affairs. Washington, DC: Government Printing Office, 1969.

Turse, Nick, and Sean D. Naylor. "Revealed: The U.S. Military's 36 Code-Named Operations in Africa." *Yahoo News*, April 17, 2019. https://www.yahoo.com/now/revealed-the-us-militarys-36-codenamed-operations-in-africa-090000841.html.

U.S. Congress. House of Representatives. Committee on Armed Services. "The Defense Department's Posture for September 11, 2013: What are the Lessons of Benghazi?," Hearing before the Subcommittee on Oversight and Investigations of the Committee on Armed Services United States House of Representatives, September 19, 2013, H.A.S.C. No. 113–59.

U.S. Congress. House of Representatives. Committee on Foreign Affairs. "Benghazi: Where is the State Department Accountability?," Hearing before the Committee on Foreign Affairs House of Representatives, September 18, 2013, Serial No. 113–93.

———. *Benghazi: Where is the State Department Accountability?: Majority Staff Report.* Washington, DC: House Foreign Affairs Committee, 2014.

———. "Foreign Assistance Act of 1968," Hearings before the Committee on Foreign Affairs House of Representatives, Ninetieth Congress Second Session on H.R. 15263, A Bill to Amend Further the Foreign Assistance Act of 1961, as Amended, and for Other Purposes, March 26, 27, 28, April 1, 2, 1968, Part IV. Washington DC: Government Printing Office, 1968.

———. "Terrorist Attack in Benghazi: The Secretary of State's View," Hearing before the Committee on Foreign Affairs House of Representatives, January 23, 2013, Serial No. 113–11.

U.S. Congress. House of Representatives. Committee on Oversight and Government Reform. *Benghazi Attacks: Investigative Update Interim Report on the Accountability Review Board: Staff Report.* 113th Congress, September 16, 2013.

———. "Benghazi: Exposing Failure and Recognizing Courage," Hearing before the Committee on Oversight and Government Reform House of Representatives, May 8, 2013, Serial No. 113–30.

———. "Benghazi, Instability, and a New Government: Success and Failures of U.S. Intervention in Libya," Hearing before the Committee on Oversight and Government Reform House of Representatives, May 1, 2014, Serial No. 113–110.

———. "Review of the Benghazi Attacks and Unanswered Questions," Hearing before the Committee on Oversight and Government Reform House of Representatives, September 19, 2013, Serial No. 113–59.

———. "The Security Failures of Benghazi," Hearing before the Committee on Oversight and Government Reform House of Representatives, October 10, 2012, Serial No. 112–193.

U.S. Congress. House of Representatives. Select Committee on the Events Surrounding the 2012 Terrorist Attack in Benghazi. "About." n.d. https://archives-benghazi-republicans-oversight.house.gov/about.

———. "Benghazi Committee Gains Historic State ARB Document Access." April 30, 2015. https://archives-benghazi-republicans-oversight.house.gov/news/press-releases/benghazi-committee-gains-historic-state-arb-document-access.

———. *Documents Provided to the Select Committee on the Events Surrounding the 2012 Terrorist Attack in Benghazi: House of Representatives.* 114th Cong., 2d sess., Volumes 1–3, 2016.

———. *Final Report of the Select Committee on the Events Surrounding the 2012 Terrorist Attack in Benghazi: House of Representatives; Together with Additional and Minority Views.* 114th Cong., 2d sess., 2016. H. Rept. 114–848.

———. "Hearing 1," Hearing before the Select Committee on the Events Surrounding the 2012 Terrorist Attack in Benghazi, Libya United States House of Representatives, September 17, 2014.

———. "Hearing 2," Hearing before the Select Committee on the Events Surrounding the 2012 Terrorist Attack in Benghazi, Libya United States House of Representatives, December 10, 2014.

———. "Hearing 3," Hearing before the Select Committee on the Events Surrounding the 2012 Terrorist Attack in Benghazi United States House of Representatives, January 27, 2015.

———. "Hearing 4," Hearing before the Select Committee on the Events Surrounding the 2012 Terrorist Attack in Benghazi United States House of Representatives, October 22, 2015.

———. "Home." n.d. https://archives-benghazi-republicans-oversight.house.gov/.

———. *Interviews of Witnesses Before the Select Committee on the Events Surrounding the 2012 Terrorist Attack in Benghazi: House of Representatives.* 114th Cong., 2d sess., Volumes 1–11, 2016.

———. "More than 10,000 Days of Delays: Obama Admin's Delays of Benghazi Documents Equivalent to Over 27 Years." May 18, 2016. https://archives-benghazi-republicans-oversight.house.gov/news/press-releases/over-10000-days-of-delays-obama-administration-s-delays-on-benghazi-documents.

———. "News." n.d. https://archives-benghazi-republicans-oversight.house.gov/news.

———. "Over One Year Later, State Department Finally Turns Over Records; Committee Still Waiting for Others." April 8, 2016. https://archives-benghazi-republicans-oversight.house.gov/news/press-releases/over-one-year-later-state-department-finally-turns-over-records-committee-still.

———. "Select Committee on Benghazi Announces Commencement of Interviews." February 6, 2015. https://archives-benghazi-republicans-oversight.house.gov/news/press-releases/select-committee-on-benghazi-announces-commencement-of-interviews.

———. "Select Committee on Benghazi Announces Scheduled Testimony of Additional Witnesses." December 3, 2015. https://archives-benghazi-republicans-oversight.house.gov/news/press-releases/select-committee-announces-scheduled-testimony-of-additional-witnesses.

———. "Select Committee on Benghazi Gowdy Opening Statement at Benghazi Select Committee Hearing." January 27, 2015. https://archives-benghazi-republicans-oversight.house.gov/news/press-releases/gowdy-opening-statement-at-benghazi-select-committee-hearing.

———. "Select Committee Joint Statement on FBI Briefing." July 31, 2014. https://archives-benghazi-republicans-oversight.house.gov/news/press-releases/select-committee-joint-statement-on-fbi-briefing.

———. "Select Committee Joint Statement on Khattala Briefing." July 9, 2014. https://archives-benghazi-republicans-oversight.house.gov/news/press-releases/select-committee-joint-statement-on-khattala-briefing.

———. "Select Committee Obtains New Blumenthal Emails Before Deposition." June 16, 2015. https://archives-benghazi-republicans-oversight.house.gov/news/press-releases/select-committee-obtains-new-blumenthal-emails-before-deposition.

———. "Select Committee Releases Interim Progress Update." May 8, 2015. https://archives-benghazi-republicans-oversight.house.gov/news/press-releases/select-committee-releases-interim-progress-update.

———. "Speaker Boehner Names Republican Members." May 5, 2014. https://archives-benghazi-republicans-oversight.house.gov/news/press-releases/boehner-names-republican-members-of-select-committee.

———. "Statement from the Communications Director on Clinton Email Addresses." March 4, 2015. https://archives-benghazi-republicans-oversight.house.gov/news/press-releases/statement-from-the-communications-director-on-clinton-email-addresses.

U.S. Congress. House of Representatives. Select Committee to Investigate the January 6th Attack on the United States Capitol. "Thompson Announces Additional Select Committee Senior Staff Members." August 6, 2021. https://january6th.house.gov/news/press-releases/thompson-announces-additional-select-committee-senior-staff-members.

———. "Thompson Announces Senior Staff for Select Committee to Investigate the January 6th Attack on the U.S. Capitol." July 22, 2021. https://january6th.house.gov/news/press-releases/thompson-announces-senior-staff-select-committee-investigate-january-6th-attack.

U.S. Congress. Senate. "Military Procurement Authorizations for Fiscal Year 1967," Hearings before the Committee on Armed Services and the Subcommittee on Department of Defense of the Committee on Appropriations United States Senate, Eighty-Ninth Congress Second Session on S. 2950 Department of Defense Programs, and Authorization of Appropriations during Fiscal Year 1967 for Procurement of Aircraft, Missiles, Naval Vessels, and Tracked Combat Vehicles, and Research, Development, Test, and Evaluation for the Armed Forces, February 23, 25, 28, March 8, 9, 10, 24, 25, 29, 30, and 31, 1966.

———. "Richard Russell: A Featured Biography." *United States Senate*, n.d. https://www.senate.gov/senators/FeaturedBios/Featured_Bio_Russell.htm.

———. "Supplemental Military Procurement and Construction Authorizations, Fiscal Year 1967," Hearings before the Committee on Armed Services and the Subcommittee on Department of Defense of the Committee on Appropriations United States Senate, Ninetieth Congress First Session on S. 665 to Authorize Appropriations during Fiscal Year 1967 for Procurement of Aircraft, Missiles, Tracked Combat Vehicles, Research, Development, Test, Evaluation, and Military Construction for the Armed Forces, and for Other Purposes, January 23, 24, and 25, 1967.

———. Committee on Armed Services. "Department of Defense's Response to the Attack on U.S. Facilities in Benghazi, Libya, and the Findings of its Internal Review Following the Attack," Hearing before the Committee on Armed Services United States Senate, February 7, 2013, S Hrg. 113–164.

———. Committee on Foreign Relations. "Benghazi: The Attacks and the Lessons Learned," Hearing before the Committee on Foreign Relations United States Senate, January 23, 2013, S. Hrg. 113–184.

———. Committee on Governmental Affairs. *Final Report of the Committee on Governmental Affairs: United States Senate: Together with Additional and Minority Views: Investigation of Illegal or Improper Activities in Connection with 1996 Federal Election Campaigns.* 105th Cong., 2d sess., 1998. Rept. 105-167.

———. Committees on Appropriations and Armed Services. "Supplemental Defense Appropriations for Fiscal Year 1966," Hearings before the Committee on Appropriations and the Committee on Armed Services United States Senate, Eighty-Ninth Congress Second Session on H.R. 13546, Making Supplemental Appropriations for the Fiscal Year ending June 30, 1966, and for Other Purposes. Washington DC: Government Printing Office, 1966.

———. Select Committee on Intelligence. *Report of the U.S. Senate Select Committee on Intelligence Review of the Terrorist Attacks on U.S. Facilities in Benghazi, Libya, September 11–12, 2012 together with Additional Views.* 113th Cong., 2d sess., 2014. S. Report. 113–134.

U.S. White House. *The National Security Strategy of the United States of America.* Washington, DC: President of the U.S., 2010.

Van Evera, Stephen. *Guide to Methods to Students of Political Science.* London: Cornell University Press, 1997.

Washington Post-ABC poll. May 29– June 1, 2014. https://www.politico.com/story/2014/06/benghazi-poll-51-percent-support-panel-hillary-clinton-107362.

Watson, Kathryn. "How Members of Congress Voted on the Impeachment of President Trump." *CBS News*, December 19, 2019. https://www.cbsnews.com/news/impeachment-roll-call-vote-how-members-of-congress-voted-on-impeachment-of-president-trump-who-voted-for-against/.

Wehrey, Frederic. *The Burning Shores: Inside the Battle for the New Libya.* New York: Farrar, Straus and Giroux, 2018.

Weiss, Carol H. "Congressional Committees as Users of Analysis." *Journal of Policy Analysis and Management* 8, no. 3 (1989): 411–31.

Werner, Erica. "Fiscal Hawk Ryan Leaves Behind Growing Deficits and a Changed GOP." *Washington Post*, April 11, 2018. https://www.washingtonpost.com/power-post/fiscal-hawk-ryan-leaves-behind-growing-deficits-and-a-changed-gop/2018/04/11/827b68d4-3d93-11e8-a7d1-e4efec6389f0_story.html.

West, William F. *Controlling the Bureaucracy: Institutional Constraints in Theory and Practice.* Armonk: M.E. Sharpe, 1995.

Wolff, Lester L. *Report of Special Study Mission to Asia.* Washington, DC: Government Printing Office, 1971.

Younger, Irving. "Congressional Investigations and Executive Secrecy: A Study in the Separation of Powers." *University of Pittsburgh Law Review* 20 (1959): 755–84.

Zegart, Amy B. "The Domestic Politics of Irrational Intelligence Oversight." *Political Science Quarterly* 126, no. 1 (2011): 1–25.

Zelizer. Julian. *On Capitol Hill: The Struggle to Reform and Its Consequences, 1948–2000.* Cambridge: Cambridge University Press, 2004.

Zoellick, Robert B. "Congress and the Making of US Foreign Policy." *Survival* 41, no. 4 (1999–2000): 20–41.

Index

Page references for figures are italicized.

About the Author

Bradley F. Podliska is a former investigator for the U.S. House of Representatives Select Committee on Benghazi. He has PhD in political science (international relations major) from Texas A&M University, MA in national security studies from Georgetown University, and BA (with honors) in international relations from the University of Wisconsin-Madison. He is assistant professor of military and security studies with the Air Force and a retired U.S. Air Force Reserve intelligence officer with the rank of lieutenant colonel. Prior to working for the Benghazi Committee, he worked as an intelligence analyst for the Department of Defense. His publications include a book, *Acting Alone: A Scientific Study on American Hegemony and Unilateral Use-of-Force Decision Making* (2010), a book chapter on congressional oversight, and articles on national security and the military.